Area Handbook for Albania

Eugene K. Keefe, Sarah Jane Elpern, William
Giloane, James M. Moore, Jr. Stephen Peters,
Eston T. White

Alpha Editions

This Edition Published in 2021

ISBN: 9789355756480

Design and Setting By
Alpha Editions
www.alphaedis.com
Email – info@alphaedis.com

TABLE OF CONTENTS

FOREWORD

This volume is one of a series of handbooks prepared by Foreign Area Studies (FAS) of The American University, designed to be useful to military and other personnel who need a convenient compilation of basic facts about the social, economic, political, and military institutions and practices of various countries. The emphasis is on objective description of the nation's present society and the kinds of possible or probable changes that might be expected in the future. The handbook seeks to present as full and as balanced an integrated exposition as limitations on space and research time permit. It was compiled from information available in openly published material. An extensive bibliography is provided to permit recourse to other published sources for more detailed information. There has been no attempt to express any specific point of view or to make policy recommendations. The contents of the handbook represent the work of the authors and FAS and do not represent the official view of the United States government.

An effort has been made to make the handbook as comprehensive as possible. It can be expected, however, that the material, interpretations, and conclusions are subject to modification in the light of new information and developments. Such corrections, additions, and suggestions for factual, interpretive, or other change as readers may have will be welcomed for use in future revisions. Comments may be addressed to:

The Director
Foreign Area Studies
The American University
5010 Wisconsin Avenue, N.W.
Washington, D.C. 20016

PREFACE

Albania, or, as it proclaimed itself in 1946, the People's Republic of Albania, emerged from World War II under the control of the local Communist movement, which later adopted the name Albanian Workers' Party. The most remarkable feature of Albanian life during the 1960s was the rigid alignment with Communist China in that country's ideological struggle with the Soviet Union. In mid-1970 the country continued to be Communist China's only European ally and its mouthpiece in the United Nations. Propaganda broadcasts in several languages, extensive for such a small, undeveloped country, continued to emanate from the capital city of Tirana, constantly reiterating the Chinese Communist line and making Radio Tirana sound like an extension of Radio Peking.

Albania's most notable tradition from ancient times has been one of foreign domination. Brief periods of independence have been overshadowed by long centuries of subjection to alien rule. Foreign rulers never seemed able or willing to subject the Albanian peasants to the complete authority of a central government. Throughout their history Albanians, protected by the remoteness of their mountain villages, often enjoyed a measure of autonomy even though they lacked national independence. The foreign domination plus the limited autonomy developed in the people a spirit of fierce independence and a suspicion of neighboring states that might have designs on their territorial integrity.

Militarily undeveloped but unwilling to submit to partition by its neighbors, Albania has held on precariously to autonomy since World War II by becoming a client state—first to Yugoslavia, then to the Soviet Union, and then to Communist China. In all three relationships Albania has maintained its independence but it has not been able to establish itself as a viable economic entity.

The *Area Handbook for Albania* seeks to present an overview of the various social, political, and economic aspects of the country as they appeared in 1970. The leaders of the Communist Party have gone to extremes to maintain an aura of secrecy about their nation and their efforts to govern it. Material on Albania is scanty and some that is available is not reliable but, using their own judgments on sources, the authors have striven for objectivity in this effort to depict Albanian society in 1970.

The spelling of place names conforms to the rulings of the United States Board on Geographic Names, with the exception that no diacritical marks have been used in this volume. The metric system has been used only for tonnages.

COUNTRY SUMMARY

1. COUNTRY: People's Republic of Albania (Albania). Called Shqiperia by Albanians. A national state since 1912. Under Communist control after 1944.

2. GOVERNMENT: Functions much like Party-state model of Soviet Union. Constitution designates People's Assembly as highest state organ; its Presidium conducts state affairs between Assembly sessions. People's Council highest organ at district and lower echelons. Communist Party (officially, the Albanian Workers' Party) organizations parallel government organizations and control them from national to local levels. Party members hold all key positions in government.

3. SIZE AND LOCATION: Area, 11,100 square miles; smallest of the European Communist states. Extends 210 miles from southern to northern extremities; 90 miles on longest east-west axis. Bordered on north and east by Yugoslavia; on southeast and south by Greece; and on west by Adriatic and Ionian seas.

4. TOPOGRAPHY: A narrow strip of lowland borders Adriatic Sea; remainder of country is mountainous and hilly, intersected by streams that flow in westerly or northwesterly direction. Terrain is generally rugged.

5. CLIMATE: Unusually varied. Coastal lowlands have Mediterranean-type climate. Inland fluctuations common, but continental influences predominate. Annual precipitation is 40 to 100 inches according to area; highly seasonal; summer droughts common. Temperatures vary widely because of differences in elevation and the changes in prevailing Mediterranean and continental air currents.

6. ADMINISTRATIVE DIVISIONS: Twenty-six districts. Economic and social factors played important role in shaping delineations. Control and direction is from Tirana.

7. POPULATION: Estimated 2.1 million in January 1970. Growth unusually rapid; at 1970 rate, would double in twenty-six years. Two-thirds live in rural areas. Inhabitants are 97-percent ethnic Albanian. About 106 males per 100 females.

8. LABOR: In 1967 the working-age population numbered about 932,000, of which approximately 745,000 were employed. About 66.7 percent were in agriculture; 14.1 percent in industry; 5.4 percent in construction; and 13.8 percent in trade, education, health, and others.

9. LANGUAGE: Albanian spoken by everyone. Some of the 3-percent minority use tongue of country of family origin as a second language.

10. EDUCATION: Nearly all persons under age forty are literate, according to Albanian statistics. Communist ideas and principles emphasized with strict controls by centralized authority. Production of capabilities and skills required for modernization and industrialization considered to be a major goal.

11. RELIGION: Organized religion destroyed by government action in 1967. Party-directed antireligious campaign aims to eliminate religious thought and belief. Pre-World War II data indicated population to be 70-percent Muslim, 20-percent Eastern Orthodox, and 10-percent Roman Catholic.

12. HEALTH: Many diseases, but reportedly greatly reduced or eliminated. Health improved substantially after 1950, as reflected in Albanian reports. Malnutrition, poor sanitary-hygienic conditions, and lack of trained personnel are continuing problems.

13. JUSTICE: System of people's courts from national to village level; purportedly independent of administrative system but guided by Party policy. Supreme Court elected by the People's Assembly. District judges popularly elected from among Party-approved candidates. Jury system not used. Persons are subject to military law and tried in military courts.

14. ECONOMY: Government controlled. Follows planning model of Soviet Union. Per capita gross national product lowest in Europe. Lack of accessible resources, arable land, and trained work force make for slow growth.

15. INDUSTRY: Poorly developed despite heavy emphasis since 1950s, with priority to means of production. Extractive industries most productive. Growth rates high in 1950s, slowed in 1960s.

16. AGRICULTURE: Production low because of lack of arable land and inefficient methods. Cereal crops for domestic use and exportable items, such as tobacco, fruits, and vegetables, most important.

17. IMPORTS: Largely items for industrial development and unfinished materials for processing. Some food, but quantity decreasing.

18. EXPORTS: Mostly at the expense of domestic needs, except for some metals and minerals. Low in proportion to imports, but increasing.

19. FINANCE: Currency: The lek is standard unit; lacks solid backing. Banks are state owned and operated. National income consistently less than expenditures, requiring supplement from foreign sources.

20. COMMUNICATIONS: Government owned and controlled. Press and radio as instruments to indoctrinate effectively reach the masses. Other media poorly developed.

21. RAILROADS: Approximately 135 miles standard-gauge. None cross international borders.

22. ROADS: Approximately 3,000 miles have improved surface. Rugged terrain makes travel difficult on others. None part of important international routes.

23. PORTS: Durres, largest and most important, alone links with hinterland. Vlore only other major port.

24. AIR TRANSPORTATION: Extremely limited within country and with foreign cities. Long-distance international flights require connections through intermediate points. Facilities for all but small aircraft limited to Tirana area.

25. INTERNATIONAL AGREEMENTS AND TREATIES: Member, United Nations after 1955. Member, Council for Mutual Economic Assistance (COMECON) and Warsaw Treaty Organization, 1955-68; participation all but ceased after 1961 split with Soviet Union.

26. AID PROGRAMS: United Nations Relief and Rehabilitation Agency (UNRRA) 1945-46; Yugoslavia 1947-48, as an integrated economy; Soviet Union 1948-61; and Communist China after 1961.

27. SECURITY: Party-controlled agencies closely watch people's activities and secure borders. Security forces total approximately 12,500.

28. ARMED FORCES: The People's Army, approximately 40,000, includes army, navy, and air elements. Most conscripts serve two years. Cost, about 10 percent of total budget.

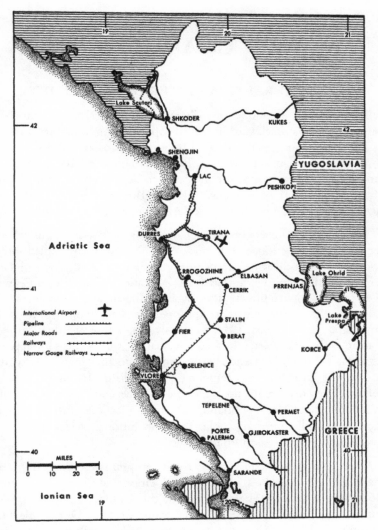

Figure 1. Transportation Systems in Albania

CHAPTER 1

GENERAL CHARACTER OF THE SOCIETY

The People's Republic of Albania was, in 1970, the smallest and economically most backward of the European Communist nations, with an area of 11,100 square miles located between Yugoslavia and Greece along the central west coast of the Balkan Peninsula. Its population of approximately 2.1 million was considered to be 97-percent ethnic Albanian, with a smattering of Greeks, Vlachs, Bulgars, Serbs, and Gypsies. Practically the entire population used Albanian as the principal language.

The country officially became a Communist "people's republic" in 1946 after one-party elections were held. Actually, the Communist-dominated National Liberation Front had been the leading political power since 1944, after successfully conducting civil war operations against non-Communist forces while concurrently fighting against Italian and German armies of occupation. The Communist regime operated first under the mask of the Democratic Front from 1944 to 1948 and, subsequently, through the Albanian Workers' Party; it asserted that it was a dictatorship of the proletariat—the workers and the peasants—and that it ruled according to the Leninist principle of democratic centralism. In practice, a small, carefully selected Party group, which in 1970 was still under the control of Enver Hoxha and Mehmet Shehu, the partisan leaders of the World War II period, made all important policy and operational decisions (see ch. 6, Government Structure and Political System).

In order to gain broad support for its programs the Party utilized mass social organizations. These included the Democratic Front, the successor in 1945 to the National Liberation Front; the Union of Albanian Working Youth; the United Trade Unions; and others. Direct election of governmental bodies, from the people's councils in villages to the People's Assembly at the national level, gave the appearance of representative institutions. While seemingly democratic, these assemblies met infrequently and for short periods and had no real power.

The average citizen has never had any influence in national politics. During the 1920-39 period vested interests, mostly landowners and clan chiefs, were the predominant influence. A middle class was lacking, and the great bulk of the population, the rural peasantry, was held in a state of subservience by local leaders. Under Communist rule political power has been concentrated completely in the Party leadership (see ch. 2, Historical Setting; ch. 6, Government Structure and Political System).

The system of controls circumscribed individual freedoms and reached nearly every facet of day-to-day life. The Communist regime, by its totalitarian rule, extended and increased obedience to, and fear of, centralized authority. A new ruling elite, that of the Party, was substituted for the *beys* (see Glossary) and *pashas* (see Glossary) of pre-Communist times (see ch. 6, Government Structure and Political System).

The goals of the Communist regime as revealed during the 1944-70 period were to strengthen and perpetuate the Party's hold on the reins of government, to maintain Albanian independence, and to modernize society according to the Leninist-Stalinist model. By capitalizing on the divisions among the Communist nations and by eliminating or rendering harmless internal opposition, the Party had a firm grip on the instruments of control, and by 1961 independence was reasonably well secured. Only modest progress had been made by 1970 toward modernization. The lack of extensive natural resources and continued reliance on foreign aid caused much strain and required sacrifices by the ordinary citizen (see ch. 2, Historical Setting; ch. 9, Internal and External Security).

Albania tended to be highly aggressive and partisan in the ideological struggles between the Communist and Western democratic states and those between the Communist nations. The successive close relationships with Yugoslavia (1944-48), the Soviet Union (1949-60), and China after 1961 reflected the inherent insecurity of a weak state. Although these coalitions frequently seemed to place Albania in a subservient role, the ultimate goals of the Hoxha-Shehu regime were to develop political autonomy and economic self-sufficiency, thus reducing dependence on foreign aid to a point where Albania could be truly independent (see ch. 6, Government Structure and Political System).

In many respects Albania was a closed society. Government controls over all internal communications media ensured that only Party-approved information was disseminated; however, foreign transmissions were not jammed, probably because funds were not available. The individual's activities were closely watched by security police or other Party watchdogs. Travel into and out of the country was restricted and closely controlled (see ch. 7, Communications and Cultural Development; ch. 9, Internal and External Security).

Pre-Communist Albania gained independence in 1912 after 4-1/2 centuries of rule by the Ottoman Turks. The movement toward nationhood during the latter part of the nineteenth century and the early twentieth took advantage of the disintegration of Turkish power and the rivalry between European nations vying for control over the Balkans. The opportunity for independence came when a group of Balkan nations attacked Turkey and proclaimed their intention of seizing the European part of the Ottoman Empire. A group of Albanian patriots, under the leadership of Ismail Qemal bey Vlora, thwarted the desires of Albania's neighbors to partition the country by declaring independence on November 28, 1912. The new nation sought and received backing from the great powers of Europe, thus forcing the weaker Balkan nations to give up their plans for the annexation of Albanian territory.

Under the cruel, corrupt, and inefficient Ottoman rule, institutions and capabilities for self-government were not allowed to develop, and the country was ill prepared for statehood when it arrived. Development had hardly begun when World War I brought chaos to the country as the opposing powers used it as a battleground. After the war, as Albania struggled to assert itself as a national entity, the lack of natural resources and a poorly developed economy created a heavy requirement for foreign aid. Excessive reliance on Fascist Italy during the 1920s and 1930s eventually led to annexation by that expansionist power.

After regaining its independence during World War II, Albania again compromised its sovereignty by excessive reliance on outside powers: first on Yugoslavia, which was heavily involved in the establishment of the Communist Party in Albania, and then on the Soviet Union. Catastrophe was averted in each instance by a split between Communist nations. When Joseph Stalin expelled Yugoslavia from the Communist bloc of nations in 1948, Enver Hoxha switched his allegiance to the Soviet Union and ended his country's economic reliance on Yugoslavia, which had all but incorporated Albania into its federation. For the next several years Albania was a Soviet satellite but, as the rift between the Soviet Union and Communist China widened, Hoxha continually sided with the Chinese and, when the break came in 1961, Albania severed its Soviet ties and became an ally of Communist China.

The lack of resources and an undeveloped economy, the same economic problems that had plagued newly independent Albania in the 1920s, continued to be problems in 1970, and foreign aid was still a necessity. Communist China provided an undetermined amount of assistance during the 1960s and into 1970 but, from the Albanian point of view, the danger of loss of sovereignty to distant China was much less than it had been during the periods when the country was a client state of nearby Italy, Yugoslavia, and the Soviet Union.

The lack of easily defended national boundaries was an additional concern in the maintenance of territorial integrity. Although the boundaries originally established in 1913 remained relatively unchanged and were not officially disputed in 1970, they were not considered satisfactory in some sectors. About 1 million Albanians lived in adjacent areas of Yugoslavia, mostly in the Kosovo region, and Albania revealed her dissatisfaction that they were not included within its territory. Neither Albania nor Greece was content with the demarcation along the two most southerly districts of Albania. The lack of sharply defined terrain features in most places along the northern and eastern borders with Yugoslavia and the southeastern and southern delineation between Albania and Greece increased the potential for dispute (see ch. 2, Historical Setting; ch. 3, Physical Environment).

The topography of the land is generally rugged, and access to inland areas is difficult. Except for the narrow strip of lowlands along the Adriatic coast, the country is made up of mountains and hills, intermittently intersected by streams that flow in a generally westerly or northwesterly direction. Valleys in the hinterland are narrow, and slopes of mountains and hills tend to be steep (see ch. 3, Physical Environment).

Considering Albania's small area, climatic conditions are quite varied. Along the coastal lowlands Mediterranean-type weather prevails. In the interior there are rapid fluctuations in many areas, but continental influences predominate. Despite annual precipitation ranging from 40 to 100 inches, droughts are common because rainfall is unevenly distributed (see ch. 3, Physical Environment).

Few places offer good conditions for large-scale settlement. Localities with good soil and a dependable water supply are small and scattered. The coastal lowlands, inundated or desert-like according to the season, are lightly populated. The region generally bounded by Durres, Tirana, Elbasan, and Fier grew most rapidly and had the highest population density in the late 1960s. Inland, the mountain and upland basins offer the best conditions for settlement (see ch. 3, Physical Environment; ch. 4, The People).

The extensive networks of rivers are of little value for transportation because waterflow fluctuates, currents tend to be violent, and estuaries are heavily sedimented. Road and railroad construction is difficult because of the uneven character of the terrain. Improved land transportation routes are exceedingly limited. Mountain homesteads and villages frequently have only a footpath to connect them with the outside world. The lack of communications routes results in isolation for many areas and helps to place Albania on a byway of international travel (see ch. 3, Physical Environment; ch. 4, The People).

Remote and isolated areas had a significant influence in shaping Albanian society. During the long period of Turkish rule they provided sanctuaries for the preservation of ethnic identity. After 1912 the people in these areas were the primary residuary for antiquated customs and attitudes.

Communist leaders made a major effort in the 1960s to eliminate old customs and other vestiges of the past that detracted from the collectivization and modernization of society. Comments of high officials in early 1970 indicated that their efforts still had not been entirely successful (see ch. 2, Historical Setting; ch. 4, The People).

The Albanians are descendants of the Illyrians, an Indo-European people who lived in the Balkans in antiquity. Their history before the eleventh century is linked with, and not easily separated from, that of the other Illyrian tribes. The written language did not develop until the fifteenth century, and then for more than four centuries under Turkish rule it was forbidden. Although Albanians distinguished themselves as soldiers under Turkish suzerainty and some held high office in the Ottoman ruling hierarchy, they were little known as a people before the nineteenth century. As members of clans or feudal estates they lived an outmoded life style and were relatively untouched by the forces of industrialization and democratization that changed much of western and southern Europe in the nineteenth and early twentieth centuries (see ch. 2, Historical Setting).

For centuries after the death in 1468 of Skanderbeg, the Albanian national hero and symbol of resistance to Turkish rule, many Albanian mountain communities lived unto themselves. Local control rested with *pashas* and *beys*, and some became virtually independent of Turkish rule. About two-thirds of the people accepted, or were forcibly converted to, the Muslim faith under the Turks. Since eligibility to participate in political life rested on religious affiliation, some Albanians thus became a part of the ruling hierarchy of the Ottoman Empire, but the masses were indifferent politically. Activities or attitudes that would tend to strengthen nationalism were suppressed. When considered in its entirety the heritage from Ottoman rule contributed almost nothing toward the development of capabilities required for a viable government and a modernized society (see ch. 2, Historical Setting).

Kinship, customs, and attitudes related to family life, and strong attachments to community and language were strong influences in the preservation of ethnic identity through the many centuries of foreign domination. The Albanians are divided into two major subgroups—the Gegs, who occupy the area north of the Shkumbin River, and the Tosks, who inhabit the territory to the south. Differences in physical appearance persist, but the breakup of clans and moves toward collectivization of society after World War II diminished the most distinguishing feature, their social system. Antiquated customs and blood feuds that were frequently initiated by offenses against women were more prevalent among the Gegs than the Tosks before the Communist takeover (see ch. 4, The People).

The family continued to be a strong social force in 1970. It was the primary residuary of customs, practices, and attitudes that detracted from Communist programs to create a monolithic and modernized society. Older persons, particularly males, who traditionally held positions of authority in the family, were considered to be the strongest force against change. In their efforts to eliminate outmoded customs, Party and government leaders placed special emphasis on youth and women, the latter having suffered much discrimination under the clan system. Large extended families, which sometimes numbered sixty or more persons and included several generations, were in most cases broken up under Communist rule as a means to decrease family influence (see ch. 5, Social System).

Party leaders, realizing the importance of education in developing attitudes and loyalties favorable to communism and in training the work force required for a modern industrial economy, placed heavy emphasis on school programs. By 1970 the level of schooling completed by the people had been significantly increased over the 1946 level, but the pool of scientific and skilled personnel fell far short of requirements (see ch. 5, Social System).

The most noteworthy improvement in the people's welfare, as reflected by Albanian data, was in the area of health. The incidence of disease was greatly reduced; the death rate decreased; and life expectancy increased by approximately 12.5 years between 1950 and 1966 (see ch. 4, The People).

Albanian art, literature, and music have gained little recognition among world cultures. After 1944 the Communist regime instituted mass participation in education and social and cultural activities to instill ideals of socialism and Communist morality and gain the capabilities required for modernization of the economy. Illiteracy, once prevalent among all age groups, was reportedly eliminated among persons under the age of forty and some, but not nearly all, of the skilled work force required has been produced. Despite these efforts Albania's cultural heritage was still meager in the late 1960s (see ch. 5, Social System; ch. 7, Communications and Cultural Development).

Albanians as individuals tended to take religion lightly, and the Muslim, Eastern Orthodox, and Roman Catholic religions that had been brought by conquerors did not play major roles in shaping national traditions or in strengthening national unity. In 1967, after the government's withdrawal of approval for religious bodies to function, an accelerated campaign was undertaken to eradicate religious thoughts and beliefs. The fact that the campaign was continuing in early 1970 indicated that it had not entirely succeeded (see ch. 5, Social System).

The major economic objective is to develop a modern economy with a strong industrial base. Before World War II there was practically no industry, and the system of agriculture was primitive and inefficient. Substantial aid from the Soviet Union during the 1950s resulted in modest growth of the economy, with rapid rates of industrial growth and improvements in education and health. Chinese aid on a lesser scale and heavy sacrifices by the masses sustained the growth trend in industry during the 1960s but at a slower pace.

The major source of national income changed from agriculture to industry during the early 1960s, but the country was still by all appearances predominantly rural and agricultural. Two-thirds of the people lived in rural areas, and more than half were engaged in agriculture. Socialization of the economy, which began in 1944, was completed in the late 1960s. The model of planning borrowed from the Soviet Union that was adopted in the late 1940s continued in use with only slight modifications. The trend was toward greater centralization and governmental control (see ch. 8, Economic System).

The provision of adequate and proper food, clothing, and housing was a constant major problem. Little improvement was made in the standard of living between 1950 and 1970, largely because of sustained rapid population growth and priority to the means of production sector of industry in the allocation of resources (see ch. 4, The People; ch. 8, Economic System).

CHAPTER 2

HISTORICAL SETTING

Historical works and official documents published in Tirana as late as 1970 stressed two major themes: the importance of patriotism and nationalism and the achievements, real or fancied, of the Communist regime since it assumed control of the country in November 1944. The appeal to nationalism always strikes a responsive chord among the Albanians not only because their history is replete with humiliations and injustices heaped upon them by long domination of foreign powers but also, and especially, because of the territorial aspirations and claims of its neighbors—Italy, Yugoslavia, and Greece. The political scene in Albania since it formally won an independent existence from Turkey in 1912 has indeed been dominated by attempts of one, or a combination, of its neighbors to dismember it.

The boundaries of Albania in 1970 were essentially the same as those delineated by representatives of the Great Powers after Albania had declared its independence. Ethnic problems raised by the drawing of the boundaries have never been solved to the satisfaction of the countries involved. The Albanians hold that in 1913 about 40 percent of their territory, with a population at that time of about 600,000 ethnic Albanians, was unjustly assigned to Serbia. The area has been a continuing source of friction between Albania and Yugoslavia.

A source of tension between Albania and Greece has been the status of Albania's two southernmost districts. Known to the Greeks as Northern Epirus, this region was awarded to Albania by the boundary delineations of 1913, but the Greeks have never relinquished their claims to the area.

Italy, located only about forty-five miles across the narrow Strait of Otranto, has attempted on several occasions to impose its hegemony over Albania. The extreme influence exercised on Albanian affairs by Italy between 1925 and 1939 that culminated in a military invasion in April of 1939 has been a source of great resentment by the Albanian people.

The Communist Party of Albania assumed control of the country in 1944. The fact that the Communist regime installed itself in the capital city of Tirana on November 28, Albania's traditional Independence Day, was an indication that originally it did not intend to cut off all ties with the past, although its declared intention was to create a new social order. A year later, however, on November 29, the regime proclaimed a new national holiday, which it called Liberation Day. Until about 1960 the traditional Independence Day was mentioned only in passing, whereas Liberation Day was celebrated with considerable publicity.

A basic change of attitude, however, occurred when the regime broke with the Soviet Union in the 1960-61 period. The ruling elite, apparently feeling insecure both for their personal safety and for the future of the country, launched an intensive campaign to win popular support by appealing to the people's nationalist and patriotic sentiments. The country's major patriots who were responsible for the national awakening in the second half of the nineteenth and the early part of the twentieth centuries had been forgotten after the Communist seizure of power. In 1961 and 1962, however, books and pamphlets began to be published praising nearly all those, irrespective of their social backgrounds, who had played a role in the national awakening and in the declaration of the country's independence in 1912.

Intensive preparations were made in 1962 to celebrate the fiftieth anniversary of the country's independence, and on November 28, 1962, all the top leaders of the party and government went to Vlore, where independence had been declared, to stage one of the biggest patriotic celebrations in the country's modern history. Among the many books and documents published on this occasion to glorify the country's past was one entitled *Rilindja Kombetare Shqipetare* (Albanian National Awakening), which included photographs of most patriots who had taken part in winning the country's independence, even those of the landed aristocracy (*beys*—see Glossary), whom the regime had previously branded as the "blood-suckers" of the peasants.

This appeal to the past was also accentuated in 1968 in connection with the 500th anniversary of the death of the country's national hero, Skanderbeg. The regime sent a number of scholars and historians to search for historical documents in Vienna and Rome in preparation for the celebration.

With the exception of these efforts to resurrect the past after a hiatus of fifteen years, the primary function of the country's historians, all under the control of the Party, is to glorify the country's achievements in the period under communism. The Party is given credit for all that has been done in the economic development of the country, in improvements in the people's health, and in expansion of educational and cultural facilities, all of which have been considerable. In 1970 Enver Hoxha, first secretary of the Party, like Stalin in his day and Mao Tse-tung in 1970, was daily quoted and glorified.

ANTIQUITY AND THE MIDDLE AGES

The modern Albanians call their country Shqiperia and themselves Shqipetare. In antiquity the Albanians were known as Illyrians, and in the Middle Ages they came to be called Arbereshe or Arbeneshe, and their country Arberia or Arbenia. The present European forms, Albania and Albanians, are derived from the names Arbanoi and Albanoi or Arbaniti, which appeared in the eleventh century.

In antiquity the Albanians formed part of the Thraco-Illyrian and Epirot tribes that inhabited the whole of the peninsula between the Danube River and the Aegean Sea. Until 168 B.C. the northern and central part of present-day Albania comprised parts of the Kingdom of Illyria, whose capital was Shkoder. The Illyrian Kingdom was conquered by the Romans in 168-167 B.C., and thereafter it was a Roman colony until A.D. 395, when the Roman Empire was split into East and West, Albania becoming part of the Byzantine Empire.

Under the Roman Empire, Albania served as a key recruiting area for the Roman legions and a main outlet to the East. The present port of Durres (the ancient Durrachium) became the western terminum of Via Egnatia, an actual extension of Via Appia, by which the Roman legions marched to the East. It was during the Roman rule that Christianity was introduced into Albania.

From the fifth century to the advent of the Ottoman Turks in the Balkans in the fourteenth century, invasions from the north and east, especially by the Huns, the Bulgarians, and the Slavs, thinned the indigenous Illyrian population and drove it along the mountainous Adriatic coastal regions. During the crusades in the twelfth and thirteenth centuries, Albania became a thoroughfare for the crusading armies, which used the port of Durres as a bridgehead. By this time the Venetian Republic had obtained commercial privileges in Albanian towns and, after the Fourth Crusade (1204), it received nominal control over Albania and Epirus and took actual possession of Durres and the surrounding areas. In the middle of the thirteenth century Albania fell under the domination of the kings of Naples, and in 1272 armies of Charles I of Anjou crossed the Adriatic and occupied Durres. Thereupon, Charles I issued a decree calling himself Rex Albaniae and creating Regnum Albaniae (the Kingdom of Albania), which lasted for nearly a century.

OTTOMAN TURK RULE

In the period after the defeat of the Serbs by the Ottoman Turks in 1389 in the battle of Kosovo, most of Albania was divided into a number of principalities under the control of native tribal chieftains, most of whom were subsequently forced into submission by the invading Turks. Some of these chieftains, however, were allowed their independence under Turkish suzerainty. One of the most noted of these was John Kastrioti of Kruje, a region northeast of Tirana, whose four sons were taken hostage by the sultan to be trained in the Ottoman service. The youngest of these, Gjergj, was destined to win fame throughout Europe and to be immortalized as the national hero of his country. Gjergj (b. 1403) soon won the sultan's favor, distinguished himself in the Turkish army, converted to Islam, and was bestowed the title of Skander Bey (Lord Alexander), which, in Albanian, became Skanderbeg or Skenderbey.

In 1443 Hungarian King Hunyadi routed at Nish the sultan's armies, in which Skanderbeg held command; Skanderbeg fled to his native land and seized from the Turks his father's fortress at Kruje. His defection and reconversion to Christianity and the creation in 1444 of the League of Albanian Princes, with himself as its head, enraged the Ottomans, who began a series of intense campaigns that lasted until Skanderbeg's natural death in 1468. In his wars against the Turks, Skanderbeg was aided by the kings of Naples and the popes, one of whom, Pope Nicholas V, named him Champion of Christendom.

Skanderbeg's death did not end Albania's resistance to the Turks; however, they gradually extended their conquests in Albania and in time defeated both the local chieftains and the Venetians, who controlled some of the coastal towns. The Turkish occupation of the country resulted in a great exodus of Albanians to southern Italy and Sicily, where they preserved their language, customs, and Eastern Orthodox religion.

One of the most significant consequences of Ottoman rule of Albania was the conversion to Islam of over two-thirds of the population. As the political and economic basis of the Ottoman Empire was not nationality but religion, this conversion created a new group of Muslim Albanian bureaucrats, who not only ruled Albanian provinces for the sultans but also served in important posts as *pashas* (governors) in many parts of the empire. A number of them became *viziers* (prime ministers), and one, Mehmet Ali Pasha, at the beginning of the nineteenth century founded an Egyptian dynasty that lasted until the 1950s.

Some of the Albanian beys and pashas, especially in the lowlands, became almost independent rulers of their principalities. One of these, Ali Pasha Tepelena, known in history as the Lion of Yannina, whose principality at the beginning of the nineteenth century consisted of the whole area from the Gulf of Arta to Montenegro. By 1803 he had assumed absolute power and negotiated directly with Napoleon and the rulers of

Great Britain and Russia. The sultan, however, becoming alarmed at the damage Ali Pasha was doing to the unity of the empire, sent his armies to surround him in Yannina, where he was captured and decapitated in 1822.

Under the Turks, Albania remained in complete stagnation and, when the Turks were expelled from the Balkans in 1912, they left it in about the same condition as they had found it. The Albanian highlanders, especially in the north, were never fully subjected, and their tribal organizations were left intact. Turkish suzerainty affected them only to the extent that it isolated them from the world. Thus, they preserved their medieval laws, traditions, and customs. As a result, Western civilization and development did not begin to penetrate Albania in any meaningful way until it became independent in 1912.

NATIONAL AWAKENING AND INDEPENDENCE

The Albanian national awakening made rapid strides after the Treaty of San Stefano in 1877, imposed on Turkey by the Russians, gave the Balkan Slavic nations large parts of Albania. The Western powers, refusing to accept Russia's diktat on Turkey, met in Berlin the following year to consider revision of the Treaty of San Stefano. Albanian leaders in the meantime convened at Prizren and founded the League for the Defense of the Rights of the Albanian Nation. Although the league was unable to bring sufficient pressure on the Congress of Berlin to save Albania from serious dismemberment, it set in motion a political movement that had tremendous influence on Albanian nationalist activity for decades to come.

Most of the league leaders held high positions in, or were influential members of, the ruling Turkish elite and were fully aware of the shaky position of the Ottoman Empire; they therefore demanded from the Turks administrative and cultural autonomy for all Albanian lands united in a principality. The Turkish government refused and in 1881 forced the dissolution of the league. Meanwhile, Russia, Italy, and Austria-Hungary began to take an active interest in Albania. Russia aimed at blocking expansion of Austrian influence in the Balkans and supported the territorial demands of Serbia and Montenegro. Italy and Austria-Hungary, on the other hand, concerned over Russia's influence extending to the Adriatic, attempted to influence developments in Albania.

The advent of the Young Turks regime (1908), in whose establishment Albanian officials in the service of the empire played a major role, encouraged the Albanians to found cultural and political clubs for the propagation of Albanian culture and the defense of Albanian rights. In 1908 a congress of intellectuals from all parts of Albania and the Albanian colonies abroad, especially the Italo-Albanian colonies in Italy, convened in Monastir (Bitolj) to decide on an Albanian alphabet; it adopted the Latin one as most suitable for the country. This decision marked a great advance toward Albanian unification and eventual statehood.

In the summer and fall of 1912, while Serbia, Bulgaria, Montenegro, and Greece, prodded by Russia, were waging war against Turkey, the Albanians staged a series of revolts and began to agitate for the creation of an autonomous and neutral Albania. Accordingly, a group of Albanian patriots, led by Ismail Qemal bey Vlora, a member of the Turkish Parliament, proclaimed Albania's independence at Vlore on November 28, 1912, and organized an Albanian provisional government. Supported by Austria and Italy, Albania's independence was recognized on December 12, 1912, by the London Conference of Ambassadors, but its boundaries were to be determined later. In March 1913 agreement was reached on the northern frontiers, assigning Shkoder to Albania but giving Kosovo and Metohija (Kosmet), inhabited then chiefly by Albanians, to Serbia. This frontier demarcation was very similar to the frontiers between Yugoslavia and Albania as they existed in 1970.

The boundaries in the south were more difficult to delineate because Greece laid claim to most of southern Albania, which the Greeks call Northern Epirus. The Conference of Ambassadors appointed a special commission to draw the demarcation line on ethnographic bases and in December 1913 drafted the Protocol of Florence, which assigned the region to Albania. The 1913 boundaries in the south, like those in the north, were almost the same as those that existed between Greece and Albania in 1970. The Albania that emerged from the Conference of Ambassadors was a truncated one; as many Albanians were left out of the new state as were included in it.

The Conference of Ambassadors also drafted a constitution for the new state, which was proclaimed as an autonomous principality, sovereign, and under the guarantees of the Great Powers; created an International Control Commission to control the country's administration and budget; and selected as ruler the German Prince Wilhelm zu Wied. Prince Wied arrived in March 1914 but had to flee the country six months later because of the outbreak of World War I and the difficulties caused by the unruly feudal beys. As a consequence, Albania's independence came to an end, and for the next four years the country served as a battleground for the warring powers.

CREATION OF MODERN ALBANIA

At the end of World War I Albania was occupied by the Allied armies, mostly Italian and French. The Secret Treaty of London, concluded in 1915 and published by the Russian Bolsheviks after the October 1917 Revolution, provided for the partition of nearly all Albania among Italy, Serbia, Montenegro, and Greece. Another accord, known as the Tittoni-Venizelos Agreement, concluded between Italy and Greece in 1919, also called for the dismemberment of Albania. At the 1919-20 Paris Peace Conference Greece laid claim to southern Albania; Serbia and Montenegro, to the northern part; and Italy, to the port of Vlore and surrounding areas. But President Woodrow Wilson's principle of self-determination and his personal insistence on the restoration of an independent Albania saved the country from partition. In the summer of 1920 an Albanian partisan army drove the Italians from Vlore, and the Italian government recognized Albania's independence.

In the meantime, in January 1920 a congress of representatives met in Lushnje, in central Albania, and created a government and a Council of Regency composed of representatives of the four religious denominations prevailing in Albania: the two Muslim sects (Sunni and Bektashi), Roman Catholic, and Eastern Orthodox (see ch. 5, Social System).

From 1920 to 1924 there was political freedom in the country along with extreme political strife. A group of statesmen and politicians, mostly from the old Turkish bureaucracy, attempted to lay the foundation of a modern state, but there was a bitter struggle between the old conservative landlords and Western educated or inspired liberals. The landowners, led by Ahmet Zogu, advocated the continuance of feudal tenure and opposed social and economic reforms, especially agrarian reforms. The liberals, led by Bishop Fan S. Noli, a Harvard University graduate who had founded the Albanian Autocephalous Orthodox Church in Boston in 1908 and had returned to Albania in 1920, favored the establishment of a Western-type democracy. The country was torn by political struggles and rapid changes of government revealed considerable political instability.

In June 1924 the liberals staged a successful coup against the conservative landlords, forcing their leader, Ahmet Zogu, to flee to Yugoslavia, and formed a new government under Bishop Noli. But Noli was too radical to command the support of the disparate coalition that had ousted Zogu. Internally he proposed radical agrarian reforms, the purging and reduction of the bureaucracy, and the establishment of a truly democratic regime. In foreign affairs he extended recognition to the Soviet Union, a move that alienated some of his supporters at home and alarmed some neighboring states. As a consequence, Zogu, having secured foreign support, led an army from Yugoslavia and in December 1924 entered the capital city of Tirana and became ruler of the country. Bishop Noli and his closest supporters fled abroad; some eventually went to Moscow, and others fell under Communist influence in Western capitals.

Zogu's rule in the 1925-39 period, first as President Zogu and after September I, 1928, as Zog I, king of the Albanians, brought political stability and developed a national political consciousness that had been unprecedented in Albanian history. To secure his position both internally and externally, he concluded in 1926 and 1927 bilateral treaties with Italy, providing for mutual support in maintaining the territorial status quo and establishing a defensive alliance between the two countries. These two treaties, however, assured Italian penetration of Albania, particularly in the military and economic spheres.

King Zog ruled as a moderate dictator, his monarchy being a combination of despotism and reform. He prohibited political parties but was lenient to his opponents unless they actually threatened to overthrow his rule, as happened in 1932, 1935, and 1937. But even during these open revolts, he showed a good deal of leniency and executed only a few ringleaders. He effected some substantial reforms both in the administration and in society, particularly outlawing the traditional vendetta and carrying of arms, of which the Albanians were very fond. The most significant contribution of Zog's fourteen-year rule, the longest since the time of Skanderbeg, was the development of a truly national consciousness and an identity of the people with the state, although not necessarily with the monarchy, and the gradual breakdown of the traditional tribal and clan systems.

In April 1938 Zog married Geraldine Apponyi, a Hungarian countess with an American mother. Italian Foreign Minister Count Ciano was the best man. On Ciano's return to Italy from the wedding, he proposed to his father-in-law, Benito Mussolini, Fascist dictator of Italy, the annexation of Albania. The following year, on April 7, 1939, Ciano's suggestion was consummated. Italian forces invaded Albania on that day, forcing Zog to flee the country, never to return. In the next few months rapid steps were taken to unite Albania with Italy under the crown of King Victor Emanuel III and to impose a regime similar to that of Fascist Italy. Albania as an independent state disappeared.

COMMUNIST SEIZURE AND CONSOLIDATION OF POWER

Resistance to the Italian invaders began soon after the invasion, but the few insignificant Communist groups that existed at that time did not join the fray until after Nazi Germany, under Adolf Hitler, attacked the Soviet Union in June 1941. These Communist groups, acting generally independently of each other, were composed chiefly of young intellectuals who had revolted against the country's medieval society. Educated mostly in the West, they felt that their country's economic development and their desire to use their Western education for their own and their country's advancement were frustrated by Zog's concept of personal rule, by the hostility of traditional chieftains and *beys*, and by the lack of opportunities in the country's underdeveloped society and economy.

The leaders of these disparate groups convened clandestinely in Tirana on November 8, 1941, and under the guidance of two emissaries from the Yugoslav Communist Party, Dusan Mugosha and Miladin Popovic, founded the Albanian Communist Party—known since 1948 as the Albanian Workers' Party. Enver Hoxha, a young schoolteacher who had studied in France and Belgium, was elected provisional and, subsequently, permanent secretary general. In 1970 he still held the same position, under the title of first secretary. From the outset the strategy of the Party was to conceal its true Marxist program and orientation and to stress nationalism and patriotism. To this end, the front technique, through the National Liberation Movement, was used.

The National Liberation Movement was created by the Conference of Peze that was convened, also clandestinely, on September 16, 1942, for the purpose of creating a militant organization to coordinate and intensify the activities of a number of guerrilla bands then active against the Italian occupiers. It was sponsored by the Party and attended by the Party leaders, who at that time paraded as patriots and vehemently denied in public that they were Communists, and by a number of nationalist resistance chieftains. The National Liberation Movement was dominated from the beginning by the Communists, as were its military formations, known as partisans.

The movement was further strengthened in July 1943 at the Conference of Labinot, when the General Staff of the Army of National Liberation of Albania was created, with Enver Hoxha as chief commissar. Thereafter, under the guise of the National Liberation Movement, the Communist leaders devoted all their energies to obtaining complete control of the partisan formations and to preparing the ground for a seizure of power as soon as the Axis powers should be defeated. Their prime objectives in the 1943-44 years were to immobilize the nationalist elements who were still in the movement by surrounding them with loyal commissars and, at the same time, to try to annihilate other nationalist groups that had refused from the outset to collaborate with the movement. There was a full-scale civil war in the country from September 1943 to November 1944.

The civil war was fought between the partisan formations and the two principal anti-Communist organizations—Balli Kombetar (National Front) and the Legality Movement. The Balli Kombetar emerged as an organization soon after the National Liberation Movement was founded; it was led by Midhat Frasheri, a veteran patriot who had formed a clandestine resistance movement during the early days of Italian occupation. The Balli Kombetar extolled the principles of freedom and social justice and championed the objective of an ethnic Albania; that is, the retention of the Yugoslav provinces of Kosovo and Metohija, which the Italians had annexed to Albania in 1941. For some time it made efforts to collaborate with the National Liberation Movement, but to no avail.

In July and August 1943 representatives of the two movements finally met at Mukaj, a village near Tirana, to try to work out an agreement of collaboration against the Axis forces. The chief obstacle to an accord was the disposition of Kosmet. The Balli Kombetar refused to consider collaboration unless the movement joined in the demand that Kosmet remain a part of Albania after the war. Finally an agreement was reached for collaboration, with the provision that the question of Kosmet be resolved after the war.

The emissaries of the Yugoslav Communist Party interpreted the agreement as a victory for the nationalists and demanded that the Albanian Communist Party not only denounce the agreement but also launch a full-scale attack on the Balli Kombetar. The Albanian Communists bowed to this demand and, in September 1943, launched the attack against Balli Kombetar and subsequently against the Legality Movement. This movement was founded in November 1943 by Abas Kupi, who until August 1943 had been a member of the Central Council of the National Liberation Movement but broke away from it after the Mukaj agreement was denounced.

In May 1944 the National Liberation Front, as the movement was by then called, sponsored the Congress of Permet for the purpose of creating the necessary machinery to seize power. The Congress appointed Hoxha commander in chief of the Army of National Liberation and elected the Albanian Anti-Fascist Liberation Council, which in turn created the Albanian Anti-Fascist Committee, under the presidency of Hoxha, as the executive branch of the council. The Congress of Berat, convened by the front in October of the same year, converted the committee into a coalition provisional "democratic" government, which in the following month seized control of the whole country and on November 28, Albania's traditional Independence Day, installed itself in Tirana.

In many respects the 1943-44 civil war in Albania followed a course similar to that which took place between the partisan forces (Communist) of Josip Broz (Tito) and General Mihailovich's Chetniks (loyalist) in Yugoslavia. The Communist operations and final seizure of power in Yugoslavia played a major role in the Communist takeover in Albania. Albania was the only European Communist country that was freed from the Axis invaders without the actual presence of Soviet forces and without direct military assistance from the Soviet Union. Political direction was supplied by the emissaries of the Yugoslav Communist Party attached permanently to the Albanian Communist Party after its founding in 1941. The Anglo-American command in Italy supplied most of the war material to the Albanian partisan forces.

Albania's future was never specifically discussed by the Big Three— Great Britain, the Soviet Union, and the United States—at either the Teheran or the Yalta conferences. Nor did Albania figure in the discussions in Moscow in October 1944 between Churchill and Stalin, when they informally agreed to divide Eastern Europe into spheres of influence, at least for the duration of the war. Accordingly, when the last German troops were driven out of Albania, there was a kind of political vacuum that the Communists, with superior political organizations and substantial armed partisan groups, were able to fill.

In August 1945 the first congress of the National Liberation Front was held, and the name of the organization was changed to the Democratic Front in an effort to make it more palatable to the public. Contending that the Democratic Front represented the majority of the population because all political opinions and groups except Fascists were included in it, the Communist rulers allowed only Democratic Front Candidates for the first postwar national elections held in December 1945.

The Constituent Assembly elected at this polling was originally composed of both party members and some nationalist elements. The latter apparently continued to feel that cooperation with the Communists was possible but, within a year after the elections, they were summarily purged from the Assembly, and subsequently a number of them were tried and executed on charges of being "enemies of the people." All national and local elections since 1945 have been held under the aegis of the Democratic Front.

Even after the "liberation," the Party continued its conspiratorial nature and did not come into the open until the First Party Congress was held in November 1948. Before that time all its meetings were held in closest secrecy, and no statements, communiques, or resolutions were published in its name. The Party thus continued to use the front technique effectively even after it became the undisputed ruler of the country.

THE COMMUNIST PERIOD

The Constituent Assembly, elected on December 2, 1945, proclaimed on January 11, 1946, the People's Republic of Albania; and on March 14 it approved the first Albanian Constitution, based largely on the Yugoslav Communist Constitution. In this first Constitution no mention of any kind was made of the role played by the Party or any other political organizations. The Constitution was, however, amended after the break with Yugoslavia in 1948, and revisions of the Constitution published since 1951 have cited in Article 12 the Albanian Workers' Party as the "vanguard organization of the working class."

The Communist regime quickly consolidated its power through a ruthless application of the dictatorship of the proletariat. The first measures were both political and economic. In the political field a large number of nationalist leaders who had chosen to remain in the country when the Communists seized power rather than flee to the West, as many of them did, were arrested, tried as "war criminals" or "enemies of the people," and were either executed or given long-term sentences at hard labor. All families considered potentially dangerous to the new regime, especially families of the landed aristocracy and the tribal chieftains, were herded into concentration or labor camps, in which most of them perished from exposure, malnutrition, and lack of health facilities. Some of these camps were still in existence in 1970.

In the economic field a special war-profits tax was levied, which amounted to a confiscation of the wealth and private property of the well-to-do classes. A large number of those who could not pay the tax, because it was higher than their cash and property assets, were sent to labor camps. All industrial plants and mines were nationalized without compensation, and a radical agrarian reform law was passed providing for the seizure of land belonging to the *beys* and other large landowners and its distribution to the landless peasants.

The 1944-48 period was characterized by an increase of power and influence of the Yugoslavs over the Party and the government. This in turn engendered resentment even among some top Party Leaders, who were kept in check or purged by Koci Xoxe, minister of interior and head of the secret police. Backed by the Yugoslavs, he had become the most powerful man in the Party and government but was tried in the spring of 1949 as a Titoist and executed. By the beginning of 1948 preparations had been completed to merge Albania with Yugoslavia, but the plan was not consummated because of the Stalin-Tito conflict, which resulted in Tito's expulsion from the Communist Information Bureau (Cominform—see Glossary) on June 28, 1948.

The Stalin-Tito rupture offered Enver Hoxha and his closest colleagues in the Albanian Party Political Bureau (Politburo) the opportunity to rid themselves of both their internal enemies, such as Koci Xoxe, and of Yugoslav domination. A few days after the Cominform resolution against Tito, the Albanian rulers expelled all Yugoslav experts and advisers and denounced most of the political, military, and economic agreements. Albania immediately established close relations with Moscow, although Stalin never signed a mutual assistance pact with Tirana, as he had done with all the other European Communist countries. The Party leadership was now concentrated in the hands of Enver Hoxha and Mehmet Shehu. Shehu had been dismissed in January 1948 as Chief of Staff of the Albanian People's Army, because he had opposed the integration of the Yugoslav and Albanian armed forces and the stationing of two Yugoslav divisions on Albanian soil. He was rehabilitated immediately after the break with Yugoslavia.

The period of direct Soviet influence in Albania began in September 1948, when the first joint economic agreement was signed. After the establishment of the Council for Economic Mutual Assistance (CEMA) in February 1949, of which Albania became a member, the other Soviet bloc countries began to extend economic aid. As a result, an intensified program of economic development began. From 1951 to 1955 industrial and agricultural production increased rapidly, and the basis was laid for transforming Albania from a backward agricultural economy to a more balanced agricultural-industrial one.

The de-Stalinization campaign in the Soviet Union had serious repercussions in the internal situation in Albania. Although Hoxha vetoed any relaxation of police controls and stamped out any dissenting voice within the Party after Stalin's death, by 1956 there was a significant minority in the Party elite that hoped to profit by de-Stalinization. The opposition reached its peak at a Party conference in Tirana in April 1956, held in the aftermath of the Soviet Twentieth Party Congress. Some of the delegates, including Central Committee members, criticized openly the conditions in the Party and requested that the topics of discussion be concerned with such topics as the cult of personality, the rehabilitation of Koci Xoxe and other top Party leaders purged since 1948, Party democracy, and the people's standard of living.

Hoxha silenced the dissident elements, however, and had most of them expelled from the Party or arrested. Some were subsequently executed. Among those executed were Lira Gega, formerly a member of the Politburo, and her husband, Dalli Ndreu, a general in the Albanian People's Army. Soviet Premier Khrushchev charged at the Soviet Twenty-second Congress that Gega was pregnant when she was executed.

Workers' riots in Poland and full-scale revolt in Hungary in late 1956, followed by general uneasiness throughout Communist East Europe, gave Hoxha additional reasons to increase his control over the Party apparatus and to sidestep all pressures from Khrushchev for reconciliation with Tito. Indeed, in an article published in the November 8, 1956, issue of the Soviet newspaper *Pravda* (Truth), Hoxha accused Yugoslavia of being at the root of the Hungarian Revolution and implied that the relaxation of internal tensions in some of the Soviet-bloc countries had endangered the existing regimes. In a speech to the Party's Central Committee in February 1957 he came openly to the defense of Stalin and lashed out against "those who attempt to discount the entire positive revolutionary side of Stalin."

Hoxha did, however, pay lip service to the collective leadership principle enunciated in Moscow after Stalin's death. In July 1954 he relinquished the premiership to Mehmet Shehu, keeping for himself the more important post of first secretary of the Party. But aside from this he made no changes in his Stalinist method of rule. He demonstrated this after the Party conference in Tirana in April 1956, when he suppressed ruthlessly all those demanding the elimination of personal rule.

Hoxha showed the same determination in the summer of 1961, when Khrushchev apparently enlisted a number of Albanian leaders, including Teme Sejko, a rear admiral and commander of the navy who had been trained in the Soviet Union to overthrow the Hoxha-Shehu duumvirate and replace it with a pro-Moscow group. Sejko and his colleagues were arrested, and he and two others were later executed.

In September of the same year Hoxha arrested a number of other top Party leaders who were suspected of pro-Moscow sympathies. Among these were Liri Belishova, a member of the Politburo, and Koco Tashko, head of the Party's Auditing Commission; these two were also cited by Khrushchev as examples of the alleged reign of terror that prevailed in Albania.

After the break with Moscow, Albania remained nominally a member of both the CEMA and the Warsaw Pact. It did not, however, attend any meetings, and it withdrew officially from the Warsaw Pact after the Soviet invasion of Czechoslovakia in 1968.

Unlike Albania's relations with the Communist world, which have been varied and fluctuating, those with the Western countries have been, with minor exceptions, static and rigid, particularly toward the United States. Only two major Western powers, France and Italy, initially recognized the Communist regime and established diplomatic relations with it. Proposals made in November 1945 by the American and British governments to normalize relations with the Tirana regime were never consummated, chiefly because of the regime's consistent inimical attitude toward them.

There have been three distinct periods in the history of the country under Communist rule. The first, from 1944 to 1948, was characterized by Yugoslav domination. The country's rulers, however, had no difficulty extricating themselves from this domination once Stalin broke with Tito.

In the second period, 1948 to 1961, Soviet predominance was evident everywhere in the country. All the armed and security forces wore Soviet-type uniforms. The regime copied much of the Soviet governmental system. The same kind of bureaucracy and the same secret police, functioning with the same supervision as in the Stalinist era in the Soviet Union, prevailed. In major branches of the government, the military, and the security forces, there were Soviet advisers and experts. The economic and cultural fields were also patterned after those of the Soviet Union. But despite this widespread penetration, the Soviets were in the last analysis unable to impose their will on the Albanian rulers, and in 1961 they withdrew completely from that country.

The third period, begun in 1961, saw the penetration of Communist Chinese influence in many aspects of political, military, and economic life. Like the Yugoslavs and Soviets before them, the Chinese introduced their advisers and experts in various governmental organs and economic enterprises, and probably in the military and security forces as well, but they were there at the invitation of the Albanian regime (see ch. 6, Government Structure and Political System).

CHAPTER 3

PHYSICAL ENVIRONMENT

Albania has land borders on the north and east with Yugoslavia and on the south and southeast with Greece. Tirana, the capital, is less than an hour by aircraft from eight other European capitals and barely more than two hours from the most distant of them. The coastline is adjacent to shipping lanes that have been important since early Greek and Roman times. Nevertheless, partly because of its rugged terrain and partly because of its political orientation, the country remains remote and isolated from its European neighbors (see ch. 6, Government Structure and Political System).

The large expanses of rugged and generally inaccessible terrain provided refuge for the Albanian ethnic group and permitted its distinctive identity to survive throughout the centuries. Although the country was almost always under foreign domination, it was never extensively colonized because of the lack of arable land, easily exploitable resources, and natural inland transportation routes. It has been, and continues to be, poorly developed. Agricultural and pastoral pursuits have been the primary means of livelihood, and only after 1950 did industry begin to be developed to any appreciable degree.

Until recently, the coastal lowlands supported few people and did not provide easy access to the interior. The mountains that constitute 70 percent of the country's area are difficult to traverse and generally inhospitable. Rivers are almost entirely unnavigable, and only in the south are there valleys wide enough to link the coast with the interior. By 1970 no railway and only three good roads crossed the national borders.

The physical characteristics of the land have contributed to differing living conditions and social relationships in the various sectors of the country. Before independence in 1912, the area of modern Albania had never been politically integrated, nor had it ever been an economically viable unit. It owes its existence as a state to the ethnic factor, and survival of the ethnic group is attributable to the natural isolation of the country.

The area is 11,100 square miles. The boundaries, established in principle in 1913 and demarcated in 1923, were essentially unchanged in 1970, although Greece had not dropped its claim to a large part of southern Albania. The eastern boundary divides the Macedonian lake district among three states—Albania, Greece, and Yugoslavia—that have ethnic populations in the area and follows high mountain ridges wherever possible to the north and south of the lakes. The northern and southern borders were drawn to achieve a separation between the Albanians and neighboring nationalities, although there is a large group of Albanians in the Kosovo area of Yugoslavia across the northeastern border, and Greeks and Albanians intermingle in the southeast (see fig. 1).

Resources are insufficient to make the country wealthy, and some that are available have not been thoroughly exploited. Interior regions have been inaccessible. Agricultural land has been inefficiently used for centuries because people having large landholdings preferred to maintain more profitable livestock herds rather than cultivate the earth for foodstuff production. Malaria, until the 1930s, prevented development or reclamation of the coastal lowlands. Lacking the capital investment necessary, extensive development projects had not been undertaken by 1970.

The lowlands and the lower mountains of the south have a Mediterranean climate; weather in the northern and eastern highlands is dominated by the continental air masses that persist over central and Eastern Europe. Overall rainfall is plentiful throughout the country, but most areas receive it seasonally.

Apart from the bare rock mountains and portions of the alluvial lowlands that are alternately parched and inundated, most of the land encourages a wide variety of wild vegetation. Areas suitable for cultivation, however, are small. There are good soils on about 5 percent of the land surface, but land three or four times that percentage is considered arable. Forests cover nearly one-half of the land. About one-fourth is suitable for grazing animals.

The citizen relates closely to the land. Although he has been nationally independent for only a few years in the twentieth century and very seldom earlier, his property has been so difficult to reach that occupying powers have often left him alone. The land has had beauty that has fostered pride and loyalty, and a hardy breed has survived the constant struggle to derive an existence from it.

NATURAL REGIONS

The 70 percent of the country that is mountainous is rugged and often inaccessible. The remaining alluvial plain receives its precipitation seasonally, is poorly drained, is alternately arid or flooded, and much of it is devoid of fertility. Far from offering a relief from the difficult interior terrain, it is often as inhospitable to its inhabitants as are the mountains. Good soil and dependable precipitation occur, however, in river basins within the mountains, in the lake district on the eastern border, and in a narrow band of slightly elevated land between the coastal plains and the higher interior mountains (see fig. 2).

North Albanian Alps

The mountains of the far north of Albania are an extension of the Dinaric Alpine chain and, more specifically, the Montenegrin limestone (karst) plateau. They are, however, more folded and rugged than the more typical portions of the plateau. The rivers have deep valleys with steep sides and do not furnish arable valley floors; most of the grazing and farming are done on the flatter mountaintops. The rivers provide little access into the area and are barriers to communication within it. Roads are few and poor. Lacking internal communications and external contacts, a tribal society flourished within this Alpine region for centuries. Only after World War II were serious efforts made to incorporate the people of the region into the remainder of the country.

Southern Mountains

The extent of the region occupied by the southern mountains is not settled to the satisfaction of all authorities. Some include all of the area in a large diamond shape roughly encompassing all the uplands of southern Albania beneath lines connecting Vlore, Elbasan, and Korce. Although this area has trend lines of the same type and orientation, it includes mountains that are associated more closely with the systems in the central part of the country. Other authorities confine the area to the mountains that are east of Vlore and south of the Vijose River. These have features generally common to southern Albania and the adjacent Greek Epirus. This demarcation is considered preferable because it more nearly defined a traditional area that tends to lose some of the more purely national character of the lands north of it.

The southern ranges revert again to the northwest to southeast trend lines characteristic of the Dinaric Alps. They are, however, more gentle and accessible than the serpentine zone, the eastern highlands, or the North Albanian Alps. Transition to the lowlands is less abrupt, and arable valley floors are wider. Limestone is predominant, contributing to the cliffs and clear water along the Albanian Riviera. An intermixture of softer rocks has eroded and become the basis for the sedimentation that has resulted in wider valleys between the ridges than are common in the remainder of the country. This terrain encouraged the development of larger landholdings, thus influencing the social structure of the area (see ch. 5, Social System).

Source: Adapted from Norman J. G. Pounds, *Eastern Europe*, Chicago, 1969, p. 824.

Figure 2. Landform Regions in Albania

Lowlands

A low coastal belt extends from the northern boundary southward to about Vlore. It averages less than ten miles deep but widens to about thirty miles in the Elbasan area. In its natural state it is characterized by low scrub vegetation, varying from barren to dense. There are large areas of marshland and other areas of bare eroded badlands. Where elevations rise slightly and precipitation is regular—in the foothills of the central uplands, for example—the land is excellent. Marginal land is being reclaimed wherever irrigation is possible.

The land itself is of recent geological origin. It has been, and is being, created by sediments from the many torrents that erode the interior mountains. New alluvial deposits tend to be gravelly, without humus, and require many years before sufficient vegetation to make them fertile can be established. The sedimentation process, moreover, raises river channels above the level of the nearby terrain. Channels change frequently, devastating areas that have not been stabilized and creating marshes in others by blocking off the drainage. Road builders are confronted with difficult and constantly changing conditions.

Rainfall is heavy during the winter and is infrequent to nonexistent during nearly half the year. Mosquitoes thrive in the hot, humid, and marshy land. Only since about 1930 have there been effective measures to control malaria. Before then no extensive working of areas near the marshes could be seriously considered. For these reasons the coastal zone, in addition to supporting few people, has until relatively recently acted as a barrier, hindering, rather than encouraging, contact with the interior.

Coastal hills descend abruptly to Ionian Sea beaches along the Albanian Riviera from Vlore Bay southward to about Sarande. The 500- and 1,000-foot contour lines are within a mile or so of the water along nearly the entire distance. In the northern portion a 4,000-foot ridge is frequently only two to three miles inland. South of Sarande is another small area of coastal lowlands fronting on the Ionian Sea and separated from the Greek island of Corfu (Kerkira) by a mile-wide channel. Climate and soil conditions permit the cultivation of citrus fruits in this southernmost area of Albania.

Central Uplands

The central uplands region extends south from the Drin River valley, which marks the southern boundary of the North Albanian Alpine area, to the southern mountains. It is an area of generally lower mountain terrain immediately east of the lowlands. In the north, from the Drin River to the vicinity of Elbasan, it constitutes an area about twenty miles wide. It narrows to practically nothing in the vicinity of Elbasan, then widens into a broader triangular shape with its base against the southern mountains. Earth shifting along the faultline that roughly defines the western edge of the central uplands causes frequent and occasionally severe earthquakes. Major damage occurred over wide areas in 1967 and 1969.

Softer rocks predominate in the uplands. The most extensive are flysch, a soft crumbly rock that is usually sandstone but frequently contains shales, sandy limestones, and marl. This type of formation erodes rapidly and is the basis of much of the poor alluvial lowland soil. The ridges of the uplands are extensions of the Dalmatian coastal range that enters Albania from Yugoslavia. Elevations are generally moderate, between 1,000 and 3,000 feet with a few reaching above 5,000 feet.

Serpentine Zone

Although there are rugged terrain and high points in the central uplands, the first major mountain range inland from the Adriatic is an area of predominantly serpentine rock. The serpentine zone extends nearly the length of the country, from the North Albanian Alps to the Greek border south of Korce, an area 10 to 20 miles wide and over 125 miles in length lying generally between the central uplands and the eastern highlands. At Elbasan, however, it makes nearly direct contact with the coastal plain, and it reaches the eastern border for nearly 50 miles in, and north of, the lake region. Within its zone there are many areas in which sharp limestone and sandstone outcroppings predominate over the serpentine, although the ranges as a whole are characterized by rounded mountain features.

The serpentine rock derives its name from its dull green color and often mottled or spotted appearance. It can occur in several states. Iron, nickel, or other metals can substitute in its chemical formula for the more prevalent magnesium and will cause color variations.

Eastern Highlands

The mountains east of the serpentine zone are the highest in the country and are the basis for part of the eastern boundary. They occupy a narrow strip south of Lakes Ohrid and Prespa, and a similar one, also running north and south, lies between the White Drin River and the Yugoslav city of Debar. A peak in the Korab range, on the border north of Debar, exceeds 9,000 feet. The ranges have north-south trend lines. Geologically young and composed largely of hard limestone rocks, the eastern highlands, together with the North Albanian Alps and the serpentine zone, are the most rugged and inaccessible of any terrain on the Balkan Peninsula.

Lake Region

The three lakes of easternmost Albania are part of the Macedonian lake district. The Yugoslav border passes through Lake Ohrid; all but a small tip of Little Lake Prespa is in Greece; and the point at which the boundaries of all three states meet is in Lake Prespa. The two larger lakes have areas of about 100 square miles each, and Little Lake Prespa is about one-fifth as large. These are total surface areas, including the portions on both sides of the national boundary lines. The surface elevation is about 2,285 feet for Lake Ohrid and about 2,800 feet for the other two. The lakes are remote and picturesque. Lake Ohrid is fed primarily from underground springs and is blue and very clear. At times its transparency can approach 70 feet. A good percentage of the terrain in the vicinity of the lakes is not overly steep, and it supports a larger population than any other inland portion of the country.

NATIONAL BOUNDARIES

The distinct ethnic character of the people and their isolation within a fairly restricted and definable area brought support for their demands for independence in the early twentieth century. There were places where different ethnic populations intermingled, and there were other pressures that affected the definition of the borders. The Kosovo area across the northeastern border is a part of modern Yugoslavia, but it contains a substantial Albanian population. There are Greeks and Albanians in the mountains on both sides of the southeastern boundary. Albania is not content with the Kosovo situation, and neither Greece nor Albania is satisfied with the division effected by their mutual border.

The country is the smallest in Eastern Europe and has a perimeter of only 750 miles. The border shared with Yugoslavia runs northward from Lake Prespa, around northern Albania, to the Adriatic Sea for a total of just under 300 miles. Forty miles of this border follows river courses, and an almost equal distance is within lakes. The Greek border from the common point in Lake Prespa southwest to the Ionian Sea is about 160 miles long. Twelve miles of this border are within lakes but, because it crosses the trend lines of the southern mountain ranges, only four miles are along rivers.

The Adriatic and Ionian coastline is just under 300 miles long. The lowlands of the west face the Adriatic Sea and the Strait of Otranto, which is a mere 47 miles from the heel of the Italian boot. The Albanian Riviera, the coastline that runs southeast from Vlore, is on the Ionian Sea.

With the exception of the coastline, all Albanian borders are artificial. They were established in principle at the 1913 Conference of Ambassadors in London. The country was occupied by the warring powers during World War I, but the 1913 boundaries were reaffirmed at Versailles in 1921. Finally demarcated in 1923, they were confirmed by the Paris Agreement of 1926 and were essentially unchanged in 1970. The original principle was to define the borders in accordance with the best interests of the Albanian ethnic group and the nationalities in adjacent areas. The northern and eastern borders were intended, insofar as possible, to separate the Albanians from the Serbian and Montenegrin peoples; the southeast border was to separate Albanians and Greeks; and the valuable western Macedonia lake district was to be divided among the states whose populations shared the area.

When there was no compromise involving other factors, borderlines were chosen to make the best possible separation of national groups, connecting the best marked physical features available. Allowance was made for local economic situations, to keep from separating a village from its animals' grazing areas or from the markets for its produce. Political pressures also were a factor in the negotiations, but the negotiations were subject to approval by powers having relatively remote interests, most of which involved the balance of power rather than economic ambitions.

Division of the lake district among three states required that each of them have a share of the lowlands in the vicinity. Such a distribution was artificial but, once made, necessarily influenced the borderlines to the north and south. The border that runs generally north from the lakes, although it follows the ridges of the eastern highlands, stays some ten to twenty miles west of the watershed divide.

Proceeding counterclockwise around northern Albania, the watershed divide was abandoned altogether along the northeast boundary. In the process a large Albanian population in Kosovo was incorporated into Yugoslavia.

In the extreme north and the northeastern mountainous sections, the border with Yugoslavia connects high points and follows mountain ridges through the North Albanian Alps where there is little movement of the people. There is no natural topographic dividing line from the highlands, through Lake Scutari, to the Adriatic, but the lake and a portion of the Buene River south of it were used. From the lake district south and southwest to the Ionian Sea, the boundary runs perpendicular to the terrain trend lines and crosses a number of ridges instead of following them.

LOCAL ADMINISTRATIVE AREAS

The twenty-six districts that are the primary administrative subdivisions of the country have evolved from divisions that have existed for many years or have developed over a period of time (see fig. 3). In the northern third of the country, district lines were based on the territory occupied by tribal groups. In the part of the country south from about Tirana, they were based on the large landholdings controlled by those who in earlier years had governed the areas for the Ottomans.

Upon independence most of the old local boundaries, long understood if not always precisely defined, were retained, and the areas became prefectures. Before World War II there were ten prefectures, which in turn were divided into about forty subprefectures. The Communist regime did not abandon the prefectures immediately but eventually replaced them with districts that were, generally, based on the old subprefectures. In a series of changes, the latest of which were made in December 1967, the districts were consolidated into the twenty-six that existed in 1970. The districts are much the same size. Sixteen of them have areas ranging between 300 and 600 square miles. The largest, Shkoder, has about 980 square miles; the smallest, Lezhe, has about 180.

Changes in the areas and boundaries of the districts made during the 1960s were based chiefly on economic considerations, although political and security considerations also played a part. A major factor has been the collectivization of agriculture. In 1968 and 1969, for example, when the government decided to enlarge the collective farms, district lines were shifted in order to keep all of the land in a collective within the same district (see ch. 6, Government Structure and Political System).

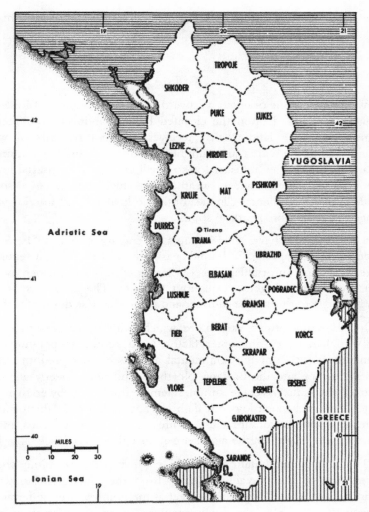

Source: Adapted from *Vjetari Statistikor i R. P. Sh., 1967-1968*, Tirana,
1968, frontispiece.

Figure 3. Administrative Districts in Albania

Although there are natural barriers to almost all movement in the
country, there are few, if any, that contribute to the boundaries of the
districts. Eight districts border on the seashore, but only three of them have
more lowland than mountainous terrain. The Shkoder District, for
example, has all of the lowlands in the vicinity of the city and almost half of
the most mountainous portion of the North Albanian Alps. In a few
instances the borders of interior districts follow the river valleys, but it is

more usual for them to contain segments of the rivers and, when this is the case, their boundary lines stay in the higher regions.

CLIMATE

With its coastline oriented westward onto the Adriatic and Ionian seas, its highlands backed upon the elevated Balkan landmass, and the entire country lying at a latitude that receives different patterns of weather systems during the winter and summer seasons, Albania has a number of climatic regions highly unusual for so small an area. The coastal lowlands have typically Mediterranean weather; the highlands have a so-called Mediterranean continental climate. Both the lowland and interior weather change markedly from north to south.

The lowlands have mild winters, averaging about 45°F. Summer temperatures average 75°F., humidity is high, and the season tends to be oppressively uncomfortable. The southern lowlands are warmer, averaging about five degrees higher throughout the year. The difference is greater than five degrees during the summer and somewhat less during the winter.

Inland temperatures vary more widely with differences in elevation than with latitude or any other factor. Cold winter temperatures in the mountains result from the continental air masses that predominate over Eastern Europe and the Balkans. Northerly and northeasterly winds blow much of the time. Average summer temperatures are lower than in the coastal areas and much lower at high elevations, but daily fluctuations are greater. Daytime maximum temperatures in the interior basins and river valleys are very high, but the nights are almost always cool (see table 1).

The average precipitation over the country is high resulting from the convergence of the prevailing airflow from the Mediterranean with the continental air mass. They usually meet at the point where the terrain rises. Arriving at that line, the Mediterranean air meets increasing ground elevations that force it to rise and an air mass that tends to resist its further progress. This causes the heaviest rainfall in the central uplands. Vertical currents initiated when the Mediterranean air is uplifted also result in frequent thunderstorms. Many of them in this area are violent and are accompanied by high local winds and torrential downpours.

Table 1. Temperature and Precipitation Averages for Selected Locations in Albania

Average Temperatures*	Annual

Place	Location	Elevation (in feet)	Annual	Coldest month	Warmest month	precipitation (in inches)
Shkoder	Northern coastal lowlands	50	59	40	78	80
Durres	Central coastal lowlands	Sea level	61	47	77	38
Vlore	Southern coastal lowlands	Sea level	62	48	77	39
Sarande	Albanian Riviera	Sea level	63	—	—	55
Tirana	Mid-Albania at base of central uplands	360	58	42	76	49
Puke	North-central uplands	2,850	51	34	70	72
Kruje	Central uplands	2,000	55	39	71	67
Korce	Eastern highlands	2,850	51	—	—	30

* In degrees Fahrenheit.

Source: Adapted from *Vjetari Statistikor i R. P. Sh., 1967-1968*. Tirana, , pp. 18-19; and Great Britain, Admiralty, Naval Intelligence Division, *Albania*, London, 1945, p. 93.

When the continental system is weak, Mediterranean winds drop their moisture farther inland. When there is a dominant continental air mass, it spills cold air onto the lowland areas. This occurs most frequently in the winter season. Since the season's lower temperatures damage olive trees and citrus fruits, their groves and orchards are restricted to sheltered places with southern and western exposures, even in areas that have seemingly high average winter temperatures.

Lowland rainfall averages from forty to nearly sixty inches annually, increasing between those extremes from south to north. Nearly 95 percent of the rain falls during the rainy season.

Rainfall in the upland mountain ranges is higher. Adequate records are not available, and estimates vary widely, but annual averages are probably about 70 inches and are as high as 100 inches in some northern areas. The seasonal variation is not quite as great as in the coastal area, with the most nearly even distribution in the north, largely because of summer thunderstorms.

The higher inland mountains receive less precipitation than the intermediate uplands. Terrain differences cause wide local variations, but the seasonal distribution is the most consistent of any area. In the northern mountains, for example, the months that usually have the highest averages are November and June.

DRAINAGE

All but a very small portion of the precipitation drains through the rivers to the coastline without leaving the country. With the exception of a few insignificant trickles, only one small stream in the northern part of the country escapes Albania. In the south an even smaller rivulet drains into Greece. As the divide is on the eastern side of the borders with Yugoslavia and Greece, however, a considerable amount of water from those countries drains through Albania. A quite extensive portion of the White Drin River basin is in the Kosovo area across the northeastern Yugoslav border. The three lakes shared with Yugoslavia and Greece, as well as all the streams that flow into them, drain into the Drin River. The watershed divide in the south also dips nearly forty miles into Greece at one point. Several tributaries of the Vijose River rise in that area (see fig. 4).

Figure 4. Rivers and Lakes in Albania

With the exception of the Drin River, which flows northward and drains nearly the entire eastern border region before it turns westward to the sea, most of the rivers in the northern and central parts of the country flow much more directly westward to the sea. In the process they cut through the ridges rather than flowing around them. This apparent impossibility came about because the highlands were originally lifted without much folding. The streams came into existence at that time and antedate the ridges because the compression and folding of the plateau occurred later. The folding process was rapid enough in many instances to block the rivers temporarily, forming lakes that existed until the downstream channel was cut sufficiently to drain them. This sequence created the many interior basins that are typically a part of the landforms. During the lifetimes of the temporary lakes enough sediment was deposited in them to form the basis for fertile soils. Folding was only infrequently rapid enough to force the streams to radically different channels.

The precipitous fall from higher elevations and the highly irregular seasonal flow patterns that are characteristic of nearly all streams in the country reduce the immediate value of the streams. They erode the mountains and deposit the sediment that created, and continues to add to, the lowlands, but the rivers flood during the seasons when there is local rainfall. When the lands are parched and need irrigation, the rivers are usually dry. Their violence makes them difficult to control, and they are unnavigable. The Buene is an exception. It is dredged between Shkoder and the Adriatic and is navigable for small ships. In contrast to their histories of holding fast to their courses in the mountains, the rivers have constantly changed channels on the lower plains, making wastes of much of the land they have created.

The Drin River is the largest and most constant stream (see table 2). Fed by melting snows from the northern and eastern mountains and by the more evenly distributed seasonal precipitation of that area, its flow does not have the extreme variations characteristic of nearly all other rivers in the country. Its normal flow varies seasonally by only about one-third. Along its length of about 175 miles it drains nearly 2,300 square miles within Albania. As it also collects from the Adriatic portion of the Kosovo watershed and the three border lakes (Lake Prespa drains to Lake Ohrid via an underground stream), its total basin is around 6,000 square miles.

The Seman and Vijose are the only other rivers that are more than 100 miles in length and have basins larger than 1,000 square miles. These rivers drain the southern regions and, reflecting the seasonal distribution of rainfall, are torrents in winter and nearly dry in the summer, in spite of their relatively long lengths. This is also the case with the many shorter streams. In the summer most of them carry less than a tenth of their winter averages, if they are not altogether dry.

Table 2. Drainage Basins in Albania

Drainage basin	Length of river (in miles)	Area of basin (in square miles)
Drin	174	2,263*
Seman	157	2,305
Vijose	147	1,682
Shkumbin	91	918
Mat	65	964

Erzen	56	301
Ishm	43	244
Buene**	27	623

* Within Albania only.

** Includes Lake Scutari.

Source: Adapted from Athanas Gegaj and Rexhep Krasniqi, *Albania*, New York, 1964, p. 8.

The sediment carried by the mountain torrents continues to be deposited but, having created the lowlands, new deposits delay their exploitation. Stream channels rise as silt is deposited in them and eventually become higher than the surrounding terrain. Changing channels frustrate development in many areas. Old channels become barriers to proper drainage and create swamps or marshlands. It has been difficult to build roads or railroads across the lowlands or to use the land.

Irrigation has been accomplished ingeniously by Albanian peasants for many years, to the degree that they and their expertise have been sought after throughout Europe. Projects required to irrigate or to reclaim large areas of the lowlands, however, are on a scale that probably cannot be accomplished without financial assistance from outside the country.

Although water is available in quantities adequate for irrigation and it has the amount of fall necessary for hydroelectric power production, terrain and seasonal factors are such that major capital investment would be required for both irrigation and power projects. Snow stabilizes drainage of the higher northern and eastern mountains but, unfortunately, the only major snow accumulations are in the Drin basin, influencing only the one river system.

NATURAL RESOURCES

Soils

Soil resources are small. Arable land figures notwithstanding, good agricultural land amounts to only about 5 percent of the country's area. Soils over limestone are thin or altogether lacking. Serpentine rock erodes slowly and produces clays of little agricultural value. The softer rocks of the intermediate mountains crumble easily into course and infertile sands and gravels that take many years to acquire humus. The alluvial soil of the lowland plains, therefore, tends to be sterile in addition to receiving its precipitation seasonally and being poorly drained. There is little land along the narrow valley floors. The best soils, those within the inland basins, are excellent. The narrow margin of slightly elevated land between the coastal plains and the mountains also provides excellent arable fields.

Vegetation

Western sources have estimated that, in 1969, 11 percent of the land area was arable, of which nearly one-half was in use as vineyards and olive groves. Forests covered just over one-third of the land, and pastures just under one-third. About 22 percent of the land was unproductive, but one-half of the unproductive areas had a potential for development. Albanian government pronouncements have stated that about 20 percent of the land was arable in 1968 and that this figure would be increased to 22 percent in 1970. The discrepancies in land use statistics arise from varying interpretations as to the amount of pastureland that is arable. Much that Albanian sources have claimed as newly arable almost certainly is marginally so.

Dependence upon corn as the primary staple crop in much of the country and limited amounts of arable land tended, until about 1950, to prevent proper crop rotation. The government is attempting to introduce more scientific agricultural practices and has claimed improved crop yields.

Although the amount of land that can be cultivated for the production of foodstuffs is meager, the remoteness of the interior has allowed natural flora to exist over fairly extensive areas with little disturbance. A large variety of species flourishes, and an unusual number of them are found in that vicinity only. Of some 2,300 seed-bearing plants, over 300 appear in the Balkans alone, and more than 50 occur only in Albania.

The land considered forest includes areas that contain little more than scrub ground cover and others that have been ravaged by unsystematic cutting. More than half of the forests, however, contain mature trees and, owing largely to their inaccessibility, have escaped the reckless harvesting that destroyed many lower elevation forests during the first years of the country's independence.

Maquis, a Mediterranean scrub tree, grows to about fifteen or twenty feet, can be extremely dense, and is the most frequent ground cover at low elevations. It withstands dry weather and, although it is of little value as a tree and does not of itself build a rich soil, it stabilizes the alluvial lowlands and provides cover for better humus-producing vegetation. Maquis can survive at slightly higher elevations in sheltered conditions, but it is usually found below 1,000 or 1,300 feet. Most maquis species are evergreen. Deciduous scrub, usually Christ's-thorn, or *shiblijak*, is also common in the lowlands, but it occurs much less frequently than maquis.

The oaks are the most important of trees. Oak forests have never reattained the majesty they had during the days of Venice's power when they could be called upon to furnish 400 shiploads of straight oak stems for Venetian fleets, but in 1970 they still constituted nearly half of all forests. The oaks are valuable not only for their economic worth as fuel and lumber but also because the leaves of deciduous varieties and the undergrowth encouraged beneath them are excellent soil builders. Occurring at moderate elevations, however, they have been accessible and overexploited. Lowland oak forests contain poorer species that rarely grow in excess of thirty feet tall, but the thick undergrowth they usually allow provides stability and improves the alluvial soil. The finer and more valuable species occur at middle and higher elevations. Oak forests predominate between 1,000- and 3,000-foot elevations but occur up to about 4,000 feet.

Beech trees appear at all elevations between 3,000 feet and the timberline. They predominate in northern areas between about 3,500 and 6,000 feet. In the south they flourish at the same elevations but are usually outnumbered by conifers. Beech is excellent hard wood, and its leaves are among the best of soil builders. The trees generate most of the humus themselves, as their canopies interlace tightly in mature forests, permitting relatively little undergrowth to flourish on the forest floors beneath them. Mature forests have survived in many of the remote, inaccessible areas that beech species prefer. The most copious forests are in cloud forest regions where cloud cover is almost constant, rainfall is frequent, and temperatures do not usually reach the extreme highs.

The better conifers, usually including several pine species in the north and fir, with lesser numbers of pine and spruce, in the south, coexist with beech but tolerate poorer soils and tend to predominate at the highest elevations. Although they tend to have less continuous canopies than beech forests, they do not encourage undergrowth. Their needles, along with rapid decay of their softer dead wood, however, can create deep humus. The poorer quality lowland pines do well at elevations down to sea level and will tolerate certain conditions, although not overly poor drainage, in which the oak will not survive. Its woods usually have discontinuous canopies and allow dense maquis and other lower shrubs to flourish beneath them.

True mixed woods, sometimes referred to as karst woods, occur at medium elevations. They are usually almost entirely deciduous but have wide varieties of species. The larger trees include maple, ash, beech, and oak, but these are vastly outnumbered. Intermediate varieties of hawthorne, dogwood, hazel, and cherry flourish among the larger trees, and hundreds of smaller plants, ranging from bushes, shrubs, and ferns to grasses and moss, provide ground cover. With a profusion of varieties in constant competition for available space and soil, those that do best in a particular soil mixture prosper in a given locality. Because the soil in the uplands relates closely to the base rock and the mountains were created by geologically recent folding that has exposed the edges of layered rock formations, there are abrupt changes in the basic surface rock. This is reflected immediately in mixed woods by equally abrupt changes in the species that appear.

Of the more abundant smaller flora families, the daisy, pea, grass, pink, nettle, mustard, parsley, figwort, rose, buttercup, and lily groups has more than fifty species that can be found within Albania. Flowering plants flourish especially well in limestone areas where there are masses of vividly colored wild flowers during the springtime. Must less brilliant colors appear on serpentine outcroppings and, as is the case with the mixed woods, the difference is abrupt where limestone and serpentine are the surface rocks in closely adjacent areas.

Wildlife

Summer livestock grazing in the mountains and uncontrolled hunting reduced wildlife to insignificance. Some deer, wild boar, and wolves remain in the more remote forests. Chamois were plentiful in the area but are now extremely rare. Wild fowl, however, are abundant in the lowland swamps and lower forests.

Minerals

Exploitation of the country's minerals generates the largest share of the gross industrial product and provides employment for the largest number of the industrial labor force. This does not indicate, however, that the country is rich in mineral resources, but it serves to underscore the still poorer state of its agricultural and industrial sectors and indicates that the country engages in relatively little international commerce.

There are considerable reserves in oil and natural gas. Oil can be extracted in quantity sufficient to meet domestic demands and to export. A pipeline from the oilfields at Stalin (formerly Kucove) transmits the oil to the port of Vlore. The crude oil, however, has a high sulfur content and is expensive to refine.

Chrome is the most important export commodity. Albania is the largest chrome source in Eastern Europe, and its mines have at times supplied about 2 percent of the world's total. Good-quality copper ore is also available in export quantities.

No hard coal veins are known, but lignite is plentiful and its deposits are accessible. Asphalt (bitumen) occurs in a concentrated deposit in one small area. This source has been actively worked for centuries. Some of it has been exported.

Iron, nickel, gold, and silver ores occur in less important deposits. Iron is plentiful, but the ores are of low grade. The other deposits are minor. Bauxite appears in quantity deposits in several areas. Sufficient year-round power sources, however, are not available to process it. Magnesite, arsenic, pyrites, and gypsum sources are worked. Clay and kaolin suitable for pottery are also extracted. Salt is abundant. Limestone is available throughout the country and quarried wherever it is needed.

TRANSPORTATION

Even when its territory sat astride a direct route between two points, Albania was usually bypassed because there was nearly always a longer way around that was easier and safer. As a result, its transportation links with the rest of the world are very few. Its internal systems are also inadequate for good communications within the country. All railways are short, internal routes, and the lines that were complete in 1970 connected only three of the major cities. Two primary roads, one of which was originally constructed by the Romans, cross into Greece, and a third crosses into Yugoslavia. Only a dozen more roads, all of them secondary, lead out of the country. There is little air traffic with the outside world; it usually involves connecting flights to major airlines in neighboring countries (see fig. 1).

Roads

Until the twentieth century only two major roads crossed what is now Albania. The Romans built the Via Egnatia, which makes an east-west transit from Durres (known as Dyrrhachium in Roman times), via the Shkumbin River valley, to the lake district. It continued eastward across the Balkan Peninsula to Thessaloniki and Constantinople (now Istanbul), and the Romans used it to move forces overland to the eastern portions of their empire. A north-south route, the Via Zenta, was built by Ragusan merchants during the period when Ragusa (now Dubrovnik) was a Balkan mercantile power and needed access to the interior of the peninsula. The road followed the Drin River valley. Both the Via Egnatia and the Via Zenta fell into disuse during the centuries of Ottoman control, but the basic course of the Roman road is followed by one of the few major highways that has been constructed in the twentieth century.

Independent Albania was slow to begin construction of roads that would better conform to the country's national requirements. During World War I Austrian forces built some 400 miles of strategic roads while they occupied the area. The Italians did the same during World War II. In both cases the objective was to improve communications with external points. There was no attempt to construct a network that would integrate the country.

The Hoxha regime has placed more emphasis on internal communications, and in 1969 it claimed that the principal road network had been expanded by three times over what it had been in 1938. Perhaps 3,000 miles could be classed as improved roads. These are considered all-weather roads, although those in the mountains may be closed by snows. Most of the surfaces are hardened with compacted stone or gravel, and a few have a tarry stabilizer. Better roads have asphalt surfaces. Road construction in almost all parts of the country is difficult, especially in bridge building, and some roads are construction masterpieces. Once built, however, routine maintenance has ordinarily not been properly accomplished, and surfaces have deteriorated.

Railways

The first standard-gauge railroad construction began in 1947. The Italians had started roadbeds during their World War II occupation but had abandoned their projects in 1943. By 1970 there were only about 135 miles of completed lines. These included basic lines between Durres and Tirana and between Durres and Elbasan. There is difficult terrain between Tirana and Elbasan and, although only about 20 miles apart, they are connected via Durres only.

The lines from Durres curve northward to Tirana and southward to approach Elbasan via the Shkumbin valley. A northern offshoot from the Durres-Tirana line is complete to Lac and will be extended to Shkoder. A southern offshoot from Rrogozhine on the Durres-Elbasan line is now in service to Fier and will be extended to Vlore. The combination of these two routes will constitute a coastal line from Shkoder to Vlore.

Construction was in progress in 1970 on a line that will connect Elbasan with Prrenjas, which is just over five miles from Lake Ohrid. This line follows the route of the old Roman Via Egnatia, and in later programs it will probably be extended to Lin, on the lake, and then southward to Korce. When these lines are completed, they and the road network will provide vastly improved internal communications, but many small areas within the North Albanian Alps and the higher central and eastern mountains will remain difficult to reach.

Pipeline

During the mid-1930s the Italian state-owned petroleum company constructed a forty-four-mile, eight-inch pipeline to connect the oilfields in the Stalin area with the port of Vlore. The line had a capacity of about 5,000 barrels a day and carried crude for transshipment to refineries in Italy. In the early 1950s the line was extended northward to the newly built refinery at Cerrik.

Airlines

In the early post-World War II period when Albania was practically a vassal state of Yugoslavia, regular air traffic was established between Belgrade and Tirana. After the estrangement of Yugoslavia from the Soviet Union, when Albania became a satellite of the Soviet Union, regular traffic was set up between Tirana and Moscow and, to a lesser degree, between Tirana and the capitals of the Eastern European Communist countries other than Belgrade. When Albania became aligned with Communist China, direct connections with almost all external points were severed. Even Peking flights were routed via intermediate stops in Italy, usually Bari or Rome.

Between 1967 and 1970 connections between Albania and most of the Eastern European countries, but not the Soviet Union, were gradually restored. Service is scheduled but infrequent. Weekly flights are typically connected through Belgrade. Traffic elsewhere is ordinarily routed via Italy. Albanian officials depart and reenter the country via Bari or Rome, connecting to Tirana on a scheduled Alitalia flight or by an Albanian flight. Internal air services are also limited. Those available are centered on Tirana.

Merchant Shipping

Because no railway leaves the country and border-crossing roads are inadequate, nearly all foreign trade is carried by sea. Durres and Vlore are the major ports. Durres has a first-class harbor, warehouses, petroleum storage tanks, a shipbuilding capability, and railway spurs to the docks. Vlore is a better natural port and is the terminus of the oil pipeline. It has fewer port facilities than Durres, however, and no rail connections with the rest of the country. Sarande, Shengjin, and Porte Palermo are less important ports.

Only the Drin and Buene rivers might be considered navigable to any degree and even then only for small ships and short distances. Lake Scutari and the interior lakes are navigable but are of little commercial use. Smaller oceangoing craft are used in a limited amount of coastal trade.

The government is encouraging the creation of a national merchant fleet. *Lloyd's Register of Shipping* for 1968 listed eleven Albanian vessels totaling 36,550 gross tons. Albania and Communist China maintain a jointly owned shipping line, and the number of ships with Albanian registry is increasing.

CHAPTER 4

THE PEOPLE

The population increased by about 71 percent from 1950 to 1969 and in 1970 was increasing at a rate that would double the number of inhabitants in approximately twenty-six years. The median age, about nineteen years, was increasing slowly. The abundance of rural population and the increasing tempo of industrial development provided potential for rapid urban growth, but government controls and a scarcity of housing tended to restrict population movements.

Persons of Albanian ethnic origin constituted about 97 percent of the 2.1 million population in early 1970. Of ancient Illyrian descent, they have maintained their homogeneity despite many invasions and centuries of foreign occupation. The Communist regime, in its effort to develop social and cultural solidarity, attempted to reduce consciousness of the differences between the major subgroups, the Gegs in the north and the Tosks in the south. Some progress has been made, but a continuing struggle is being carried out against customs and beliefs that are considered remnants of the past and detract from the achievement of Communist objectives (see ch. 5, Social System).

The Albanian language is a derivative of the tongues that were spoken by the ancient Illyrians and Thracians. For many centuries its continuity was maintained by only verbal means. A standardized alphabet was not developed until the twentieth century. Since World War II considerable progress has been made in making the Tosk dialect the standard written language. In the late 1960s there were still some variations in spelling.

The pattern of settlement was predominantly one of widely dispersed villages; approximately two-thirds of the people lived in communities with less than 1,000 population. Only twelve cities had more than 10,000 population in 1969. The quadrangular area formed by the cities of Durres, Tirana, Elbasan, and Fier, all of which are linked by rail and roads, was experiencing the most rapid growth in the 1960s.

There was a very slight improvement in living standards from 1950 to 1970. Despite modest growth in the economy, the per capita gross national product (GNP) in 1967 was the lowest in Europe, an estimated United States equivalent of $320. The average citizen's welfare in the allocation of resources for food, consumers' goods, and housing was sacrificed to the development of industry and the program to achieve eventual self-sufficiency in agriculture. Reduction of disease and improved health were the most important gains countrywide. Also, by 1970 electricity had been extended to over two-thirds of all villages. Consistently high levels of population growth placed severe strains on available supplies of food, consumers' goods, housing, and services.

POPULATION

The total population in January 1970 was an increase of approximately 500,000 over the 1960 official census total of 1,626,315. The distribution by age groups in 1970 was: under fifteen years of age, 42 percent; fifteen to thirty-nine years, 37 percent; forty to sixty-four years, 16 percent; and sixty-five years and over, 5 percent. With almost 60 percent of its inhabitants under forty years of age and a median age of approximately nineteen years, the population was extremely youthful, and indications were that it would remain so into the 1970s. The proportion of persons in the dependent age groups, under fifteen and over sixty-four years, to the working age group, fifteen to sixty-four years, was 887 to 1,000.

The overall ratio of males to females, 106 to 100, was the highest among the Communist countries of East Europe. The preponderance of men was greatest at ages below forty; in the age group above sixty-four there were only 77 men to 100 women. The higher ratio of men for the total population was attributed in part to the high infant mortality rate among female infants, caused by neglect and the deference accorded to male progeny. Losses in World War II, an estimated 28,800 persons, or 2.48 percent of the population, had little influence on the ratio of males to females and the population structure.

In keeping with the traditional pattern of a highly dispersed population, the country remains predominantly rural. About two-thirds live in villages and in the countryside. Urban population increased from about one-fifth to one-third of the total during the 1950-70 period and would have increased to a greater extent had the government not taken measures, beginning in the mid-1960s, to build up agriculture and to restrict city growth. During the drive to reduce the number of people involved in administration and to increase production forces in the mid-1960s, thousands of persons living in the city, including some from the bureaucracy and the Party, were sent to the country.

Housing in the cities was greatly overcrowded, and the allocation of new dwellings built by state funds and controlled by the government provided further restrictions on city growth. Indications were that the expansion of industry would continue to require urban growth but that the rate of growth would be controlled. The largest cities and their populations in 1967 were: Tirana, 170,603; Durres, 80,066; Vlore, 57,745; Korce, 53,563; and Shkoder, 49,095.

The birth rate declined only slightly from 1950 to 1970 and in 1968 was 35.5 per 1,000 population (see table 3). Fertility continued at a high level, and there were no apparent influences that tended to reduce the prevailing rate of births. No information was published concerning the effects, if any, on the birth rate of women's employment outside the home, abortions, contraceptives, or other restraints on population growth.

The expansion of medical services and improvement in the standard of health during the 1950s and 1960s resulted in a marked decline in the mortality rate, from 14 per 1,000 in 1950 to 8 per 1,000 in 1968. The age structure of the population, with a preponderance in the lower age brackets, provided the potential for a continuing low mortality rate.

A concomitant of the reduced death rate was an increase in life expectancy. Data from domestic sources indicated that the average life expectancy at birth increased from 53.5 years in 1950 to 66.1 years in 1965.

Because of the highly restrictive policies of the Communist regime, migration into and out of the country had a negligible influence on the size and composition of the population. Internal migration was controlled by requiring approval for persons to move from one location to another. Specific data on the scale and character of population movements were not available.

The pattern of sustained high birth rates and declining death rates resulted in high rates of natural increase. Total population increased by 71 percent from 1950 to 1969, whereas the average increase for all other East European Communist countries, excluding the Soviet Union, was 18 percent. The growth rate for 1970 was estimated at 2.7 percent.

Government and Party leaders, voicing the need for greater numbers of people for the building of socialism, supported a continuing high level of population growth. They were undeterred, in the face of persistent shortages of food and the requirement for foreign assistance, in their encouragement of a sustained high birth rate and the payment of an allowance for each child.

Table 3. Albanian Vital Statistics for Selected Years, 1950-68 (per thousand population)

	Natural

Year	Birth	Death	increase
1950	38.5	14.0	24.5
1960	43.3	10.4	32.9
1968	35.5	8.0	27.5

Source: Adapted from U.S. Department of Commerce, Office of Technical Services, Joint Publications Research Service (Washington), "Protection of Mother and Child Health, the High Expression of Socialist Humanism, Realized by the Party During the 25 Years of People's Power," by Vera Ngjela et al., in Shendetesia Popullore (People's Health), Tirana, 1969 (JPRS: 50,302, *Translations on Eastern Europe, Political Sociological, and Military Affairs*, Nos. 204, 1970).

ETHNIC GROUPS

Persons of non-Albanian ethnic origin—Greeks, Vlachs, Bulgars, Serbs, and Gypsies—constitute only about 3 percent of the population. Among the Albanians, the natural dividing line between the Gegs and the Tosks is the Shkumbin River, but there is some spillover on both sides. Numerically, the Gegs predominate, making up slightly over one-half of the Albanians within the country (see ch. 2, Historical Setting).

Despite successive foreign invasions and centuries of occupation, a distinctive ethnic identity was preserved. Mountains and the lack of communication routes provided isolation and opportunity to evade intruders. Nevertheless, the imprints of foreign influences were considerable. Additions and modifications to the language were made from the Latin, Greek, Slavic, and Turkish contacts. Lacking an organized religion as part of their Illyrian heritage, Albanians embraced the Muslim, Orthodox, and Roman Catholic faiths brought to them by their conquerors (see ch. 5, Social System).

Individual Albanians distinguished themselves in the service of the Roman and Turkish empires and were noted for their ability as soldiers. It was not until the nineteenth century when they began to seek autonomy that their history was recorded in writing. Kinship and tribal affiliations, a common spoken language, and folk customs served to provide continuity and common identity through the many centuries of relative obscurity.

There are marked differences in the physical appearance of the typical Geg and the typical Tosk, but until World War II the greatest contrast was in their social systems. The Geg and Tosk dialects differ, and there are also variations within subgroups. Some progress was made under the Zog regime in bringing the clans, whose authority prevailed particularly in the north, under government control and in eliminating blood feuds (see ch. 5, Social System).

After the Communists emerged victorious they imposed controls, the objective of which was to eliminate clan rule entirely; they waged a continuing struggle against customs and attitudes that, they believed, detracted from the growth of socialism. Blood feuds were brought to an end. Party and government leaders, in their effort to develop national social and cultural solidarity in a Communist society, publicly tended to ignore ethnic differences.

In practice, Enver Hoxha, the Party leader, who came from the south and received the bulk of his support during World War II from that area, frequently gave preference to persons and customs of Tosk origin. In the late 1960s Party and government leaders continued to devote considerable effort to the suppression of customs and rituals that, they declared, were vestiges of the patriarchal, bourgeois, and religious systems of the past. On one occasion in 1968 the Party announced that because of its influence 450 infant betrothals were annulled and 1,000 girls renounced ancient customs, including the taboo against females leaving their village (see ch. 5, Social System).

The Gegs, because of their greater isolation in the mountainous areas of the north, held on to their tribal organization and customs more tenaciously than the Tosks. As late as the 1920s approximately 20 percent of male deaths in some areas of northern Albania were attributed to blood feuds.

Under the unwritten tribal codes, which included the regulation of feuds, any blow, as well as many offenses committed against women, called for blood. Permitting a girl who had been betrothed in infancy to marry another, for example, could cause a blood feud. The *besa* (pledge to keep one's word as a solemn obligation) was used under various conditions and included pledges to postpone quarrels. A person who killed a fellow tribesman was commonly punished by his neighbors, who customarily burned his house and destroyed his property. As fugitives from their own communities, such persons were given assistance wherever they applied.

A man who failed to carry out prescribed vengeance against a member of another tribe or that individual's relatives was subjected to intolerable ridicule. Insult was considered one of the highest forms of dishonor, and the upholding of one's honor was a first requirement for a Geg. On the other hand, if the individual carried out the required act of vengeance, he was in turn subject to extinction by the victim's relatives. Women were excluded from the feud and, when escorted by a male, he too was considered inviolable. In other respects, women's position in society generally was one of deprivation and subjugation (see ch. 5, Social System).

The isolation from influences beyond his community and the constant struggle with nature tended to make the Geg an ascetic. Traditionally, his closest bonds were those of kinship, as a member of a clan. Obstinate and proud, the Geg proved himself, under the leadership of his compatriots, a ruthless and cruel fighter. Visitors from outside the clan were generally suspect, but every traveler was by custom accorded hospitality.

Less isolated by rugged terrain and with greater, although limited, contact with foreign cultures, the Tosk generally was more outspoken and imaginative than the Geg. Contacts with invaders and foreign occupiers had influence and, before 1939, some Tosks had traveled to foreign countries to earn sufficient funds to buy land or to obtain an education. The clan or tribal system, which by the nineteenth century was far less deeply rooted and extensive in the south than in the north, began to disappear after independence was achieved in 1912.

Of the minority ethnic groups, persons of Greek descent are the most numerous. Estimates based on World War II and earlier data indicate that they compose approximately 2 percent of the population. They are most numerous in the southwestern coastal area of Dhermi and Himare and the region extending southward to the Greek border from Gjirokaster. They have adopted Albanian folkways and dress. Although their first language is Greek, they speak Albanian as well.

Persons of Vlach, Bulgar, Serb, and Gypsy origin make up about 1 percent of the population. The Vlachs in Albania have lost much of their homogeneity and adopted the ways of their Tosk neighbors. The typical Vlach is akin to the modern Romanian. Both are descendants of Romanized Dacians or Thracians of the pre-Christian era.

Under Communist rule the Vlachs, mostly herdsmen, have been incorporated into the collectivized economy. Previously, they grazed their flocks in the mountains in the summer and then returned to the valleys in the winter. They are most numerous in the Pindus Mountains and in the Fier, Korce, and Vlore areas. Persons of Bulgar origin live mostly in the border area near Lake Prespa; a few persons of Serb derivation live in the Shkoder area; and Gypsies are scattered in various places.

There are large numbers of persons of Albanian origin living outside the country. Estimates based on Yugoslav data indicated the total number in Yugoslavia in 1970 was approximately 1 million, of which about 70 percent were in Kosovo. Data is generally lacking on the exact number in other areas, and estimates vary widely. There may be as many as 250,000 in Italy and Sicily, 350,000 in Greece, and 80,000 in the United States. They are found also in Bulgaria, Egypt, Romania, and Turkey. The degree to which persons living outside the country have retained Albanian customs and language varies. Indications are that they have retained their clannishness to a considerable degree.

LANGUAGES

Albanian, of Indo-European origin, is the only surviving language of the early Thraco-Illyrian group and is spoken by all or nearly all inhabitants. Some of the minority ethnic groups also speak the tongue of the country from which their families originated.

Modern Albanian is derived from the ancient Illyrian and Thracian, but many outside influences are evident. Additions and modifications, beginning in the pre-Christian era, were made as a result of foreign contacts. Most important of these were the Latin and Italian influences during the centuries of Roman domination and trade with the Venetian merchants and, later, in the nineteenth and twentieth centuries. Contributions also were made by the Greeks, Turks, and Slavs. The first written documents in Albanian did not appear until the fifteenth century; therefore it is difficult to trace the development of the language during the earlier period.

The repressive policies of the Ottoman rulers over a period of 450 years, beginning in the fifteenth century, further retarded language development. Written Albanian was forbidden, and only the Turkish or Greek languages could be used in schools. Emigré Albanians, particularly those in Italy after 1848, helped keep the written language alive. Until the nineteenth century continuity of the language in Turkish-dominated areas was provided largely by verbal communication, including ballads and folk tales (see ch. 7, Communications and Cultural Development).

By the early twentieth century more than a dozen different alphabets had developed. Some were predominantly either Latin, Greek, or Turko-Arabic. Many were a mixture of several forms. It was not until 1908 that a standardized orthography was adopted. The Latin-based alphabet of thirty-six letters, approved at that time by a linguistic congress at Monastir, was made official by a government directive in 1924 and continued in use in 1970.

Letters are written as they are pronounced. There have been variations in the spelling of many words because of dialectical differences, and they still persist despite the government's efforts to develop a uniform language. A dictionary was published by the Institute of Sciences in Tirana in 1954, and it indicated that the spelling of some words varied. During the 1960s the Linguistics and History Institute, which was part of the State University of Tirana, carried on studies relating to language origins and morphology, but no lexicon was known to have appeared as of early 1970 to standardize spelling or supersede the 1954 dictionary.

The two principal Albanian dialects are Geg, spoken by about two-thirds of the people, including those in the Kosovo region of Yugoslavia, and Tosk, by the remaining third. There are subvarieties of both dialects. Despite the considerable variations that developed in the many isolated communities, Albanians are able to communicate easily with each other.

Efforts were made by the government during the 1920s and 1930s to establish the dialect of the Elbasan area, which was a mixture of Geg and Tosk, as the standard and official language; but the local dialects persisted, and writers and even officials continued to use the dialect of their association. After the Communists, most of whose leaders had come from southern Albania, acceded to power, the Tosk dialect became the official language of the country. In 1952 the Albanian Writers' Union, a Party-controlled organization, took action to make Tosk the only dialect to be used in publications.

SETTLEMENT PATTERNS

Some two-thirds of the people live in rural areas in a widely dispersed pattern of small villages. The urban population, according to 1969 data, lived in forty cities with 1,000 to 10,000 inhabitants and twelve cities with over 10,000 dwellers; of the latter group, six had 10,000 to 30,000 inhabitants; two had 30,000 to 50,000; three had 50,000 to 100,000; and one, Tirana, was approaching 200,000.

The heaviest concentrations of settlement in the late 1960s were in the districts of Tirana with a density of 528 persons per square mile, Durres with 469, Fier with 323, and Lushnje with 298. The area surrounding Korce and the area immediately around, and to the south of, Shkoder were among the most thickly settled even though the administrative districts of Korce and Shkoder were not heavily populated when considered in their entirety (see ch. 3, Physical Environment).

Several factors contributed to the pattern of settlement. Large expanses of mountains and generally rugged terrain made the building of land transportation routes difficult. Poor soil and lack of water during part of the year did not provide support to large concentrations of people. Mineral and other resources were generally not readily accessible or were difficult to exploit (see ch. 3, Physical Environment).

Coastal cities generally have a small hinterland, and their influence does not extend beyond their borders. The port of Durres, with road and rail links to Tirana, Elbasan, and Fier, is an exception. During the 1960s the area generally bounded by these cities experienced the greatest growth of industry and population of any region. Vlore, a port and naval center, increased almost fourfold between 1945 and 1967, but it lacks links with inland areas.

Tirana, the capital and largest city, increased from about 60,000 inhabitants in 1945 to 170,000 in 1967, largely because of the expansion of industry and a growing bureaucracy. It is located on the inner margin of the coastal plain and is surrounded by an area of the better soils of Albania. The streets in the central area of the city, where government buildings are clustered, are wide and attractive; many parts of the city are much like the rural villages. Tirana has become the most industrialized city and continues to be a collecting and distributing point for agricultural products of the area.

Centers for inland mountain valley or upland basin communities are Berat, Elbasan, and Korce. They, like most cities, have changed little in appearance and retain much of the flavor of nineteenth-century agricultural life.

The typical mountain village, of 70 to 100 homesteads, is located on an isolated slope among rocks and thin scrub-like vegetation. Only footpaths link it by land with the outside world. During the summer there is a drought period which requires that water use be limited to drinking. Houses are clustered in the south, whereas in the northern mountains they tend to be dispersed. Fields and pastures are located some distance from the village. Water must be carried from a common source, usually a spring. Mountain villages frequently are located at 1,300 to 1,600 feet above sea level. This is generally the line of contact between the underlying impervious serpentine rock and layer of limestone and the point where spring water comes to the surface.

At lower levels the villages are laid out around the collective or state farms or enterprises, many of which were previously estates or patriarchal settlements. Here the houses are more substantial, and the fields or other place of work are near the village. Water is carried from a common source. Open sewers run down the streets of some villages, but this condition is gradually changing. Electric power has been extended to about 70 percent of all villages, but other facilities and amenities, except medical services, have been little improved since the end of World War II.

LIVING CONDITIONS

The standard of living in 1970 was very low, and life was difficult for the masses despite very modest improvements in living conditions during the 1950s and 1960s. The standard of living was the lowest in Europe and was improving at a slow pace because priority was given to industry, to increasing the means of production, and to developing eventual self-sufficiency in food production, especially of cereal foods. The most widely felt improvements were in health services and in use of electricity, which resulted from expanding the electrical network to many villages.

Plans for the late 1960s and 1970 called for 23 to 25 percent of the state budget to be spent on social and cultural sectors. In 1967, when total planned budget spending was 3.6 billion leks (5 leks equal US$1—see Glossary), the sum for social and cultural sectors was 837 million leks, of which 189 million were for health, 167 million for social insurance, 143 million for assistance to mothers and children, and 338 million for education and culture.

The government maintained that it was improving living conditions by increasing food supplies and commodities and by construction of public facilities and structures. In February 1970 the chairman of the State Planning Commission reported that 1,200 dining rooms, 1,140 bakeries, 1,850 public baths and laundries, and 187 water mains had been built and that electricity had been supplied to 1,096 additional villages in 1968 and 1969, leaving only 663 without electricity. Although these additions added to the amenities of life, the rapid growth of population caused heavy strain on the very limited total resources available.

Medicine and Health

Medical authorities asserted that many diseases and afflictions that had taken heavy tolls of life and tended to debilitate large segments of the population before 1950 had been greatly reduced or eliminated. These successes were primarily attributable to large-scale inoculation programs, elimination or reduction in the number of disease-spreading pests, and expansion of health services. Malnutrition, unsatisfactory sanitary-hygienic conditions, and indifference to medical aid in some areas posed problems for further improvements.

The Communist regime, posing as the protector of the masses, credited itself with a revolutionary transformation in the health standards of the country. Data on health and disease from other than Albanian sources were not available. Statistics released by the Ministry of Health indicated substantial improvements during the 1960s. Responsibility for shortcomings and inadequacies relating to health care was attributed to backwardness on the part of the people or to the lack of resources. Failures on the part of the Party or government were not mentioned.

There were widespread epidemics of measles in 1948 and 1949 and 1954 and 1955, of Asiatic influenza in 1957, of typhoid in 1945 and 1950, and of poliomyelitis in 1953. Health officials stated that there were no epidemics during the 1960s.

Malaria was one of the most prevalent diseases before 1950. Health authorities, assisted by the Rockefeller Foundation beginning in the 1920s, made considerable progress in eliminating mosquitoes and reducing the incidence of malaria before World War II. The campaign was continued by the Italians during their occupation. The ravages of war greatly increased the spread of malaria from 1945 to 1947; according to Communist reports, 60 to 70 percent of the population were afflicted in those years, in comparison with 16.5 percent in 1938.

The United Nations Relief and Rehabilitation Administration provided food, medicine, and antimalarial assistance in 1945 and 1946, and the Communist regime followed up with a concerted effort against the disease, which reduced the percentage of persons afflicted to approximately 7 percent in the early 1950s. Health officials declared in 1970 that malaria had been eradicated by 1967, and no cases had been recorded after that date.

Health authorities reported that measles had been eliminated by 1970 through a program of mass vaccinations. The last major epidemic, that of 1954-55, afflicted almost 14 percent of the population. The incidence among children under three years of age was 60 percent, and 1,712 children under age fifteen died.

A broad program against tuberculosis was begun in the 1960s that included general prophylactic measures and vaccine injections. Health officials planned completion of vaccinations countrywide in 1970. It was estimated that almost 15 percent of the population had tuberculosis in the mid-1950s. Officials reported that the incidence of this disease had dropped to less than 0.2 percent in 1968.

The Health Ministry reported progress in combating many other diseases. Syphilis, once prevalent, was eliminated. A broad program of serologic examinations involving over 2.3 million persons between 1947 and 1968 was utilized to detect venereal disease and was instrumental in reducing the rate of syphilis infection from 3.14 percent in 1949 to 0.02 percent in 1968. Incidence rates per 1,000 population of other illnesses decreased from 1955 to 1968 as follows: abdominal typhoid, from 5.2 to 2.4; dysentery, from 87.7 to 14.5; diphtheria, from 2.3 to 0.5; poliomyelitis, from 0.4 to 0.1; brucellosis, from 2.4 to 0.8; and arthritis, from 2.2 to 0.8. Trachoma was eliminated, and no cases of rabies were reported in the 1967-69 period. Deaths per 100,000 population from contagious diseases, including influenza, decreased from 220 in 1950 to 43 in 1968. Data on the number of deaths from heart ailments, cancer, and other causes were not published.

Although progress was made in reducing mortality among children up to one year of age—from 121.2 per 1,000 live births in 1950 to 75.2 in 1968—the rate remained unusually high. Failure to obtain timely medical assistance was given as the primary cause of death by health authorities. Malnutrition, shortages of professional medical personnel, and insufficient health facilities were also contributing factors. The rate for cities in 1968 was 65.4 as compared with 78.0 in rural areas. Some areas in the mountains of the north ran as high as 136.9 during the 1963-67 period. About three-fourths of all infant deaths occurred during the first six months after birth. In 1960 only 34 percent of infant deaths were diagnosed; by 1967 the percentage had increased to 65. Medical aid by a physician or midwife was provided for about 99 percent of births in cities; in rural areas approximately 61 percent of births were with medical assistance.

There were indications that some segments of the population, those in remote and most poverty-stricken areas, were in poor health. A 1968-69 study of 1,580 children up to three years of age in thirteen northern localities, reported by the Ministry of Health, showed that 60 percent suffered from neuromuscular disorders in various degrees and that 47 percent suffered from rickets. The principal causes for these abnormalities, according to the official study, were malnutrition and unsatisfactory hygienic-sanitary conditions.

Health and medical organizations from national to local levels were under the Ministry of Health. In the 1960s the departments of the ministry were: epidemiology, pharmaceuticals, sanitary inspectorate, medical prophylactic institutions, personnel, administration, finance, and planning. Data for 1968 reported by the minister of health listed facilities countrywide as: 196 hospitals and other facilities with beds; 11,922 beds for medical use; 1,108 first aid stations and polyclinics; and 36 dispensaries and tuberculosis centers. The average annual increase in hospital beds from 1950 to 1968 was 323; in 1968 there was 1 bed for every 169 inhabitants.

The total number of persons employed in health and medicine increased from 9,881 in 1960 to 14,370 in 1967. The numbers of professional and semiskilled workers in 1969 were: physicians, 1,396;

stomatologists (mouth specialists), 183; pharmacists, 262; medical aides, 725; dental assistants, 139; pharmacist assistants, 334; midwives, 1,091; nurses, 4,100; and laboratory technicians, 737. Dentists were not listed as a separate category. The average number of inhabitants per doctor in the districts was approximately 2,000; however, in two districts the average was over 3,000, and in one, less than 1,000. All medical personnel were in government employ, and no private medical practice existed.

The expansion of medical services after World War II was made possible to a large extent by accelerated training programs. A school for training medical assistants was begun in 1948 and, starting in the early 1950s, the Red Cross conducted courses for semiskilled medical workers. A medical college for training professional personnel was established in 1952; in 1957 it became the Faculty of Medicine of the State University of Tirana, and the first doctors were graduated that year. During the 1950s most physicians were trained in the Soviet Union. In the late 1960s the number of persons undergoing training as midwives was increased, and the goal was to have at least one midwife in every village by June 1971.

The use of mobile medical teams and equipment played a major role in expanding and improving medical care in rural areas. Laboratory, X-ray, and other services once available only in the largest cities were established in the district and sometimes at lower levels. The regime, in its effort to build up agriculture in the mid-1960s, set as an objective the improvement of living conditions in the countryside and the elimination of the differential between city and country. Medical assistance to rural areas continued to increase in the late 1960s, but in late 1969 the minister of health stated that the differences between the center and the districts and between the cities and the villages were very pronounced. He directed that action be taken to lessen the gap but added that differences would continue to exist.

Nutrition

Food supply—perennially a problem because of poor soil, primitive methods of cultivation, and lack of readily accessible resources—did not keep pace with population growth. For the late 1960s calorie intake per capita per day probably did not exceed 2,100 to 2,200, while the estimate for the mid-1950s was 2,200 to 2,300. The diet lacked protein and other protective elements. An estimated 80 percent or more of food intake was carbohydrates. Fruits and green vegetables were in short supply, and meats were a real scarcity. Little progress had been made in increasing livestock herds during the period of Communist rule, and credits to procure adequate supplies of protective foods from sources outside the country were not available (see ch. 8, Economic System).

The diet generally depicted scarcity and, in the mountain and rural areas, was simple and routine. Dishes, high in starch content, made from corn, wheat, rice, and potatoes were basic. Yogurt, cheese, and prepared dry beans were among the most commonly found other foods. Green vegetables and fruits appeared seasonally in limited quantities.

While some progress has been made in improving sources of drinking water, the vast majority of rural families, and some in the smaller cities, must rely on unprotected sources. Central sewage systems are found in only the largest cities.

Housing

Living quarters became increasingly overcrowded as population expanded at consistently high rates. Party First Secretary Enver Hoxha stated in December 1967 that the entire country, especially urban areas, was experiencing a housing crisis. Reports on housing construction indicated that the situation further deteriorated in the late 1960s because of the necessity to divert resources to even higher priorities, to the building of industry and procurement of food and clothing. War and natural catastrophes added to the burden. In World War II some 35,000 dwellings were destroyed. Earthquakes in November and December of 1967 demolished 3,500 homes. In April 1969, when 6,500 buildings were damaged or destroyed by earthquakes, additional thousands of homes had to be replaced or repaired.

Hoxha stated in late 1969 that 185,000 flats and houses had been built since World War II. The average annual rate of construction, as indicated by incomplete reports for the 1960s, was 6,000 private dwellings and 3,000 state-owned and cooperative apartment units. Total requirements were not stated, but with annual population growth at approximately 40,000 to 50,000 persons, and considering reports relating to crowded conditions, the critical condition was unresolved. Hoxha stated in late 1967 that the housing situation had reached the point where in some instances five persons were living in one room.

Most rural houses are of one or two rooms, with a hearth, and are of simple construction. They are small and sparsely furnished. Many are made of natural rock or stones. Urban houses and apartments are usually small and lack central heating. Kitchen and toilet facilities in apartments must be shared by three or four families.

Social Insurance

The social insurance program is administered by state organizations and covers medical care, compensation for incapacities, old-age pensions, family allowances, and rest and recreation. Social insurance was introduced in 1947. Several modifications were made later to the basic program. The law of 1953 provided a program closely resembling that of the Soviet Union, and for a number of years, following the Soviet example, trade unions administered a large number of social insurance activities. In 1965 the state assumed the administration of all phases except those for rest and recreation facilities.

The social insurance program, as provided for in the Council of Ministers decision of September 13, 1966, and effective January 1, 1967, included benefits for workers, employees, and others. Peasants in the collectives were not included in this law, but similar welfare benefits were provided from funds established by their organizations. The 1966 law continued the policy announced in 1964 that free medical care was provided to everyone. Drugs, such as penicillin and antibiotics, and vitamins prescribed during outpatient treatment had to be paid for by the user. Funds for social insurance payments came from the state budget. Contributions were paid by state institutions and enterprises that were in the role of employers.

Workers who became incapacitated and had over ten years of work credit received payments at the rate of 85 percent of the average wage for the last month worked; persons with less than ten years' service received 70 percent, except that temporary or seasonal workers were given less. When disability resulted directly from work, pay was given at the rate of 95 percent for most trades and 100 percent for persons working in mines. Compensation was less when incapacity resulted from an accident unrelated to work. Payments under these circumstances depended on age and years of work credit. Veterans who served in the Army of National Liberation before May 1944 and some of the Party elite were allowed an extra 10 percent when incapacitated (see ch. 2, Historical Setting).

Pregnant women were given eighty-four days' leave under normal circumstances and 95 percent of their monthly wage if they had worked over five years. They received 75 percent if they had worked less than five years. Workers could remain at home for limited periods to care for the sick and receive 60 percent of their pay. When children under seven years of age were ill, the worker was permitted up to ten days' leave during a three-month period. A subsidy, a one-time payment, of 280 leks was provided for each child. Upon the death of a family head or his spouse, 300 leks were provided for funeral expenses.

Old-age pensions were based on age and years of work. Payments were computed at the rate of 70 percent of the worker's average monthly wage. The minimum pension was 350 leks, and the maximum was 900 leks per month; two exceptions were veterans of the Army of National Liberation who served before May 1944 and Party leaders, who were awarded an additional 10 percent. Women who reared six or more children to the age of eight were permitted to retire at age 50 when they completed fifteen years of work, instead of the usual requirement of twenty years.

Wages and Prices

The limited data available indicated that in early 1966 factory and manual workers received 400 to 800 leks in wages per month. Skilled workers were paid 400 to 1,500 leks, and senior officials received up to 1,500 leks per month. After the reduction in the size of the bureaucracy was announced in late 1966, the maximum for officials was reduced to 1,200.

Prices in leks per pound for foodstuffs in 1966 were approximately as follows: bread, 1 to 2, depending on type; flour, 2 to 2.5; sugar, 4.5; beans, 3 to 4.5; beef, 6.5; and lamb, 8.5. Prices for other commodities, in leks, were as follows: a man's suit, 400 to 1,300; a pair of men's shoes, 120 to 200; radio, 500 to 2,400; and a bicycle, 800 to 1,300.

During the late 1960s the consumer continued to feel the squeeze of the drive for greater economic self-sufficiency and the priority given to the building of means of production. Despite announcements of greater benefits to the worker, the average citizen in early 1970 continued to pay approximately 90 percent of his income for food and shelter. Basic commodities and foodstuffs were in short supply, and waiting in line at distribution points was required to obtain the most commonly used items. Manufactured items were generally of poor quality. Automobiles were owned by the government only, and bicycles, a status symbol, were available to only a few.

CHAPTER 5

SOCIAL SYSTEM

The Communist regime was still striving in 1970 to alter the traditional tribal and semifeudal social patterns of the country and to restructure the whole system to fit Marxist-Leninist principles of a socialist society. Until after World War II the strongest loyalties of the people had been toward family and larger kin groups, which have been the most important units in Albanian society. Kin groups had been held together by strong spirit and loyalties, as well as by economic factors. The head of the family, usually the eldest male member, historically exercised patriarchal authority, with general responsibility for the welfare and safety of the members. In this patriarchal society, respect for parental authority was dominant.

Local autonomy and suspicion of central authority had for centuries been a way of life for Albanian society. This way of life persisted until the twentieth century, despite the foreign cultural and political influences to which the society was subjected during the long domination by the Ottoman Turks.

Of particular social importance during this domination was the conversion of the majority of the people to the Islamic faith. Even before this conversion, however, the people had been segmented by the schism between the Roman and Eastern Orthodox churches. The people in the north were usually Roman Catholic, and those in the south, Eastern Orthodox. Tolerance, however, has been a marked feature of the people and, accordingly, religious divisiveness has had no great effect on the tribal and semifeudal structure of the society. Indeed, the three religious faiths in the country—Muslim, Roman Catholic, and Eastern Orthodox—have represented traditional loyalties rather than living creeds for the Albanians.

Until the Communist takeover in 1944, there had been two broad social classes in the country, an upper and a lower class. The upper class was composed of the landowning *beys* (see Glossary); some *bajraktars* (relatively well-to-do tribal chieftains); and a smaller number of rich Christian farmers, merchants, small industrialists, some intellectuals, and the higher clergy. The lower class, amounting to about 90 percent of the population, was composed of a small group of workers, the peasant masses, livestock breeders, and the lower clergy.

The Communist regime's political, social, and economic measures aimed at redirecting the traditional social patterns have resulted in more social transformations than at any time since the Turkish invasions in the fifteenth century. Collectivization of agriculture, industrialization and the consequent migration from rural to industrial areas, and a widespread educational system have done much to transform the tribal character of the society.

Although in 1970 the patriarchal system was still a way of life in the countryside, especially in the highlands, the authority of the master of the house had been considerably reduced. Marriage customs in particular had changed. As a result, the position of the close-knit family had been altered. Radical changes had occurred also in the life of women. Many of them have had to work outside the home to compensate for the generally low wages of their husbands. Day-care nurseries had been set up to make it easier for mothers to work and also to give the regime an early opportunity to indoctrinate the children.

Despite such transformation, however, the family was still the most significant unit in the society. The allegiance given to the family, coupled with the individualism characteristic of the people and the traditions of political autonomy in local affairs, had made it difficult for the regime to fully implement its policies for restructuring the society in general and the family in particular.

Reflecting the influence of the standard Marxist-Leninist dogma, the regime officially recognized only two classes—one composed of workers and considered the leading class and the other consisting of the working peasants, a third group usually being referred to as the people's intelligentsia. Actually, a distinct new upper class, constituting less than 10 percent of the total population, emerged under Communist rule to replace the upper ruling and middle classes that existed before the Communist takeover. This new upper class was composed of the top ruling elite that controlled all facets of society and its supporting echelons, made up of officials of the Party and state apparatus; mass organizations; and professional and technical people, such as doctors, lawyers, engineers, and managers of state enterprises.

Membership in the Party or sympathy toward communism was the chain that linked this upper class together. All its segments had benefited from the Communist system, having enjoyed considerable advantages over the rest of the population; they formed practically the only social group with a vested interest in the perpetuation of the system. The rest of the population—peasants, workers, and remnants of the upper and middle classes—were only cogs in the Communist apparatus, all used for the purpose of implementing the Party policies for the building of a Communist society.

Under Communist rule the stabilization of the class differentiations had lessened social mobility both upward and downward. In 1970 it was difficult to alter one's social status except through a long process of training and education. Educational opportunities, however, had been greatly expanded, although they were still limited in the rural areas. The best opportunities were offered to the children of the Party elite and Party faithful. But because of the great demand for qualified personnel to manage the growing socialist sectors of the economy, some children of worker and peasant backgrounds had opportunities to continue their education to the highest levels and to fully develop their abilities and capacities. The whole educational system, however, was geared to the demands of the Party, and its first objective was the inculcation of the youth with Communist ideology.

Perhaps the most radical change in the whole social system had been effected in the area of religion. By 1970 the country's three principal religious faiths had been eliminated as organizational bodies. All churches and mosques had been closed; the clergy was not permitted to function; and the country had been declared by the official media to be the first atheist nation in the world. Top Party and government officials admitted, however, that the closing of the houses of worship and the action against the clergy had not eliminated the religious feelings and beliefs of the people.

TRADITIONAL SOCIAL PATTERNS AND VALUES

The social structure of the country was until the 1930s basically tribal in the north and semifeudal in the central and southern regions. The highlanders in the north retained intact their medieval tribal pattern of life until well into the twentieth century and were considered the last peoples in Europe to preserve tribal autonomy. In the central and southern regions, however, increasing contact with the outside world and invasions and occupations by foreign armies had reduced the tribes to tenure peasants.

Traditionally, there have been two major groupings or sub-cultures in the country: the Gegs in the north, probably numbering slightly over half the total population, and the Tosks in the south. Although the terms *Geg* and *Tosk* have disappeared from the vocabulary because they connote division rather than Communist unity, Tirana officials and the press have often implied in recent years that the old differences and contrasts between the two groups still existed. These differences were marked not only in the physical appearance of the people and in dialect but also in the way of life in general.

The Gegs, partly Roman Catholic but mostly Muslim, lived until after World War II in a mountain society characterized by blood feuds and fierce clan and tribal loyalties. The Tosks, on the other hand, were considered more civilized because of centuries of Greek and other foreign influences. Coming under the grip of the Muslim landed aristocracy, the Tosks lost the spirit of individuality and independence enjoyed for centuries by the Gegs, especially in the highlands.

Until the end of World War II society in the north and, to a much lesser extent, in the south was organized in terms of kinship and descent. The basic unit of society was the extended family, usually composed of a couple, their married sons, the wives and children of married sons, and any unmarried daughters. The extended family formed a single residential and economic entity held together by common ownership of means of production and common interest in defense of the group. Such families often included scores of persons, and as late as 1944 some contained as many as sixty to seventy persons living in a cluster of huts surrounding the father's house.

Extended families were grouped into clans, the chiefs of which preserved, until the end of World War II, patriarchal powers over the members of the entire group. The clan chief arranged marriages, assigned tasks, settled disputes, and decided what courses should be followed in such basic issues as blood feuds and politics. Descent was traced from a common ancestor through the male line, and brides were usually chosen from outside the clan. Clans in turn were grouped into tribes.

In the Tosk regions of the south the extended family was also the most important social unit, although patriarchal authority had been diluted by the feudal conditions imposed by the *beys*. The clan and tribal systems had disappeared at a much earlier period in the south and were retained into the mid-twentieth century only among the northern highlanders.

Leadership of society in the lowlands was concentrated in the hands of semifeudal tribal *beys* and *pashas* (see Glossary). The general Tirana region, for example, was controlled by the Zogolli, Toptani, and Vrioni families, all being Muslim *pashas* or *beys* and all owning extensive agricultural estates. Ahmet Zogu, subsequently King Zog I, was from the Zogolli family. Originally the *pasha* class ranked slightly higher than that of the *bey*, but differences gradually diminished and all members were called *beys*. In the northern highlands the *bajraktars* were the counterparts of the *beys* and enjoyed similar hereditary rights to titles and positions.

The Geg clans put great importance on marriage traditions. Marriage customs and prohibitions designed to perpetuate these traditions were still practiced at the end of World War II. According to the custom a young man from a given clan always married a young woman from outside the clan but from within the same tribe. In some tribes marriages between Christians and Muslims were tolerated even before the advent of the Communist regime, but as a rule such marriages were frowned upon.

A variety of offenses against women served as an igniting spark for blood feuds. Many girls were engaged to marry in their infancy by their parents. If later the girl did not wish to marry the man whom the parents had chosen for her and married another, in all likelihood a blood feud would ensue. Among the Tosks, religious beliefs and customs, rather than clan and tribal traditions, were more important in regulating marriages.

The family had for centuries presented the basic, most important unit in the social structure of the country. One aspect of this was the deep devotion of a person to his parents and family. This feeling took a striking form because the family was a social unit occupying to a great extent the place of the state. Children were brought up to respect their elders and, above all, their father, whose word was law in the confines of his family.

Upon the death of the father the authority of the family devolved upon the oldest male of the family. The females of the household, with the exception of the mother, occupied an inferior position. The unwritten law of family life was based on the assumption that a daughter was part of the family until she married. When the time came for sons to set up their own households, all parental property was equally divided among them; the females did not share in this division.

Geographical conditions affected Tosk social organization. The region's accessibility led to its coming much more firmly under Turkish rule. This rule in turn resulted in the breakup of the large, independent family-type units and their replacement by large estates owned by powerful Muslim landowners, each with his own retinues, fortresses, and large numbers of tenant peasants to work the lands. Their allegiance to the sultans in the period before 1912 was secured by the granting of administrative positions either at home or elsewhere in the Ottoman Empire.

The large estates were usually confined to the plains, but the process of their consolidation was a continuing one. Landowning *beys* would get peasants into their debt and thus establish themselves as semifeudal patrons of formerly independent villagers. In this way a large Muslim aristocracy developed in the south, whose life style was in marked contrast both to that of the chieftains of the highlands in the north and to that of the peasantry, the majority of whom assumed the characteristics of an oppressed social class. As late as the 1930s two-thirds of the rich land in central and southern parts of the country belonged to the large landowners.

There was a sharp contrast between the tribal society of the Geg highlanders and the passive, oppressed Tosk peasantry, living mostly on the large estates of the *beys* and often represented in the political field by the *beys* themselves. This semifeudal society in the south survived well into the twentieth century because of the lack of a strong middle class. After independence in 1912, however, a small Tosk middle class began to develop, which in the 1920-24 period, having common interests with the more enlightened *beys*, played a major role in attempts to create a modern society. But the advent of Zogu in 1925 as a strong ruler put an end to Tosk influence and, from that time until the Italian invasion in 1939, Zog cemented his power in the tribal north by governing through a number of strong tribal and clan chiefs. To secure the loyalty of these chiefs, he placed them on the government payroll and sent several of them back to their tribes with the military rank of colonel.

In the 1939-44 period general anarchy prevailed throughout the country, and in the north the tribal chieftains assumed their old independent positions. The three major resistance movements that developed during World War II represented the principal social classes then in existence in the country. The Communist-dominated National Liberation Movement was composed chiefly of low-level Tosk intellectuals and bureaucrats, some labor leaders, and a few chieftains from the Geg areas, such as Haxhi Leshi, who was head of state in 1970. The movement derived its main support from the small working class and the poor peasants.

The nationalist Balli Kombetar (National Front) was composed of nationalist *beys* and Orthodox intellectuals and derived its support from well-to-do peasants, merchants, and businessmen. The Legality Movement, a pro-Zog organization, was headed by a chieftain from Mat, and its supporters were confined to that region. Farther north the resistance groups were led by the local chieftains, such as Muharem Bajraktari and Gani bey Kryeziu. The collaborators with the Italian authorities were composed of reactionary *beys*, Geg chieftains (both Muslim and Catholic), and a small group of intellectuals that had embraced the fascist ideology. This group had little or no popular support.

SOCIAL STRATIFICATION UNDER COMMUNIST RULE

The general class structure of the country at the advent of the Communist regime in 1944 consisted of the peasants and workers making up the lower class and a small upper class. The peasants represented over 80 percent of the total population, most of whom lived at or below subsistence level. Chiefly because of the old grievances against the

- 74 -

landowning *beys* and the promises made by the National Liberation Movement (which presented itself as a purely patriotic, democratic movement for agrarian reforms), a large number of peasants, especially the tenant and landless ones, sided with the movement (see ch. 1, General Character of the Society).

Nonagricultural workers numbered about 30,000 persons, most of whom worked in mines and in the small handicraft industries. The movement found strong support from this group also. The upper class comprised professional people and intellectuals; medium and small merchants; moneylenders; and well-to-do artisans, whose capital was invested mostly in trade, commerce, and the Italian industrial concessions. The industrialists also belonged to this class; they owned very small industries and workshops. Both the *beys* and the tribal chiefs of the north had been somewhat reduced in importance politically and economically during Zog's rule, but it was chiefly from these two groups that Zog created the ruling elite that helped him to control the country until the Italian invasion in 1939.

The clergy of the three religious denominations did not form a distinct social group. The higher clergy was intellectual and upper class in structure; it supported the ruling elite but did not mix in politics after Bishop Fan Noli, leader of a short-lived reformist government, was driven out of the country in 1924. The income from the fairly extensive church estates and the state subsidies provided a good, but not luxurious, living for the higher clergy. The rank-and-file clergy, however, were derived from peasant origins, and most of their parishes were as impoverished as the peasant households they served.

The events immediately preceding and following the Communist seizure of power forebode the doom not only of the *beys* and tribal chiefs but also of most of the upper class and intellectuals, who had refused to collaborate with the National Liberation Movement. In the summer and fall of 1944, while civil war was raging between the Communist-controlled partisan formations and anti-Communist bands, nearly all the influential *beys* and *bajraktars* either fell in battle or fled the country; those who remained were quickly rounded up by the Communist security forces and subsequently tried as "enemies of the people" (see ch. 2, Historical Setting).

The whole leadership of the two nationalist organizations, the Balli Kombetar and the Legality Movement, fled to Italy. Influential patriots and intellectuals who had remained neutral during the so-called War of National Liberation but who were considered potentially dangerous to the Communist regime were apprehended and tried en masse in the spring of

1945. Some were executed; others were sent to labor camps, where most of them died from malnutrition and lack of medical care.

A new Communist social order was legally instituted in the country with the adoption of the first Communist Constitution in March 1946, which created a "state of workers and laboring peasants." The various constitutional articles dealing with the new social order abolished all ranks and privileges that had derived from reasons of origin (such as the tribal chiefs and the *beys*), position, wealth, or cultural standing. All citizens were considered equal regardless of nationality, race, or religion.

Marriage and family were brought under the strict control of the state, which determined by law the conditions of marriage and the family. Marriages could be considered legal only when contracted before competent state organs, and only state courts had jurisdiction on all matters connected with marriage. Included in the 1946 Constitution also was the Marxist tenet "from each according to his ability and to each according to his work." Subsequent revisions to the Constitution gave legal sanction to the existing situation that the Party and its members were the leading, or vanguard, group in the country.

E Drejta Kushtetuese e Republikes Popullore te Shqiperise (The Constitutional Right in the People's Republic of Albania), published in 1963 by the Faculty of Jurisprudence of the State University of Tirana, stated that the War of National Liberation was actually class warfare, a civil war whose purpose was as much national as it was social liberation—that is, the establishment of the "people's power" and the "dictatorship of the proletariat."

Communist spokesmen listed three principal classes prevailing in the early years of the regime: the working class, the laboring peasants, and, in their terms, the exploiting class, that is, the landowners in the agricultural economy and the bourgeoisie in trade. The exploiting class was liquidated through a rapid revolutionary process in the early stages of the regime. The middle and high bourgeoisie was destroyed as a result of the nationalization of industry, transport, mines, and banks and the establishment of a state monopoly on foreign commerce and state control over internal trade. The feudal landlords disappeared with the application of the agrarian reforms in the 1945-47 period. These steps were followed by a program of rapid industrialization, with the consequent creation of a strong working class, and the collectivization of agriculture, supposedly resulting in the formation of a homogeneous peasant class.

After the destruction of the old class structure, the Communist regime claimed that only two classes existed in the country, the workers and the working peasants. A somewhat different social composition of the population, however, has been given by the government's statistical yearbooks, based on the last official census, taken in 1960. Under the title "Social Composition of the Population," for instance, the 1965 statistical yearbook listed, in order, the following groups; workers, employees (civil servants), collective and private farmers (officially called villagers), collective and individual artisans, collective and private traders, free professions, clergymen, and unemployed and unknown (see table 4).

In the 1967-70 period several of these groups disappeared. The individual farmers were all collectivized; the artisan collectives were converted to state industrial enterprises; the private traders, except the peasant open markets, were reduced to a minimum, and members of the clergy were sent to work either in industrial plants or agricultural collectives.

The number of families almost doubled in the 1945-60 period. In the cities they grew from 48,800 to 95,500 and in the countryside, from 148,000 to 184,305. The greatest rate of increase, almost 8 percent, occurred during the 1950-55 period in the urban sector; this was attributed primarily to the creation of an industrial base.

The expansion of the existing cities, especially the capital city of Tirana, caused by the establishment of a number of industrial projects, drew people from the rural regions into the urban centers. This new migration was reinforced by the relocation of entire families. In addition, new family units were formed by the younger migrants once they settled in the newly developing industrial centers. During the decade of the 1950s the trend was toward larger families.

Table 4. Social Composition of the Population of Albania*
(according to the 1960 official census)

Social Groups	Number of families	Number of persons	Males	Females	Average number per family
Workers	79,804	433,040	237,307	195,733	5.9
Employees (civil servants)	36,891	182,913	98,279	84,634	4.3
Collective farmers	105,778	670,422	331,269	339,153	6.8

Private farmers	44,419	275,169	136,683	138,486	6.4
Collective artisans	5,255	35,056	17,304	17,752	5.3
Individual artisans	1,846	8,950	4,683	4,267	5.4
Collective traders	431	2,328	1,216	1,112	5.0
Private traders	751	3,474	1,880	1,594	5.0
Free professions	166	889	498	391	4.1
Clergymen	831	2,785	1,668	1,117	n.a.
Unemployed and unknown	3,633	11,289	5,507	6,782	3.0
Total	279,805	1,626,315	836,294	791,021	5.8

n.a.—not available.

* According to 1965 data, the family of seven or eight members was then typical in the villages for the agricultural collectives that were researched and, in the peasant families as a whole in 1965, the average family had 6.2 persons.

Source: Adapted from *Vjetari Statistikor i R. P. Sh.*, Tirana, 1968, pp. 74-77; and *Ekonomia Popullore*, Tirana, November to December 1965.

Aside from the workers and peasants, the only group to which the Tirana authorities have continued to give special attention has been the so-called intelligentsia. Usually termed a layer or stratum of the new social order, the intelligentsia was considered, in 1970 to be a special social group because of the country's needs for professional, technical, and cultural manpower. To justify this special attention, the ideologists have often quoted Lenin to the effect that "the intelligentsia will remain a special stratum until the Communist society reaches its highest development."

In the development of the social structure under the Communist regime, basic transformations have occurred in the social composition of the intelligentsia. This transformation, during the 1944-48 period, involved not only the purging of a number of Western-educated intellectuals whom the regime considered potentially dangerous but also some top Communist intellectuals who were suspected of having anti-Yugoslav or pro-Western feelings. The remaining old intellectuals were reeducated and reoriented and were utilized for the preparation of new personnel for the bureaucracy and industry. Finally, a new intelligentsia was created, thoroughly imbued with the Communist ideology and recruited generally from among the children of the Party leaders, workers, and peasants.

The Communist regime created another social group at the bottom rung of the ladder. This group was composed largely of elements of the upper classes in existence before 1944. The tribulations of this class had by 1970 reduced it to a small minority, some members of which were still interned in forced labor camps. It was actually a class of outcasts, discriminated against politically, socially, and economically.

Most of the members of this group were used as so-called volunteer laborers on construction projects and in other menial tasks, and their children did not enjoy the same rights to higher education and other opportunities open to the other classes. Discriminatory measures against this class continued to be taken in the late 1960s; in 1968, for instance, the government passed a law prohibiting them from receiving money remittances or food and clothing packages from their relatives and friends abroad.

The Communist assertion of the existence of only two social classes did not correspond to the real class structure that prevailed in the country in 1970. In fact, there existed different classes and gradations of rank and privilege, beginning with an upper class, composed of the Party elite, leaders of the state and mass organizations, and the leading members of the armed and security forces. The top Party elite itself was composed of two distinct social groupings, the higher group consisting of the Political Bureau (Politburo) of eleven regular and five candidate members and the chiefs of the Directorates of the Central Committee the lower group being made up of the rank-and-file members of the Central Committee.

Family connections played a key role in the composition of the Politburo in 1970. The top three families were those of First Party Secretary Enver Hoxha and his wife Nexhmije, who headed the Directorate of Education and Culture in the Central Committee; Prime Minister Mehmet Shehu and his wife, Fiqrete, who headed the top Party school; and Party Secretary Hysni Kapo and his wife, Vito, who headed the politically and ideologically important women's organization. General Kadri Hasbiu— minister of interior, head of the security forces, and a Politburo candidate member—was a brother-in-law of Mehmet Shehu. Similar family relationships existed between the other Politburo members. About half of the sixty-one members of the Central Committee were also related.

Just below the Politburo and the Central Committee were the vast Party and government bureaucracy, professional people and intellectuals, and managers of state industrial and agricultural enterprises. There were some basic social differences between the top Party elite and the lower Party functionaries and state officials in terms of privileges, influence, authority, and responsibility. This group of lower Party and state officials was bound together by the economic privileges and prestige that went with their positions and membership in, or sympathy for, the Party; they all benefited from the regime and enjoyed educational and economic advantages denied the rest of the population. Below this group were the rank-and-file Party members, whose leadership role was constitutionally guaranteed. Aside from the prestige enjoyed as Party members, however, their privileges and economic benefits did not differ much from the next class in Communist structure of Albanian society, namely the workers.

Constituting about 15 percent of the total population, the working class, styled by the regime as the leading class, was created mostly after the Communist seizure of power and was composed almost wholly of peasant stock. This group, probably more so than the peasant masses, has been under constant pressure to work harder, to produce more, and to work longer, often even after their normal schedules were completed. Although the regular work schedule was eight hours, workers were called upon to perform volunteer labor and to overfulfill norms. There was very little chance for rest and recreation.

Before 1967 the workers could take advantage of religious holidays, which provided some time for recreation, but since then all religious holidays have been banned. The only legal holidays were New Year's Day; Republic Day, on January 11; May Day; Army Day, on July 10; and Independence and Liberation Days, on November 28 and 29, respectively. There were, however, a few local socialist holidays connected with the liberation of the areas by the partisan formations in 1944. The workers also received two-week paid vacations annually.

The largest class, that of the peasants, represented about two-thirds of the total population and, according to Communist dogma, was allied with the working class and led by it. The regime's policy of complete agricultural collectivization has been distressing for the peasant class. A lover of his land, irrespective of its size, and of his independence, the peasant was deprived of his farmland, except for a tiny plot, and herded into a collective. His income in the collective was only on the subsistence level.

Collective peasants were called upon to perform 300 to 350 workdays a year.

A constant complaint of the regime has been that the peasants have not been "freed from the psychology of the small owner, the concept of private property." As of 1970 there were actually no social differences between the workers and peasants because nearly all the workers were of peasant stock and still had close ties with relatives in their native villages, and indeed some workers continued to keep their families in the villages.

Soon after the adoption of the Constitution in 1946, a number of laws were adopted regulating marriage and divorce. The law on marriage, adopted in 1948, provided that marriages had to be contracted before an official of the local People's Council, and strong penalties were prescribed for any clergyman performing a religious ceremony before a civil ceremony had taken place. The legal age for contracting marriage was set at eighteen for both sexes, but persons as young as sixteen years of age could enter into marriage with the permission of the people's court. In such cases the minors did not need parental consent, and the law considered them "emancipated."

Marriage was based on the full equality of rights of both spouses. Thus the concept of the head of the family, recognized by pre-Communist civil law and so important for Albanian family life, was eliminated. Each of the spouses, according to the 1948 law, had the right to choose his or her own occupation, profession, and residence. Marriage with foreigners was prohibited unless entered into by permission of the government.

The laws on divorce were designed to facilitate and speed up divorce proceedings. The separation of spouses was made a ground for divorce under the law, and in such cases a court could grant a divorce without considering related facts or the causes of the separation. The basic divorce law, which was originally passed in 1948 and, after some modifications, was still in effect in 1970, provided that each spouse may ask for divorce on grounds on incompatibility of character, continued misunderstandings, irreconcilable hostility, or for any other reason that disrupted marital relations to the point where a common marital life had become impossible. Certain crimes committed by the spouse, especially political crimes, the so-called crimes against the state, and crimes involving moral turpitude, were also made causes for divorce.

In the 1950-64 period the total number of marriages averaged about 12,000 annually, except in 1961, when 18,725 marriages were registered; for the whole fourteen-year period marriages averaged about 7.8 per 1,000 population annually. During the same period there were about 1,000 divorces a year in the whole country; this represented about 0.2 percent of the total married population.

The problems still facing the Communist regime in its efforts to change the traditional character of society, especially in the countryside, were highlighted in a strong editorial in the February 8, 1970, issue of *Zeri i Popullit* (The Voice of the People), the Party's official daily. According to the article, the most dangerous antisocial phenomenon in the social life of the country was patriarchalism. This phenomenon was particularly strong in the mountainous north where it was firmly entrenched and involved people from rank-and-file villagers to Party members.

The basic difficulty derived from the fact that the local Communist leaders entertained patriarchal notions about the Party; they considered the Party organization as one in which they found a reincarnation of the clan. There was a tendency therefore for the Communists to admit to the Party organization people from their own *bajrak*, or clan, in order to have a dominant position in, and exercise command over, such socialist organizations as agricultural collectives. In a Party organization the head of one *bajrak* was put in command so that he could rule over the other, just as if he were the head of the clan. As in the old clan society, quarrels often occurred in basic Party Organizations when one *bajraktar* attempted to wrest control of the organization from another.

Entrance into the Party was considered by the patriarchal-minded highlanders as penetration into places where they could enjoy privileges and prestige. A similar situation prevailed in the agricultural collectives, in which the presidents of the collectives, imbued with the traditional idea of chieftainship, behaved toward the property of the collectives as if it were their own. The problems of the collectives were not submitted to either the basic Party organizations or to the general assembly of the collective. According to official criticism, everything was settled in the "clan style, in the spirit of family interest, of the clan, of the entity, precisely because they formed a family within which defense and support of their interests, right or wrong, had become the rule."

Enver Hoxha stated in a speech in 1968 that the position of the secretary of the Party organization or of an agricultural collective was considered in many areas as inheritable, just as the chieftainship in the tribal society has been inherited. The difficulties faced by the regime's attempts to eradicate the persistent patriarchal notions were succinctly phrased by Hoxha in his address to the Democratic Front Congress in September 1967. Declaring that the social problems in the country were complex in the towns and more so in the countryside, he lamented the fact that the rural areas:

have their own written and especially unwritten laws, which are often expressed in various regressive and harmful customs, in norms that are alien to our Communist morals. These are very dangerous and obstinate; they insistently resist the new and are liquidated with difficulty. These customs and norms have their own economic, ideological, religious, and ethical basis; they have their own class roots from capitalism to feudalism, indeed from the *bajrak* and the tribe.

In an obvious effort to root out some of the old prevailing customs and traditions, the Party inaugurated in 1967 a movement aimed at revolutionizing the family and, in Party jargon, liberating it from the remnants of bourgeois and petty bourgeois ideology. The targets have been directed toward the youth, both boys and girls. In resolutions adopted by the Party's Central Committee it was charged that in some families, because of the conservative and patriarchal mentality of the parents, the children were still not allowed to participate in parental conversations, especially the girls, on the pretext that they were too young and immature.

Discussions on morals, such as relations between boys and girls, love, and the creation of a socialist family, were particularly limited. It was the parents' view that they should not discuss such things with their children since this would undermine the traditional respect and authority of the parents. As stated in the January 30, 1970, issue of *Zeri i Popullit*, the need to strengthen the struggle against alien concepts that still plagued families became clearer when one considered some negative concepts that were evident in young people. Families of intellectuals were particularly singled out for criticism because, according to the Party journal, they manifested liberal attitudes in their attempts to satisfy every petty bourgeois craving and desire of their children; they instilled in them their own intellectual tendencies and fed and dressed them beyond their means.

Evidence of the Party's failure to detach the people completely from their traditional habits and customs was forcefully presented by the Party in a book published in 1968 under the title *Party Basic Organizations for Further Revolutionizing the Life of the Country*. It was freely admitted that much remained to be done in the struggle to emancipate the women and to draw boys and girls from the tutelage of their parents.

When the wife of a Party member decided to join the Party, for example, her husband addressed a note to the secretary of the basic Party organization saying that should the secretary enroll his wife in the Party, he would be destroying a family because he could not possibly live with his wife on an equal basis. Similarly, when a woman in a village was proposed as a member of the council of the agricultural collective, her brother-in-law objected strenuously, saying that her candidacy should be rejected since it was advanced without obtaining his permission as the head of the family and that in any case the "men of that family were not yet dead."

In a village in Kruje the first woman to become a Party candidate was asked to leave the Party because she did not belong to the same clan to which the Party secretary belonged. In another case, when a candidate was proposed for Party membership, someone reportedly stated that "we must enlist one from our clan also" in order to maintain the clan equilibrium in the Party.

The problem of social and family relations was still a major concern for the regime at the end of 1969. For example, in a major speech on family and social relations in November 1969, Hysni Kapo, the third-ranking man in the Party hierarchy, blamed the class enemy for the slow progress the Party had registered in creating a new social structure. The class enemy, Kapo admitted, was found everywhere, in and outside the Party, and it was striving hard to obstruct the path of socializing the family and emancipating the women.

Kapo bemoaned the fact that the men of the socialist society had not shaken off the vestiges of the past and that there were yet a large number of people who, with their behavior and actions at work, in society, and at home, were in contradiction to the requirements of the personality of the new man in the socialist society. Villages, agricultural collectives, artisan and trade cooperatives, and work centers daily faced such social problems as betrothals and marriages that did not follow guidelines set by the Party, conservative attitudes toward women and youth, and widespread tendencies toward clannishness.

According to Kapo, there were a large number of Communists who made little effort to implement the Party social line because the customs inherited from the old society still existed in the minds and hearts of the people and because the Party had been unable to divest people of all that was "hostile and reactionary and clothe them with the Party ideology." Kapo considered the most disturbing feature of this state of affairs to be the religious and patriarchal aspects that prevented the youth from creating a new socialist society and that continued to exist even among Communist cadres.

Western correspondents reporting from Tirana, in commenting on Kapo's speech, stated that what actually disturbed the Party most was the persistent opposition of the parents to new social standards set by the Party to regulate and control family life in general and the life of the youth in particular. Standards for dating, mixed Muslim-Christian marriages, engagement of boys and girls within socially accepted classes (the aim being to isolate the children of the former upper classes), and working and living together in various so-called volunteer construction projects were objectionable to parents.

EDUCATION

Pre-Communist Era

As late as the 1940s over 80 percent of the people were illiterate. The principal reason for this was that schools in the native language were practically nonexistent in the country before it became an independent state in 1912. Until about the middle of the nineteenth century the Ottoman rulers prohibited the use of the Albanian language in schools. The Turkish language was used in the few schools that existed, mainly in cities and large towns, for the Muslim population. The schools for Orthodox Christian children were under the supervision of the Istanbul Ecumenical Patriarchate. The teachers for these schools were usually recruited from the Orthodox clergy, and the language of instruction, as well as that used in textbooks, was Greek. The first known school to use the native tongue in modern history was in a Franciscan seminary that was opened in 1861 in Shkoder, where the Jesuits in 1877 founded a seminary in which the native tongue also was used.

During the last two decades of the nineteenth century and the first decade of the twentieth, a number of patriots who were striving to create a national consciousness founded several elementary schools in a few cities and towns, mostly in the south, but they were closed by the Turkish authorities. The advent of the Young Turks movement in 1908 encouraged the Albanian patriots to intensify their national efforts, and in the same year a group of intellectuals met in Monastir (Bitolj), Yugoslavia, to formulate an Albanian alphabet. Books written in Albanian before that date used a mixture of alphabets, consisting mostly of a combination of Latin, Greek, and Turkish-Arabic letters.

The Monastir meeting developed a unified alphabet based on Latin letters. As a result, a number of textbooks were written in the new alphabet, and elementary schools were soon opened in various parts of the country. In 1909, to meet the demands for teachers able to teach in the native tongue, a normal school was inaugurated in Elbasan. But in 1910 the Young Turks, fearing the emergence of Albanian nationalism, closed all schools that used Albanian as the language of instruction.

Even after the country became independent, schools were scarce. The unsettled political conditions caused by the Balkan wars and World War I hindered the development of a unified educational system. The foreign occupying powers, however, opened some schools in their respective areas of occupation, each using its own language. A few of these schools, especially the Italian and French, continued after the end of World War I and played a significant role in introducing Western educational methods and principles. Of particular importance was the French Lycée in Korce, founded by the French army in 1817.

Soon after the establishment of a national government in 1920, which included a Ministry of Education, the foundations were laid for a national educational system. Elementary schools were opened in the cities and some of the larger towns, and the Italian and French schools opened during the war were strengthened. In the meantime, two important American schools were founded—the American Technical School in Tirana, established by the American Junior Red Cross in 1921, and the American Agricultural School in Kavaje, sponsored by the Near East Foundation. An important girls' school was also founded by Kristo Dako, an Albanian-American, whose teaching language was English. The two top leaders of the Country in 1970, Party First Secretary Enver Hoxha and Prime Minister Mehmet Shehu, were educated in these foreign schools; Hoxha graduated from the French Lycée in 1930, and Shehu from the American Technical School in 1932.

In the 1920s, the period when the real foundations of the modern Albanian state were laid, education made considerable progress. In 1933 the Albanian Royal Constitution was amended, making the teaching and educating of citizens an exclusive right of the state. Education was thus nationalized, and all foreign-language schools, except the American Agricultural School, were either closed or nationalized. The reason for this move was to stop the rapid spread of schools sponsored directly by the Italian government, especially among the Catholic element in the north.

The nationalization of schools was followed in 1934 by a far-reaching reorganization of the whole school system. The new system provided for obligatory elementary education from the ages of four to fourteen; the expansion of secondary schools of various kinds; the establishment of new technical, vocational, and commercial secondary schools; and the acceleration and expansion of teacher training. The obligatory provisions of the 1934 reorganization law, however, were never enforced in the rural areas because of the economic conditions of the peasants who needed their children to work in the fields and because of the lack of schoolhouses, teachers, and means of transportation.

The only minority schools operating in the country before World War II were those for the Greek minority of about 35,000 living in the prefecture of Gjirokaster. These schools too were closed by the constitutional amendment of 1933, but Greece referred the case to the

International Permanent Court of Justice, which forced Albania to reopen the schools.

There was no university-level education in prewar Albania. All advanced studies were pursued abroad. Every year the state granted a number of scholarships to deserving high school graduates who were economically unable to continue their education. But the largest number of students were from well-to-do families and thus privately financed. For instance, in the 1936/37 academic year, only 65 of the 428 students attending universities abroad had state scholarships. The great majority of the students attended Italian universities because of geographic proximity and because of the special relationship between the Rome and Tirana governments. The Italian government itself, following its policy of political, economic, military, and cultural penetration of the country, granted a number of scholarships to Albanian students recommended by its legation in Tirana.

There are no reliable prewar statistics on school population. The 1967-68 Albanian official statistical yearbook placed the total 1938/39 school enrollment at 56,283. Other sources placed it at over 60,000. Soon after the Italian occupation in April 1939 the educational system came under complete Italian control. The Italian language was made compulsory in all secondary schools, and fascist ideology and orientation were inserted into the school curricula. After 1941, however, when guerrilla bands began to operate against the Italian forces, the whole educational system was paralyzed. In fact, secondary schools became centers of resistance and of guerrilla recruitment, and many teachers and students went to the mountains and became members or leaders of resistance bands. By September 1943, when Italy capitulated and German troops occupied the country, education came to a complete standstill.

Education Under Communist Rule

Immediately upon seizure of power in November 1944, the Communist regime gave high priority to opening the schools and organizing the whole educational system along Communist lines. The Communist objectives for the new school system were to liquidate illiteracy in the country as soon as possible, to struggle against "bourgeois survivals" in the country's culture, to transmit to the youth the ideas and principles of the Party, and to educate the children of all classes of society on the basis of these principles. The first Communist Constitution (1946) made it clear that the intention of the regime was to bring all children under the control of the state. The state, constitutionally, took special care for the education of youth, and all schools were placed under state management.

The Educational Reform Law of 1946 provided specifically that Marxist-Leninist principles would permeate all school texts. This law also made the struggle against illiteracy a principal goal of the new school system. A further step in this direction was taken in September 1949, when the government promulgated a law requiring all illiterates between ages twelve and forty to attend classes in reading and writing. Courses for illiterate peasants were established by the education sections of the people's councils. The political organs in the armed forces provided parallel courses for its illiterate military personnel.

The 1946 education law, in addition to providing for seven-year obligatory schooling and four-year secondary education, called for the establishment of a wide network of vocational, trade, and pedagogical schools to prepare personnel, technicians, and skilled workers for the various social, cultural, and economic fields. Another education law adopted in 1948 provided for the further expansion of vocational and professional courses to train skilled and semiskilled workers and to increase the theoretical and professional knowledge of the technicians.

A further step was taken in 1950 to expand technical education. Secondary technical schools were established along Soviet lines by the various economic ministries. In 1951 three higher institutes of learning were founded: the Higher Pedagogic Institute, the Higher Polytechnical Institute, and the Higher Agricultural Institute, all patterned along Soviet models. The Council of Ministers said that their purpose in founding these institutes was to create conditions for further development "according to the example of science, culture, and technique of the Soviet Union."

In the 1949-54 period the school system was given a thorough Soviet orientation both ideologically and structurally. Most textbooks, especially those dealing with scientific and technical matters, were Soviet translations. Soviet educators were attached to the major branches of the Ministry of Education. The Russian language was made compulsory as of the seventh grade, and Soviet methodology was applied. Large numbers of students and teachers were sent to Soviet pedagogical schools for study and training.

Courses for teacher preparation were established in which the Russian language, Soviet methods of pedagogy and psychology, and Marxist-Leninist dialectics were taught by Soviet instructors. A law adopted in 1954 reorganized the Ministry of Education, renamed it the Ministry of Education and Culture, and, among other things, provided for the dissemination of Communist principles "supported by the school experience of the Soviet Union." In 1957, when the State University of Tirana was opened, a team of Soviet educators laid its structural, curricular, and ideological foundations.

Parallel with the Sovietization of the school system in the 1950s, the government made a concerted effort to implement the idea that education must be directly connected with daily living. A large number of white-collar and blue-collar workers were registered in evening and correspondence courses in the various trade and professional schools. According to government statistics, in the late 1950s one out of every four workers was taking some kind of course. Importance was particularly given to improving polytechnical and related work experiences and to the dissemination of manual work in most of the schools. Attempts were made to build vocational workrooms in most elementary and secondary schools. Emphasis was placed on technical and agricultural subjects.

By 1960 the system of elementary and secondary education had evolved into an eleven-year program made up of schools of general education and of vocational and professional schools. The schools of general education consisted of primary grades one to four, intermediate grades five to seven, and secondary grades eight to eleven. In October 1960, however, as the Soviet-Albanian conflict was reaching the breaking point, the Party adopted a resolution calling for a reorganization of the whole school system, the real aim being to purge the schools of Soviet influence and rewrite the textbooks. One more year was added to the eleven-year general education schools, and the whole school program was integrated more closely with productive work so as to prepare youths to work in industry to replace some of the Soviet specialists should the latter be withdrawn, as they actually were in January and April 1961.

Another far-reaching school reform became effective on January 1, 1970. Two factors seemed to have accounted for the new reorganization: the apparent lack of success in completely ridding the schools of so-called revisionist Soviet influences and the decision, evidently related to the Soviet invasion of Czechoslovakia in 1968, to introduce military training in the whole school system. The reform was decreed by the Party's Central Committee in a special plenum held in June 1969. At the plenum the principal speakers were Party First Secretary Hoxha and Prime Minister Shehu, the latter in his capacity as chairman of a special education commission attached to the Central Committee. Hoxha charged that the old school system had left vestiges of the past in the consciousness of many intellectuals, teachers, professors, and men of science.

According to Hoxha the aim of the reform was to revolutionize the schools so that the new generation would be imbued with scientific and theoretical concepts of Marxism-Leninism and to combine these concepts with physical and military training. The new educational system was to persist in its struggle against old customs in society and in its efforts to inculcate youth with atheistic ideas. The new system, Hoxha declared, was intended in particular "to safeguard our schools from the Soviet revisionist school," which in a "demagogic way was degenerating into a bourgeois school." Accordingly, the Soviet concept in pedagogy was to be eradicated from the Albanian schools.

As reorganized on January 1, 1970, the system was divided into four general categories: preschool, general eight-year, secondary, and higher education (see fig. 5). On December 23, 1969, the government submitted to the People's Assembly a draft bill on educational reform, which was approved and became effective on January 1, 1970. The preamble to the law set the ideological tone of the new system. Its aim was to make "a decisive contribution to the training and education of the new man with comprehensive Communist traits, loyal to the end to the Party's cause," closely linking "learning with productive work and with physical and military education, giving absolute priority to Marxism-Leninism." In presenting the bill on the school reform to the People's Assembly, Minister of Education and Culture Thoma Deljana listed the three components of the reorganized school system as academic education, production, and military education.

The educational system in 1969 was divided into two general parts: one dealt with full-time pupils and students from the kindergarten to the university level, and the other with adult education for employed people. The eight-year education was obligatory, beginning at age six and ending at age thirteen; secondary education began with grade nine, or age fourteen, and ended with grade twelve.

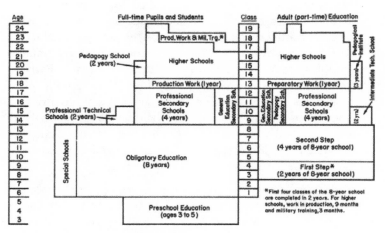

Figure 5. Educational System in Albania, 1969

Before a full-time student proceeds to higher education, he must pass a probationary period of one year in production work. The eight-year system was described as the fundamental link of the entire educational system; it was intended to provide the pupils with the primary elements of ideological, political, moral, aesthetic, physical, and military education. The new eight-year system differed from the old in that it lowered the entrance age from seven to six, and there were no longer separate primary and intermediate schools; that is, there was a single eight-year school, which was, however, completely separate from the secondary school.

The secondary schools were of many kinds, consisting of four-year general education courses and four-year vocational and professional courses (industrial, agricultural, pedagogic, trade, arts, health, and others). Some of these courses lasted only two years. In his report to the Party's Central Committee in June 1969 on the reform of the school year, Prime Minister Shehu said that the secondary schools were to have a standard curriculum for the school year. Priority was to be given to academic subjects, followed by production and by physical and military education.

Shehu formulated the structure of the academic year in all secondary schools as follows: 6-1/2 months of academic study, 2-1/2 months of productive work, 1 month of military training, and 2 months of vacation. The curriculum of the secondary schools and, with slight differences, of the higher schools was divided as follows: academic subjects, 55 to 56 percent; production work, 26 to 27 percent; and physical and military education, 17 to 19 percent. Shehu also said that terms borrowed from the Soviet school system, would be dropped, and in the future secondary schools would be known by such names as general secondary school and industrial, agricultural, construction, trade, art, and sanitation secondary schools.

The terms of study in the higher institutes lasted from three to five years. Provision was also made to expand higher education by increasing the number of full-time students, setting up new branches in places where there were no higher institutes, and organizing specialization courses for those who had completed higher education to train highly qualified technical and scientific cadres. All full-time graduate students had to serve a probationary period of nine months in production and three months in military training, in addition to the prescribed military training received while in school.

Adult education had the same structure as that for full-time students, with two exceptions: first, the eight-year general education was not compulsory and was contracted into a six-year program allowing for completion of the first four grades in two years; second, those who wanted to proceed to higher institutes after graduating from secondary school had to devote one year to preparatory study instead of engaging in production work, as did full-time students.

According to official statistics, in the late 1960s, the regime had made considerable strides, at least quantitatively, in education since it came to power in 1944 (see table 5). From a total enrollment of less than 60,000 students of all levels in the 1938/39 school year, according to the Tirana press, the number had reached over 570,000 in the 1969/70 school year, with a teaching staff of 22,000. The total enrollment included pupils in the compulsory eight-year schools and students, workers, and collective farmers in the eight-year general education, secondary, trade, and professional schools, the State University of Tirana, and other higher institutes of learning.

Nearly half of the total enrollment represented adults attending evening and correspondence courses. An article in the April 5, 1970, issue of *Zeri i Popullit* admitted that, of those originally enrolled in September 1969 in evening elementary, secondary, higher education, trade, and vocational courses, from 25 to 50 percent either dropped out or were often absent.

According to available official statistics, nearly 500,000 people were enrolled in schools and courses in the 1967/68 academic year; this included all adults who registered for, but did not necessarily attend regularly, technical and vocational courses, evening classes, or correspondence courses. In the same academic year the State University of Tirana and five other higher institutes of learning had a total enrollment of 12,435 students, of whom nearly 8,000 attended the State University of Tirana (see table 6). Of the total enrollment, over 4,000 were adults or part-time students.

In the 1945-56 period, that is, before the founding of the State University of Tirana, the government sent a number of students to pursue their education in the Soviet-bloc countries, mostly the Soviet Union. When the break came with Moscow in 1961, all students were either expelled or withdrawn from all these countries. According to documents published by the Tirana government after the break, at the beginning of the 1961/62 academic year there were 1,213 Albanian students already enrolled in Soviet institutions, and an additional 100 were to enroll during that academic year. They were all expelled by the Soviets except for a few who asked for and obtained political asylum. In 1970 an unknown number of students were attending schools in the People's Republic of China (Communist China), and a few in Romania and Italy.

Table 5. Summary of Educational Institutions, Pupils, and Teachers in Albania, for Selected Years

	1938/39	1950/51	1960/61	1967/68
Primary and Secondary Education				
Schools	649	2,222	2,990	3,597
Pupils	55,404	172,831	290,728	455,557
Teachers	1,477	4,942	9,071	16,758
Secondary Professional Schools				
Schools	5	17	34	25
Pupils	879	4,818	14,105	21,005
Teachers	34	171	511	638
Normal Schools				
Schools	(3)	(8)	(11)	(5)
Pupils	(675)	(2,525)	(5,591)	(2,708)
Teachers	(18)	(61)	(200)	(115)
Technical Schools				
Schools	(2)	(9)	(23)	(20)
Pupils	(204)	(2,253)	(8,514)	(18,297)
Teachers	(16)	(110)	(311)	(522)
Higher Education				
Institutes	—	1	6	6
Students	—	304	6,703	12,436
Professors and assistants	—	13	288	606

All Educational Systems*

Schools	654	22,240	3,030	3,628
Pupils and students	56,283	177,953	311,536	498,997
Teachers and instructors	1,511	5,126	10,942	18,001

* The lower vocational schools are not included.

Source: Adapted from *Vjetari Statistikor i R. P. Sh.*, 1967-68, Tirana, 1968, p. 115.

The chain of command in the organization of the educational system in 1970 ran from the Party Politburo to the education sections in the district people's councils. The Politburo set the general policy guidelines and directives. In 1968 the Politburo created a Central Commission on Education attached to the Central Committee and headed by Prime Minister Mehmet Shehu. The commission's function was to elaborate the Politburo's directives on reforming the school system. When Mehmet Shehu submitted the report on behalf of the commission to the plenum of the Central Committee in June 1969 concerning the reorganization of the school system, it was decided to continue the commission for an indefinite period.

A more permanent body in the Party's Central Committee was the Directorate of Education and Culture, headed by Nexhmije Hoxha, wife of Party First Secretary Enver Hoxha. This body, guided by the directives prescribed by the Politburo, supervised the Ministry of Education and Culture in implementing the Party's ideological and political guidelines.

Table 6. Students Attending Higher Institutes in Albania
(academic year 1967/68)

	Total Number of Students		Full-Time Students	
	Total	Female	Total	Female
State University of Tirana				
Faculties				

Economics	1,275	271	437	137
Geology	255	10	255	10
History and Philology	1,944	701	984	462
Engineeering	1,259	139	1,102	120
Law	504	62	163	29
Medicine	1,034	378	1,034	378
Natural Sciences	1,683	529	1,262	440
Total	7,954	2,090	5,237	1,576
Higher Agricultural Institute				
Faculties				
Agronomy	1,234	62	839	58
Forestry	174	10	150	8
Veterinary	324	23	324	23
Total	1,732	95	1,313	89
Higher Institute of Arts	239	60	232	60
Higher Institute of Physical Culture	191	39	169	37
Two-Year Higher Institute of Pedagogy, Tirana	1,113	458	331	140
Two-Year Higher Institute of Pedagogy, Shkoder	1,206	446	859	316
Grand Total	12,435	3,188	8,141	2,218

Source: Adapted from *Vjetari Statistikor i R. P. Sh., 1967-1968*, Tirana, 1968, p. 125.

The Ministry of Education and Culture was responsible for executing Party policies and for administering the whole school system. It had education sections in all the district people's councils, which administered and, through their inspectors, controlled the teachers and the teaching programs. Party control at all levels was exercised either directly by the Party's basic organizations, as was the case in the higher institutes, or through the branches of the Union of Albanian Working Youth, the Party's most powerful front organization. The majority of the teachers in secondary schools and higher institutes were Party members.

By the beginning of 1970 the regime seemed to have scored substantial progress in the field of education. Illiteracy had been reduced considerably, if not actually eliminated. Through an intensive program to train elementary and secondary school teachers, build schoolhouses, and make schooling obligatory up to the eighth grade, the government had enabled all the country's children to obtain some kind of rudimentary education. It had also instituted a system of higher education and had founded the first university in the history of the country and was thus no longer dependent on foreign universities to train people in the various professions. It had also instituted a widespread network of professional and vocational schools intended to train badly needed technicians and skilled workers.

The whole education network, however, was a one-track system geared to serve the ideological and political objectives of the Party. The Party, through the Central Commission on Education and the Directorate of Education and Culture, both attached to the Party's Central Committee, controlled every facet of the school system: programs, curricula, administration, teaching staffs, and funds. The schools, students, teachers, and professors were so organized as to form a monolithic establishment centrally directed and completely immersed in Marxism-Leninism.

The entire system was dedicated to the education of the new man with Communist traits and morality. As defined by the Party leaders and Party theoreticians, these traits and morality meant the development of a "revolutionary spirit and responsibility for one's tasks for society and the cause of socialism, the defense of the basic principles of the Party and the implementation of its correct policy." The whole school system, as developed in the past twenty-five years, therefore, was for the building of communism as defined and interpreted by the Albanian Communists. All other ideologies, beliefs, cultures, and thoughts were banned from the country's schools.

RELIGION

Situation Before the Communist Takeover

One of the major legacies of nearly five centuries of Ottoman rule was the conversion of over 70 percent of the population to Islam. When independence came, therefore, the country emerged as a predominantly Muslim nation, the only Islamic state in Europe. No censuses taken by the Communist regime since it assumed power in 1944 have shown the religious affiliations of the people. It has been estimated that of a total population of 1,180,500, at the end of World War II, about 826,000 were Muslims, 212,500 Eastern Orthodox, and 142,000 Roman Catholics. The Muslims were divided between adherents of the Sunni branch and over 200,000 followers of a dervish order known as Bektashi, an offshoot of the Shia branch.

Christianity was introduced early in Albania, having been brought in during the period of Roman rule. After the division of the Roman Empire into East and West in 395, Albania became politically a part of the Eastern, or Byzantine, Empire but remained ecclesiastically dependent on Rome. When, however, the final schism occurred in 1054 between the Roman and Eastern churches, the Christians in the southern part of the country came under the jurisdiction of the Constantinople Ecumenical Patriarchate. This situation prevailed until the Turkish invasions of the fourteenth century, when the Islamic faith was introduced. The apostasy of the people took many decades.

In the mountainous north the propagation of Islam met strong resistance from the Catholics. Gradually, however, backwardness, illiteracy, the absence of an educated clergy, and material inducements weakened resistance. Coerced conversions occurred, especially when Catholic powers, such as the Venetian Republic and Austria, were at war with the Ottoman Empire. By the close of the seventeenth century the Catholics in the north were outnumbered by the Muslims.

Large-scale forced conversions among the Orthodox in the south did not occur until the Russo-Turkish wars of the eighteenth century. Islamic pressure was put on the Orthodox Christians because the Turks considered them sympathetic to Orthodox Russia. The situation of the Orthodox improved temporarily after a Russo-Turkish treaty of 1774 in which Russia was recognized as the protector of the Orthodox Christians in the Ottoman Empire. The most effective method employed by the Turks in their missionary efforts, especially in the central and southern parts of the country, was the creation of a titled noble Muslim class of *pashas*, *beys*, and *agas* (Albanian tribal chiefs in Turkish service), who were endowed with both large estates and extensive political and governing powers. Through their political and economic influences these nobles controlled the peasants, large numbers of whom were converted to Islam either through coercion or through promise of economic benefits.

In the period from independence to the Communist seizure of power, the Muslim noble class composed the country's ruling elite, but this elite never interfered with religious freedom, which was sanctioned by the various pre-World War II constitutions. The church and state were separate. These constitutions had declared that the country had no official religion, that all religions and faiths were respected, and that their freedom of exercise was assured. These provisions had expressed the true feelings of the people who, whether Muslim, Eastern Orthodox, or Roman Catholic, were tolerant on religious matters.

Tolerance has been a marked characteristic of all Albanians, as indicated in part by the fact that even after accepting Islam, many people privately remained practicing Christians, or so-called crypto-Christians. As late as 1912 in a large number of villages in the Elbasan area, most men had two names, a Muslim one for public use and a Christian one for private use. A characteristic remark on the religious tolerance of the Albanians was made by Lord Byron, who observed in one of his diaries that elsewhere in the Ottoman Empire a man would declare himself to be either a Muslim or a Christian when asked what he was, but the Albanian would reply that he was an Albanian.

Situation Under Communist Rule

The Communist regime has exhibited in its attitude toward religion a wide gap between precept and practice. The Communist Constitution, adopted in March 1946 and as subsequently amended, contains liberal provisions with regard to religion. Freedom of conscience and religion is guaranteed to all citizens; the church is separate from the state; religious communities are free to exercise and practice their creeds; it is forbidden to use the church and religion for political purposes, and political organizations based on religion are outlawed; and the state may give material assistance to religious organizations.

Even before the adoption of the Constitution, however, legislative measures had already been taken to curb the freedom and power of all religious bodies. For example, the agrarian reform law of August 1945 made special provision for the confiscation of all their wealth, especially the estates of monasteries, orders, and dioceses, and the seizure of their libraries and printing presses. But the first major law aimed specifically at the control and regulation of all religious bodies and at the elimination of all distinguished clergymen was enacted two years after the promulgation of the Constitution. This law is known as Decree No. 743 On Religious Communities, approved by the Council of Ministers on November 26,

1949, converted into Law No. 773 on January 16, 1950, and amended by Decree No. 3660 of April 10, 1963.

The law provided that religious communities through their activities had to develop in their followers a sentiment of loyalty toward the People's Republic of Albania. In order to organize and function, religious communities had to be recognized by the state, such recognition taking place as a result of the approval of their statutes by the Council of Ministers. All regulations and bylaws issued on the basis of such statutes had also to be approved by the Council of Ministers, and the heads of religious communities and sects had to be approved by the Council of Ministers after being elected or appointed by the proper religious organs. Religious communities or branches, such as the Jesuit and Franciscan orders, that had their headquarters outside the country were henceforth prohibited and ordered to terminate their activities within a month of the enactment of the decree.

All religious communities were obliged to send at once to the Council of Ministers all pastoral letters, messages, speeches, and other instructions of a general character that were to be made public in any form. Religious institutions were forbidden to have anything to do with the education of the young since this was the exclusive right of the state, and all religious communities were prohibited from operating philanthropic and welfare institutions and hospitals or from owning real estate.

On the basis of Decree No. 743 the Council of Ministers on May 4, 1950, issued Decrees Nos. 1064, 1065, and 1066, approving respectively the statutes of the Sunni, Orthodox, and Bektashi religious communities. A common provision of all three decrees was that each religious community had to develop the "sentiment of loyalty in their followers toward the people's power and the People's Republic of Albania, as well as their patriotic feelings." The Statute of the Independent Catholic Church of Albania was approved by Decree No. 1322 of July 30, 1951.

The regime's policy toward each of the three religious denominations, although differing somewhat in tactics, aimed from the outset at the eventual destruction of all organized religion. The regime achieved control over the Muslim faith by dealing with each sect separately. The first measure aimed at dividing the Sunni and Bektashi, which was effected, officially, in May 1945, when the two were declared completely independent of each other.

In dealing with the Sunni clergy, the government arrested and executed as "enemies of the people" those members of the top hierarchy who were reluctant to toe the Communist line, while others were imprisoned or sent to concentration camps. It named as head of the Sunni community Hafez

Musa Haxhi Ali, who in 1950 led a delegation of the Sunni clergy to the Soviet Union, visiting Uzbekistan and the Muslim religious shrines of Samarkand and Tashkent and meeting with many Soviet Muslim leaders. He was also used in appeals for world peace and other slogans directed at the Muslim countries in the Middle East.

The policy followed toward each group differed somewhat. The Bektashi group had always been much more liberal and forward looking than the Sunni. During the war a few leading Bektashi clergymen had joined the National Liberation Movement, and three of them—Baba Mustafa Faja Martaneshi, Baba Fejzo, and Sheh Karbunaro—played major roles in bringing about close collaboration between the Bektashi order and the regime. In March 1947, however, Baba Faja and Baba Fejzo were assassinated at the group's headquarters in Tirana, where they had gone to meet with the World Bektashi Primate Dede Abazi (the Bektashi had moved their world headquarters in the 1920s from Ankara to Tirana). As the Tirana press reported the event: "The leaders of the Bektashi, Baba Faja and Baba Fejzo, cooperating with the people's government, visited Dede Abazi to discuss the democratization of the religious organization. Dede Abazi answered with bullets, killing them both. Later he shot himself." Taking advantage of this incident, the regime eliminated those leaders of the Bektashi clergy it considered disloyal.

Because of the traditionally nationalistic character of the Albanian Orthodox Church, the regime has attempted from the outset to use it as an instrument for mobilizing the Orthodox population behind its policies. Using the church for its own ends, the regime took steps to purge all those elements within it that were considered unreliable. Clergymen who did not yield to the demands of the regime were purged.

Among the purged Orthodox leaders was the primate of the church, Archbishop Kristofor Kisi, who was deposed in the late 1940s and subsequently died in jail. The regime replaced Kisi with Pashko Vodica, a renegade priest who had joined the ranks of the partisan formations. On assuming the office of primate, under the name of Archbishop Paisi, he stated that it was the church's duty to be faithful to the People's Republic of Albania and to the people's power and added: "Our Church must be faithful to the camp of Peace, to the great anti-imperialist and democratic camp, to the unique camp of socialism led brilliantly by the glorious Soviet Union and the Great Stalin...."

Archbishop Paisi brought about close ties between the Albanian Orthodox Church and the Moscow Patriarchate. These ties were further strengthened after a delegation of Soviet religious leaders, headed by

Bishop Nikon of Odessa, visited Tirana in the spring of 1951. After the 1960-61 Moscow-Tirana break, however, these ties lapsed.

The Roman Catholic Church, chiefly because it maintained close relations with the Vatican and was more organized than were the Muslim and Eastern Orthodox faiths, became a principal target of persecution as soon as the Communists assumed power. In May 1945 Monsignor Nigris, the apostolic nuncio in Albania, was arrested on charges of fomenting anti-Communist feelings and deported to Italy. In 1946 a number of Catholic clergymen were arrested and tried on charges of distributing leaflets against the regime; some were executed, others given long prison terms at hard labor.

According to Vatican sources, from 1945 to 1953 the number of Catholic churches and chapels in Albania was reduced from 253 to 100. Both seminaries in the country were closed, and the number of monasteries dropped from ten to two. All twenty convents were closed, as were fifteen orphanages, sixteen church schools, and ten charitable institutions. Both Catholic printing presses were confiscated, and the publication of seven religious periodicals ceased.

The ranks of Catholic priests were thinned from ninety-three in 1945 to ten in 1953, twenty-four having been executed, thirty-five imprisoned, ten either missing or dead, eleven drafted into the army, and three having escaped from the country. Secular officials and laymen active in church affairs also suffered execution, imprisonment, and harassment.

The Catholic school system was completely eliminated. This included five secondary schools with a total enrollment of 570 and ten elementary and vocational schools with 2,750 pupils. All Catholic associations were suppressed.

A severe blow against the Catholic church was struck in 1951, when the regime mustered a small group of clergymen to hold a national Catholic assembly to draw the statute for the church. As approved by the Council of Ministers on July 30 of that year, the statute provided that the "Catholic Church of Albania has a national character ... [and that] it shall no longer have any organizational, political, or economic relations with the Pope." The statute provided further that the church was to be directed both in religious and administrative matters by a new Catholic Episcopate, that relations concerning religious questions could be established only through governmental channels, and that the church would submit to the canon law of the world Catholic church only if the provisions of this law did not contradict the laws of the People's Republic of Albania.

Enver Hoxha himself spearheaded the campaign against the Catholic church. In 1952, for example, he purged Tuk Jakova, the only Catholic member of the Politburo and previously one of Hoxha's closest collaborators, because he had allegedly befriended the Catholic clergy. In his speech to the Second Party Congress in 1952, in an attempt to justify Jakova's purge, Hoxha said: "Comrade Tuk Jakova, in contradiction to the political line of the Party and of the state concerning religion generally and the Catholic clergy in particular, has not properly understood and has not properly acted against the Catholic clergy. Without seeing the great danger of the reactionary clergy, Comrade Tuk Jakova has not hated them in sufficient measure...."

A new policy aimed at the complete destruction of organized religion was enunciated by Hoxha in a speech to the Party's Central Committee on February 6, 1967. Calling for an intensified cultural-education struggle against religious beliefs and declaring that the only religion for an Albanian should be Albanianism, he assigned the antireligious mission to the youth movement. By May of the same year religious institutions were forced to relinquish 2,169 churches, mosques, cloisters, and shrines, most of which were converted into cultural centers for young people. As the literary monthly *Nendori* (November) in its September 1967 issue reported the event, the youth had thus "created the first atheist nation in the world."

According to Western correspondents in Tirana, the procedure employed in seizing the places of worship was to assemble the villagers or parishioners in order to discuss Hoxha's speech and to take measures to eliminate what the regime referred to as harmful survivals of religious customs. A decision was then taken to ask the government for permission to close a church, mosque, or monastery. A few days later the government, stating that it was following the will of the people, would issue orders to close the house of worship.

Drastic measures were reportedly taken in cases where the clergy opposed the government order. The strongest resistance came from the Catholic clergy, resulting in the detention of some twenty priests. The cloister of the Franciscan order in Shkoder was set afire in the spring of 1967, resulting in the death of four monks. The Catholic cathedral in Tirana had its facade removed, and on June 4, 1967, it was taken over by the government and converted into a museum. A similar fate befell the Catholic cathedrals in Shkoder and Durres.

After the seizure of the houses of worship, the younger clergymen were forced to seek work either in industry or agricultural collectives. The elder clergy were ordered to return to their birthplaces, which they could not leave without permission from the authorities. Monsignor Ernest Coba, bishop of Shkoder and acknowledged head of the Catholic church in Albania, was evicted from the cathedral in April 1967 and was forced to seek work as a gardener on a collective farm. He was still alive but ailing at the end of 1969.

By the beginning of 1970 the provision of the Constitution concerning freedom of religion was ostensibly in effect, but government decrees had made such a provision a dead issue. On November 22, 1967, a significant measure was taken that apparently aimed at delivering the coup de grace to formal religious institutions. On that day *Gazeta Zyrtare*, the government's official gazette, published Decree No. 4337 of the Presidium of the People's Assembly entitled, "On the Abrogation of Certain Decrees." Specifically, the new decree annulled all previous decrees dealing with organized religion, thus removing official sanction from religious bodies and, in effect, placing them outside the law.

The 1949 decree on religion had provided for subsidies from the state to the three religious denominations. These subsidies had become indispensable for their survival because their property and all other material means of subsistence had been confiscated and nationalized in 1945, and without state help the churches could not function. Concurrent with the official moves against religions, a number of antireligious brochures and pamphlets were prepared and distributed by the Democratic Front in an effort to prepare the people for the attacks on their religious institutions.

Even though organized religion had been destroyed by the end of 1967, the regime was still struggling as of early 1970 to eradicate religious thought and beliefs. The *Nendori* article that proclaimed the creation of the first atheist state in the world admitted that "despite the hard blows religion had suffered through the destruction of its material institutions, religious ideology is still alive."

Hoxha himself has often admitted that antireligious measures and the closing of places of worship have not sufficed to eradicate religious beliefs. Thus, addressing the Fourth Congress of the Democratic Front in September 1967, he declared that it was misleading to hold that religion consisted of church, mosque, priests, icons, and the like, and that if all of these disappeared, then automatically religion and its influence on the people would vanish. The struggle against religious beliefs, he added, had not ended because for centuries they had been deeply rooted in the conscience of the people.

Hoxha reverted to the subject again in his speech to the Party's Central Committee plenum in June 1969, devoted to reforming the school system, in which he said that one of the aims of the reorganized schools would be to bring up the new generation imbued with scientific and theoretical knowledge; for, according to Hoxha, religious beliefs could be eradicated only through the elimination of old concepts still prevalent in the minds of the people.

At the beginning of 1970 Party leaders in their speeches and in the press were continuing to call for an intensification of the struggle against religious ideology and especially for the eradication of every religious influence or belief among students, who were still under the influence of parents. The older generation, according to the leadership, continued to entertain the religious beliefs that everything in nature has been created with a predetermined purpose by God. The press has also reported on several occasions that there was strong resistance to the closing of places of worship and that the clergy resorted to all kinds of subterfuge to continue their religious activities.

CHAPTER 6

GOVERNMENT STRUCTURE AND POLITICAL SYSTEM

Political power in 1970 was solely in the hands of the ruling elite, that is, the leadership of the Communist Party (officially the Albanian Workers' Party). No political, economic, or social activity occurred without the sanction of the Party. Although the facade of a people's republic under constitutional rule was established in 1946, the reality of a rigid police state was clearly evident from the beginning, and no true democratic processes had been allowed to develop. The greatly heralded People's Assembly, people's councils, and people's courts were elected from a list of Party candidates; only one candidate was presented for each office, and there was no popular selection or popular choice. In effect, the Party was the government and directed all aspects of the lives of the people—from the cradle to the grave.

The governmental structure and political system of the Albanian People's Republic have their roots in the National Liberation Movement, which came into existence during the Italian and German occupations of World War II. Communist Party members dominated the leadership and, while combating Italian and German occupiers, fought against other national resistance groups for postwar control of the country. Enver Hoxha, first secretary of the Albanian Workers' Party in 1970, and Mehmet Shehu, premier and second ranking Party member, were wartime leaders of the Communist resistance forces. Superior organization and the establishment of crude governing bodies called national liberation councils facilitated the Communist takeover of the country after the cessation of hostilities. These councils later became the basis of the postwar governmental structure.

The Communists moved rapidly after the end of the war to prevent the reestablishment of the monarchy and to secure their own position of power. Operating under the banner of a mass organization known as the Democratic Front, the Communist Party strengthened its hold on the country and in early 1946 promulgated a Constitution based on Yugoslav and Soviet models. This Constitution provided for a unicameral legislature, a collective executive branch, and an independent judiciary. Actually, the Albanian Workers' Party, formerly the Communist Party, which is mentioned in the Constitution as "the vanguard organization of the working class," uses the formal governmental structure as the instrument for governing the nation and for implementing its own policies.

The Albanian People's Republic in its twenty-five years as a Communist nation has remained as rigidly authoritarian and Stalinist in its approach to government as it was at the end of World War II. The Party is all pervasive, the leadership is glorified to an extreme degree, and Party pronouncements are treated as infallible doctrine. The average citizen casts his ballot in periodic elections for local and national offices, but two conditions invariably exist: a candidate for office is a member of the Party, and only one name is listed for any particular office. It has become standard practice for well over 99 percent of the electorate to vote and for over 99 percent of those voting to approve the single candidate. Absolute control of the government, the economy, and the cultural life of the country is assured by a system that places the leading officers of the Party in the top positions of government.

Albanian history as a Communist state can be divided into three distinct phases based on outside influence: the Yugoslav period, the Soviet period, and the Chinese period. Yugoslav influence began with the founding in 1941 of the Albanian Communist Party, in which some Yugoslav nationals played leading roles, and lasted until Yugoslavia's expulsion from the Cominform in 1948. From 1948 until 1961 the Albanians looked to the Soviet Union for assistance and advice, and after 1961 Communist China became the foreign power wielding greatest influence in the country.

In 1970 Albania continued as the only European ally of Communist China. Hoxha and Shehu continued the harsh polemics with the Soviet Union; made tentative gestures of friendship toward Yugoslavia; continued their tirades against Western imperialism; and, in general, tried to present themselves to the world as the embodiment of true Marxism-Leninism.

FORMAL STRUCTURE OF GOVERNMENT

The People's Assembly

The Constitution established the People's Assembly as the legislative branch of the government and refers to it as "the highest organ of state power." Representatives to the Assembly are elected from a single list of Party-selected candidates for a term of four years in a ratio of 1 representative for every 8,000 inhabitants. The Assembly meets in two regularly scheduled sessions annually, and there is constitutional provision for the convening of extraordinary sessions.

All legislative power is vested in the People's Assembly, although proposals for legislation and for constitutional amendments can be made by the Presidium of the People's Assembly or the Council of Ministers, as well as by members of the Assembly itself. Bills become laws after an affirmative vote by a simple majority of the Assembly, but an amendment to the Constitution requires a two-thirds vote. In practice, the Assembly listens to the reading of bills drawn up by its Presidium and then votes unanimous approval.

The Assembly elects officers to preside over its meetings and direct its affairs. Usually a chairman, two vice chairmen, and a secretary are elected for the four-year term of the Assembly. The chairman of the People's Assembly in 1970 was Abdyl Kellezi, who was concurrently a candidate member of the Party, Political Bureau (Politburo). One of the two vice chairmen and the secretary were also members of the Party Central Committee. The Assembly has the power to appoint commissions, to carry out specific functions, or to conduct investigations.

The Presidium

The Constitution provides that the People's Assembly elect its Presidium, which is made up of a president, two vice presidents, a secretary, and ten members. The president of the Presidium becomes the titular chief of state and, in 1970, this office was held by Haxhi Leshi, a member of the Party Central Committee. Enver Hoxha was one of the ten members of the Presidium, and a majority of the other Presidium members concurrently held high Party positions. Because of the infrequent and short meetings of the Assembly and because the real power, that is Party power, is held by the Presidium, it has become the actual legislative branch of government.

The Presidium performs several functions besides that of conducting the affairs of the Assembly between sessions. It calls for the elections of representatives to the Assembly and convenes its sessions. It has the power to issue decrees and to ratify international treaties. The Presidium also appoints or recalls diplomats, receives credentials and letters of recall of foreign diplomats, and appoints and recalls the supreme commander of the armed forces. Between sessions of the Assembly, the Presidium is empowered to decree general mobilization and a state of war and to appoint and relieve ministers as proposed by the premier. The Presidium also designates ministry jurisdiction over various enterprises according to the recommendations of the premier.

The Council of Ministers

The Council of Ministers, referred to as the government in the Constitution, is the highest executive organ and constitutionally is appointed by, and responsible to, the People's Assembly or its Presidium. The chairman of the Council of Ministers, by virtue of his position, is also the premier or prime minister. Mehmet Shehu, who assumed this position in 1954, still held it in 1970. Shehu was also a member of the Politburo of the Party Central Committee. The Council of Ministers is composed of the chairman, three deputy chairmen, thirteen ministers, and the chairman of the State Planning Commission, who has ministerial rank. The Constitution provides for the establishment of new ministries and the abolishment or combining of old ones.

The Council of Ministers, as a unit, is constitutionally responsible for preparing the overall economic plan and the budget, which must then be approved by the People's Assembly. After approval, which is pro forma and usually granted without discussion or debate, the council is responsible for implementation. The council also directs the monetary system; assures protection of citizens rights and the maintenance of public order; directs the organization of the army; oversees foreign relations; and, in effect, administers the entire economic and cultural life of the nation.

The interlocking of the Party with the Council of Ministers has been standard practice since its inception. In 1970 eight of the seventeen principal officers of the council were members or candidate members of the Politburo, six were Central Committee members, and the remaining three were regular members of the Party. With every key position occupied by a Politburo member, the Party elite maintained direct control over the entire governmental structure.

Local Government

People's councils are the constitutional agencies on the local level. Elected for three-year terms to administer districts, cities, and villages, they are responsible to their constituencies as well as to the higher organs of state power. According to the Constitution, the councils are charged with economic and cultural matters and direct the affairs of the administrative organs within their jurisdictions. Councils are responsible for maintaining public order, for implementing laws, and for drawing up local budgets. The Constitution also requires that the councils call periodic meetings of their constituents to keep the people informed on council activities.

Each council chooses an executive committee from among its membership, and it is through this committee that the actual work of local government is accomplished. Other committees or departments may be established at the discretion of the executive committee for the performance of specific tasks or for the supervision of a particular enterprise. In performing such functions, the special committees and departments are constitutionally responsible to the people's councils and to corresponding sections at higher levels of the bureaucracy. The people's councils are elected from lists of the local organizations of the Albanian Workers' Party.

COURT SYSTEM

The people's court system consists of the Supreme Court and courts at each of the territorial subdivisions. Other types of courts may be created by law. The Constitution provides that the people's courts are independent of the administration. A law on the organization of the courts passed in 1968, however, specified that the "people's courts will be guided in their activities by the policy of the Party. In carrying out their responsibilities, they must strongly rely on the working masses and submit to their criticism and control."

Decisions are made collegially. In cases where the Supreme Court and district courts have original jurisdiction—that is, when a case is to be first heard by them—assistant judges participate in the ruling, unless the case is such that the law specifically states otherwise. People's courts at the village and city levels decide cases with the participation of an assistant judge from the district court and two so-called social activists, who are actually local Party members. If a case is before the Supreme Court by appeal, three judges make the verdict; when a case is before a district court by appeal, assistant judges participate.

Trials are generally open to the public. In order to facilitate the political and social education of the population, courts are held in places of employment, villages, and any other place that makes them more accessible to the people.

Assistant judges from the district courts and several social activists make up the village and city courts. The social activists are elected for one-year terms by a people's meeting. This level of the court system has jurisdiction over minor social crimes and simple civil cases.

The district courts are composed of a chairman, judges, and assistant judges. The judges are elected for three-year terms by the general population, and the People's Council appoints the chairman from among the elected judges. The district courts have original jurisdiction in all penal and civil cases unless otherwise specified by law. They also hear appeals from lower court decisions.

Military courts, called military collegiums, are appointed by the Presidium of the People's Assembly to operate at the district level. They are composed of a military judge and several military assistant judges. These courts have original jurisdiction over crimes committed by military personnel.

The highest court is the Supreme Court. It has original jurisdiction in important cases that the chairman of the Supreme court takes over from the district courts. It also hears appeals from the rulings of all lower courts.

Supreme Court judges are elected for four-year terms by the People's Assembly. The court consists of a chairman, deputy chairmen, and assistant judges, the exact number being determined by the Presidium of the People's Assembly. The Supreme Court is broken down into collegiums to handle different types of cases, such as penal, civil, and military. It also sits in a plenum in order to issue directives concerning legal practices, to hear appeals from decisions made by its collegium, and to study the operation of the court system in its entirety.

POLITICAL DYNAMICS

The Dictatorship of the Proletariat

As officially defined by the Constitution, the state is a form of dictatorship of the proletariat. The power of the state constitutionally belongs to the workers and peasants, represented locally by the people's councils, which supposedly make up the political base of the state. In legislation and in official documents dealing with elections, it has been stated that the people not only enjoy freedom of choice concerning candidates but also have the right to supervise the work of their elected representatives and the right of recall if they are dissatisfied. In practice, such people's democracy does not exist, and the dictatorship of the proletariat—that is, the rule of the people over themselves—is a facade behind which the real dictatorship of the Party elite operates.

The Constitution provides for direct, secret vote to elect representatives to all governmental bodies, from the people's councils in villages to the highest organ of the state, the People's Assembly. The voters themselves do nothing on their part to be registered in the electoral lists. These lists are drawn up for every type of election by the people's councils and are supposed to include all citizens who reach age eighteen on or before the day of the elections.

The democratic character of these elections is allegedly guaranteed by the procedure or right for nominating candidates. This right legally belongs to the Party, the Democratic Front, trade unions, and social organizations and is exercised by the central organs of these organizations and their organs in the districts. Nominations, with Party approval, also are made at the general meetings of workers and employees in the enterprises and state farms, of soldiers in their detachments, and of peasants in their agricultural collectives or villages.

All meetings for the selection of candidates are held under the auspices of the Democratic Front, in whose name all the candidates are presented for election. The only legal requirement of a candidate is that he enjoy the right to election, that the organization which proposes him confirm its intention in writing, and that he accept his candidacy for that of the Assembly was a "vivid expression of the socialist democ-him. In practice, all candidates are preselected, and the meetings simply confirm the Party choice.

Political power, according to official documents, is thus vested in the broad masses who, through various organizations to which they belong, choose the candidates to be elected to all state organs, including the people's courts. The candidate who receives one more vote than half the number of voters registered in the electoral zone is proclaimed the winner and becomes, in theory, the agent representing the sovereignty of the people.

The highest organ of state power, according to official dogma, is the People's Assembly, composed of representatives elected by direct vote who exercise the sovereignty and will of the people. The aim of the People's Assembly, this dogma alleges, is to carry out the main functions of directing and supervising the people's democratic state. The Assembly's sphere of action includes practically all the political, economic, social, and cultural fields through the passage of laws. "These laws," according to an official document published in 1964, "on their part determine the juridical form of the line pursued by the Albanian Workers' Party in building socialism in Albania." The same document that stated that the laws passed by the Assembly were but the juridical form of Party policies declared that the concentration of all state power in the hands of the Assembly was a "vivid expression of the socialist democracy of the state system of the People's Republic of Albania."

Another document, published in 1963, asserted that economic power and political power were indivisible and that a combination of the two formed the state power. The representative nature of the socialist state, the document declared, was rooted in the socialist economic basis of the country, derived from the state ownership of the means of production and from the property of the cooperative and collective organizations, principally the agricultural collectives. All mines and subsoil resources, waters, forests and pastures, industrial enterprises, the means of air, rail, and sea communications, post, telegraph, telephones, radio broadcasting stations, and banks had become the property of the people.

It is thus the contention of the regime that the creation of the socialist sector of the economy not only placed all economic levers in the hands of the people but also altered old relations in production, resulting in a planned organization of the economy. Economic planning, it is argued, makes possible the elimination of exploitation of man by man. Also, through the planned organization of the economy the people are guaranteed the right to work.

With a view to regulating relations in work, the regime passed a series of legislative acts that were subsequently embodied in the Labor Code. As a result of this legislation, it was asserted, conflicts between a worker and an enterprise were no longer possible, for the enterprise was the property of the state and the state was of and for the worker. Accordingly, both the worker and the enterprise strove to achieve the same results, namely, to increase production and improve the material and cultural conditions of all the workers. To assure their own welfare, the workers in turn had to assume certain obligations; they were duty bound to guard socialist property, which was the "sacred and inviolate basis of the people's democracy, the source of power of the homeland and of the welfare and culture of the workers."

The theoretical mechanism evolved for the exercise of power through freely elected representatives had no resemblance to the actual locus of power and the state institutions created to wield this power. The source of political and economic power was neither the workers and peasants nor the organs presumably elected by them. A perfect example was the actual power and influence of the People's Assembly, to which official documents attributed the power to appoint all the higher state organs and on which all state organs were dependent. In actual practice, the People's Assembly held only two sessions a year, each lasting about two days; the delegates heard reports made by Party and government officials, approved without debate all bills and appointments presented to them, and then adjourned. The Presidium of the People's Assembly was also given wide constitutional powers in the fields of legislation and control of the state apparatus, but in reality its main function was to promulgate draft laws submitted to it by the Council of Ministers.

The Albanian Workers' Party

National Organization

The real source of all power was the Party, whose all-powerful Politburo was the country's top policymaking body. But even this body, composed of eleven regular and five candidate members, was under the firm control of Party First Secretary Enver Hoxha, who has headed the Party since it was founded on November 8, 1941, and Prime Minister Mehmet Shehu, who emerged as the military strategist in the Communist-dominated Army of National Liberation during World War II.

Although Hoxha, as first secretary and as the only surviving member of the small group of Communists who founded the Party, was considered the leader and the foremost Albanian Marxist-Leninist, he and Shehu have shared almost equal power since 1949 (see ch. 2, Historical Setting). The real base of their power has rested in the security and armed forces, and Hoxha and Shehu have divided this power. As minister of defense until 1953, Hoxha personally controlled the armed forces, and since then he has controlled them through Beqir Balluku, his lieutenant (see ch. 9, Internal and External Security).

Shehu, as minister of the interior from 1948 to 1954, personally controlled the security forces, composed of the Directorate of State Security (Drejtorija e Sigurimit te Shtetit, commonly known as the Sigurimi), the People's Police, and the Frontier Guards. Since then he has controlled them through his brother-in-law Major General Kadri Hasbiu, who succeeded Shehu as minister of the interior in 1954 and who still held that position in 1970.

The top executive branches of the Politburo were the four-man Secretariat and the various directorates of the Central Committee. In 1970 the Secretariat was composed of Hoxha as first secretary and Ramiz Alia, Hysni Kapo, and Xhafer Spahiu as secretaries. Hoxha supervised the whole work of the Secretariat; the other three secretaries were responsible for general areas of operation. Alia was responsible for ideological affairs, Kapo for organizational matters, and Spahiu for the state administration.

Policy guidelines adopted by the Politburo were passed by the Secretariat to the appropriate directorate, which elaborated and drafted them in final form for implementation by the respective Party and state organs. The directorates had direct connections with all implementing bodies. For instance, the Directorate of Agitation and Propaganda, known as Agitprop, issued directives not only to the Agitprop sections of the District Party Committees but also to all propaganda outlets in the government, mass organizations, and the armed and security forces.

The most important directorates were the: Directorate of Cadres and Organizations, headed by Hysni Kapo, the third ranking man in the Party hierarchy; Directorate of Agitation and Propaganda, headed by Ramiz Alia; Directorate of Education and Culture, headed by Nexhmije Hoxha, wife of the first secretary; Directorate of State Administrative Organs, headed by Llazi Stratoberdha; and Directorate of Mass Organizations, headed by Politburo member Adil Carcani.

When important policy issues were decided by the Politburo, special commissions were created in the Central Committee to draft implementing guidance for a specific decision. Thus, for instance, in the spring of 1968 the Politburo decided on a complete reorganization and reorientation of the country's educational system. A Central Commission on Education was immediately created in the Party Central Committee; the commission was headed by Prime Minister Mehmet Shehu and included some fifty experts in the ideological, academic, and military aspects of education.

After a year's work the commission completed its report and, in June 1969, submitted it to the Central Committee, which gave its formal stamp of approval. In December of the same year the government submitted a bill to the People's Assembly for the reorganization of the educational system; in its preamble the bill said that it was based on the report of the previous June as approved by the Party Central Committee (see ch. 5, Social System).

The Central Committee was the next highest echelon in importance in the Party organization. In 1970 it was composed of sixty-one regular and thirty-six candidate members. It was to the Central Committee that the Politburo submitted its policy decisions for formal approval. As a rule, in recent years the Central Committee has approved Politburo reports and decisions with little, if any, debate. But there have been occasions when the Central Committee has been called upon to decide on issues of the utmost importance for the country. For example, in February 1948 the Central Committee was convened to discuss and decide the issue of a possible merger of Albania with Yugoslavia. Although the forces favoring such a merger were in the majority, the dissenting voices were sufficient to block the proposed merger. Another Central Committee meeting, held in September of the same year, purged the top Party group that had advocated the merger with Yugoslavia. A similar crucial issue arose in the fall of 1961 on the question of relations with the Soviet Union. The Central Committee approved the Politburo decision to break with Moscow and issued a declaration to that effect.

The Party's ideological principles, tasks, and organizational structure were delineated in the Party's statute, originally adopted by the First Party Congress in 1948 and amended several times since then. In it, control by the Party was detailed specifically, and the statute rather than the Constitution was the fundamental law of the land. According to the statute, the highest leading organ of each organization was: the general meeting for the basic Party organizations; the conference for the Party organizations of districts and cities; and the congress for the entire Party.

The guiding principle of the ideological and organizational structure of the Party was the Leninist dictum known as democratic centralism. As described in the statute, this principle provided in theory that the leading organs of the Party were elected from bottom to top at general meetings, conferences, and congresses; these organs were obliged from time to time to give account of their activities before their Party organizations.

Strict Party discipline was to be maintained under any circumstances, the minority being subject to the majority; decisions were to be reached on the basis of so-called free discussions but, from the moment a decision was reached, unanimously or by a majority of votes, all Party members were obliged to execute it without question; and the decisions of the higher Party organs were binding on the lower organs. The statute also provided that collective leadership was the highest principle of the leadership of the Party and that the elected organs as well as the basic Party organizations examined and solved collectively all Party problems.

The Party statute considered the Party Congress as the highest Party organ. The congress, usually called every four years, heard, examined, and approved the reports of the Central Committee and of other central Party organs; reviewed and made changes in the Party program and statute; determined the Party's tactical line on major policy problems; and elected the Central Committee and the Central Control and Auditing Commission and fixed the number of members of these two bodies. In actual practice, however, the Party Congress merely heard and approved reports submitted by the Politburo.

According to the statute, the Central Committee, which should meet in plenum at least once every four months, performed such formal functions as electing both the Politburo for guiding the affairs of the Central Committee between sessions and the Secretariat for "guiding the day-to-day affairs of the Party, especially for organizing the control of the execution of decisions and for the selection of cadres." During the period between two congresses the Central Committee guided the activities of the Party; represented the Party in its relationships with other parties, organizations, and institutions; organized and guided different Party institutions; named the editors of the Party's central press organs and granted permission for publication of the local Party press; distributed the cadres and the means of the Party and administered the central treasury; and guided and controlled the activities of the central organs of the people's democratic authority and social organizations by means of Party groups in them.

Regional Organization

Regionally, the highest Party organ is the Party Conference at district and city levels, which is supposed to meet once a year and is comparable to the Party Congress at the national level. In practice, the periodic Party Conference becomes a pro forma meeting held for the purpose of displaying unanimity of opinion. Between conferences, operations are conducted by Party committees, and real power is exercised by a bureau of each committee that usually consists of about eleven members, who must first be approved by the Party Central Committee in Tirana. Bureau membership includes two secretaries who are the leading Communist officials in the city or district and, by virtue of their positions, the most powerful individuals.

The principal functions of the district or city committees are to guide the activities of all Party organizations in the district or town so as to assure the precise application of the Party line; approve the establishment of basic Party organizations; maintain records on members and look after their ideological and political education; distribute within the district or city the Party cadres; and administer the Party finances. More importantly, the district or city committee guides and regulates the activities and work of the local governmental bodies and social organizations by means of Party groups within them.

The statute describes the basic Party organizations as the foundations of the Party because they serve to link the working masses of the town and village with the Party. The basic Party organizations are established in factories and plants, agricultural enterprises, machine tractor stations, villages, units of the armed and security forces, state administration, schools, and other work centers where there were no less than three Party members. When deemed necessary and where there are less than three Party members, there can be created joint groups of the Party and of the Union of Albanian Working Youth. These groups are directed by a Party member chosen by the district or city committee.

The basic Party organizations are assigned a multitude of duties and responsibilities. They must ensure that Party orders are fully implemented, the masses are politically oriented, the Communists obtain the required ideological and political education, new members are accepted into the Party, the masses are mobilized in production work, the activities of the mass organizations are checked and guided, and control is exercised over all economic sectors and over all local governmental bodies.

The statute provides that in the armed forces Party affairs are to be directed by the Political Directorate of the Ministry of People's Defense and in the Ministry of the Interior they are to be directed by appropriate political organs. Party organizations in the armed forces operate on the basis of special instructions issued by the Party's Central Committee. All chiefs of political branches in military units and installations must be Party members with no less than five years of membership. The political organs in the military units are required to maintain close contact with the local Party committees (see ch. 9, Internal and External Security).

The latest official figures for Party membership were given by Party First Secretary Hoxha in his report to the Fifth Party Congress in 1966. He placed the total membership at 66,327, of which 3,314 were candidate members. Since the Fourth Party Congress in 1961 the membership had grown by 12,688. According to Hoxha, the social composition of the Party membership was as follows: workers, 32.9 percent; collective farmers, 25.8 percent; private farmers, 3.2 percent; state, Party, and mass organization officials and armed forces personnel, 37.2 percent; and students and housewives, 0.9 percent. Of the total Party membership, women comprised 12.5 percent. Hoxha also said that nearly 68 percent of all Communists lived in cities and only 32 percent in villages, despite the fact, he commented, that the rural population was three times as large as that of the cities.

Party Operations

A fundamental factor in the Party's exercise of political power and control is the selection of candidates for all elected positions. Although the candidates for such elective organs as the People's Assembly, the people's courts, and the people's councils at all levels are formally nominated by the meetings of mass organizations or of workers and peasants, they have been, in fact, handpicked by the local Party organizations and approved by the Party Central Committee.

The procedure at all nominating meetings is standard and simple: a list of candidates, previously prepared by the Party district or city committee, is read; the qualifications of each candidate are described; and the list is unanimously approved. Since the first national and local elections held in 1945 in which the list of candidates included non-Party people, lists have been restricted to Party members only. Veterans of Hoxha's partisan forces of the so-called War of National Liberation still predominate among candidates for office.

A similar situation prevails with regard to the appointment of government officials. After each national election, the People's Assembly has appointed a new government. The procedure for this appointment has never varied: at the first meeting of the new People's Assembly the Party First Secretary has submitted for approval the list of the new ministers, which invariably has received unanimous approval. Because of purges in the top echelons of the Party, especially in the late 1940s and early 1950s, the government list has undergone several changes. Since the elimination of the pro-Yugoslav faction in 1948, however, these changes have affected mostly the technical and economic ministries. The three key posts in the government, however—namely, those of prime minister, minister of the interior, and minister of defense—have been consistently held by Enver Hoxha and Mehmet Shehu or their trusted lieutenants.

The appointment of all government officials as well as the managers of the state economic enterprises rested formally with the agencies involved, but no official has been appointed without the prior approval of the appropriate Party organization. In reality, all key positions are held by Party cadres who have been selected and appointed by the Party district or city committees. The Party statute empowers the basic Party organizations in all governmental organs and economic enterprises to check and guide the activities of all officials and to see that they are properly oriented in the political and ideological fields. The prime requisite in filling these positions is Party loyalty.

Party Schools

In 1970 the Party operated a number of schools and courses for its cadres as well as three research and study institutes, attached to the Central Committee. The highest school was the V.I. Lenin Institute, headed by Fiqrete Shehu, wife of the prime minister. It was attended by the higher and more promising Party members.

The three Party institutes were the Institute of Marxist-Leninist Studies, headed by Nexhmije Hoxha, wife of Enver Hoxha; the Institute of Party History, headed by Ndreci Plasari, who was also editor in chief of the Party's theoretical monthly, *Rruga e Partise* (Party Path); and the Institute for Economic Studies, under the direction of Myqerem Fuga. In addition, there were a number of secondary Party schools for training low-level Party functionaries and one-year schools for refresher ideological courses, attended both by Party officials and leaders of mass organizations.

The Party also operated intermittently, as the need arose, political courses and study groups for its activists and propagandists. In 1969, for example, more than 20,000 study centers were organized throughout the country for the study of the official, newly published *History of the Workers' Party of Albania*. The teaching program of all the Party schools and study centers included such topics as the importance of Communist education; the origins and development of Communist morality; socialist attitudes toward work and property; the importance of patriotic education; the history, theories, and tactics of the international Communist movement; and the history and statutes of the Party.

Mass Organizations

In its exercise of power and control over every phase of the people's lives, the Party also utilizes several mass, or social, organizations, the most important of which are the Democratic Front, the Union of Albanian Working Youth, the Union of Albanian Women, and the United Trade Unions of Albania. In a speech at the Fourth Congress of the Democratic Front held in September 1967, Enver Hoxha said that the mass organizations, as components of the system of the dictatorship of the proletariat were "levers of the Party for its ties with the masses" and that they carried out their political, executive, and organizational work in such a way as to enable the Party directives to be correctly understood and implemented by all segments of the population.

Party Secretary Hysni Kapo, in a speech delivered at a Party seminar in January 1970, declared that the Party carried out its mission through its own organizations and through the activities of its "levers, the mass organizations, such as the trade unions, youth, Democratic Front, women's, and the people's councils," thus revealing that even the people's councils were mere Party levers. By relying on these powerful levers, Kapo added, the Party guaranteed its links with the masses and obtained their support for its policies. He remarked further that, although there were not Communists in every family in the country, everyone in the family belonged to some kind of organization.

The Party has set the implementation of its line as a general primary goal for all mass organizations. Considered as powerful Party levers, they are required to convey the Party line to the people and to bring to the Party the people's attitudes and grievances. As Party instruments they must mobilize, organize, and orient the people during the process of the building of socialism. The mass organizations also assist the Party in its control over the administration and management of state enterprises and initiate new actions and new movements in all work centers.

The Party places particular importance on the Union of Albanian Working Youth, described officially in such terms as the "greatest revolutionary force of inexhaustible strength," a "strong fighting reserve of the Party," and a "vital force of our revolution." According to the Party statute, the union operates directly under the guidance of the Party, and the union's local organizations are guided and checked by the appropriate district or city Party committees. Organized in the same way as the Party, the union has parallel basic organizations, district and city committees, a Central Committee, a Politburo, and a Central Control and Auditing Commission. In 1967 official reports credited the youth organization with 210,000 members, ranging in age from fifteen to twenty-five and, in a few cases, even older.

The main function of the union is to select and prepare future Party members. It is also required by the Party to control all Pioneer organizations, which embrace all children from seven to fourteen years of age; to see to it that all Party directives and policies are implemented by the country's youth, especially in schools and in military units; and to mobilize the youth into so-called voluntary labor brigades to work on production projects. The Party often gives the union special storm trooper or Red Guard types of missions to perform. For example, in February 1967 Enver Hoxha assigned to the organization the mission of shutting down all places of worship in the country; within a period of a few months, the union had accomplished its mission.

The Democratic Front, successor to the National Liberation Front, was defined by Enver Hoxha, who has headed it since 1945 and was still its president in 1970, as the greatest political revolutionary organization of the Albanian people and as a powerful weapon of the Party for the political union of the people. In 1970 the Democratic Front continued to be a key element in the Party's control mechanism. Considered officially as the broadest mass organization, it was supposed to give expression to the political views of the entire population and to serve as a school for mass political education.

The tasks and objectives of the Democratic Front, as set forth in its statute and as constantly reiterated by Party leaders, include the strengthening of political unity among the people and the mobilizing of the people for the implementation of Party policies. The spreading of the Marxist-Leninist ideology is also a task of the front, as is the purging of any attitudes that are considered backward and reactionary. In essence, the front is an instrument of the Party, expressly designed for the political control of the entire population. Enver Hoxha declared in a speech to the Fourth Congress of the Democratic Front in 1967 that all citizens over age eighteen were members of the front, including Party members and members of all other mass organizations.

The Union of Albanian Women is also referred to as a powerful weapon of the Party. The union, headed in 1970 by Vito Kapo, wife of Secretary of the Party Central Committee Hysni Kapo, controls and supervises the political and social activities of the country's women, handles their ideological training, and spearheads the Party's campaign for the emancipation of women. The campaign was launched by Hoxha in June 1967 and renewed in October 1969 in a Hoxha speech to the Party Central Committee.

The Union of Albanian Women, according to reports by visitors has a good record of assistance to the Party in making legal, economic, and social equality for women a reality. By 1970 women shared responsibility in the government at all levels, had entered all the professions, and worked side by side with men for equal pay in most occupations.

By 1967 the union was able to boast that more than 284,000 women took part in production in some way, mostly in industrial plants and agricultural collectives. In the same year there were about 40 women, out of a total of 240 deputies, in the People's Assembly; 1,878 women in the people's councils; and 1,170 in the people's courts.

Since 1967 task forces of women from the cities have been dispatched to tour backward regions, particularly the highlands, explaining the Party's line on the emancipation of Albanian women. Reforms such as giving women equal rights to inherit property, an equal voice in the people's councils, and equal political rights, however, have created considerable hostility in a country where man has traditionally been the master of the family.

The tasks of the United Trade Unions are similar to those of the Democratic Front, albeit on a more limited scale. During ceremonies in February 1970 marking the twenty-fifth anniversary of the founding of the trade unions, it was stated that they were created by the Party, that they had since struggled to implement the Party line, and that they recognized the Party leadership as the "decisive factor of their force and vitality." It was stated further that they were created jointly with the dictatorship of the proletariat for its consolidation and defense and as an important component part of this dictatorship.

In a conference in Tirana on February 10, 1970, Gogo Nushi, then president of the trade unions, boasted that they had become powerful levers of the Party in implementing the Party line among all the country's workers, who had grown from some 30,000 in February 1945 to about

400,000 in February 1970. At the same conference Politburo member Adil Carcani, in a speech dealing with the functions of the trade unions, attributed to them the task of exercising control over all workers.

Other duties and responsibilities of the trade unions in 1970, according to Tonin Jakova, General Secretary of the General Council of the United Trade Unions of Albania, were to carry out the political and ideological education of the workers; to influence all the other strata of the population so that the class ideology should gradually become the sole ideology of the society; to broaden their control and sphere of action in all fields of life— political, ideological, cultural, artistic, social, economic, and educational; to increase labor productivity by increasing work norms; and to struggle against old traditions and backward customs, with emphasis on religious beliefs. In listing the duties and responsibilities of the trade unions not a word was said about their safeguarding the interests of the workers, such as improving their living and bargaining with the management.

Organizationally, the United Trade Unions of Albania was composed in 1970 of three general unions—the Trade Union of Workers of Industry and Construction, consisting of workers in industry, mines, construction, and transportation; the Trade Union of Workers of Education and Trade, made up of the workers in the state administration, trade, health, education, and culture; and the Trade Union of Workers of Agriculture and Procurements, composed of workers in agriculture, forestry, and procurements. Over 2,000 individual trade union organizations existed in enterprises, factories, plants, offices, schools, and other work centers and cultural and social institutions.

In the exercise of political power through the Party, the mass organizations, the state organs, and the security and armed forces, the Tirana rulers have consistently followed Stalinist methods of rule. In major policy speeches these rulers have in recent years often praised Stalin's political system and have consistently attempted to emulate it in Albania. As *Zeri i Popullit* (Voice of the People) phrased it on April 13, 1963, "without reinstating Stalin and his work, [throughout the Communist world] our revolutionary movement and the cause of Marxism-Leninism can make no headway."

FOREIGN RELATIONS

After centuries of foreign domination, Albania in 1912 was ill prepared for independence, and the chaos brought by the Balkan wars and by World War I allowed little opportunity for the development of statehood. One of its first moves in foreign relations was to secure support for its independence from some of the great powers of Europe. In the years between World War I and World War II, Albanian foreign policy was dominated by the Italians.

In the years immediately after World War II, Albania was a satellite of Yugoslavia, which in turn was a satellite of the Soviet Union. This situation deprived Albania of any initiative in foreign affairs, and it remained out of the mainstream of Eastern European affairs until 1948, when ties with Yugoslavia were broken and Albania became a full-fledged satellite of the Soviet Union. Albania's position vis-à-vis the other satellite countries was improved when it came under the direct tutelage of the Soviet Union; it then became the recipient of economic aid, military assistance, and military and economic advisers, not only from its powerful sponsor but also from the other Communist nations. In time it also became a member of the Warsaw Pact and the Council for Economic Mutual Assistance.

Soviet influence in Albanian affairs was pervasive from 1948 to 1960 but, from a material point of view, Albania benefited from the relationship. The Soviets canceled a large debt and sent aid and advisers to help develop the backward Albania economy. Internally, the ruling elite, headed by Enver Hoxha, maintained a rigid regime of the Stalinist type. In foreign affairs the country became a cold war participant completely accepting directions from Moscow.

Its thirteen years as a Soviet satellite were years of turmoil for Albania, particularly after the death of Joseph Stalin and the rise of Nikita Khrushchev to the Soviet leadership. Khrushchev's policy of seeking a rapprochement with Yugoslavia worried both Hoxha, the Party leader, and Shehu, the premier, because of the difficulties they had encountered in purging their Party of a strong pro-Yugoslav faction while in the process of securing their own positions of power. In the Albanian view Stalin had been a great hero, and Tito of Yugoslavia, a great villain. Khrushchev's denunciation of Stalin and wooing of Tito brought consternation to Tirana, but reliance on Soviet aid apparently tempered Albanian reactions.

During the 1950s the Albanian leadership, coaxed by Moscow, made some attempts at restoring normal relations with Yugoslavia. After the riots in Poland and the revolt in Hungary in 1956, however, the Albanians raised strident voices against Yugoslavia's so-called revisionism—that is the alleged perversion of Marxism-Leninism—which they asserted was the basis for the troubles afflicting Eastern Europe. According to official Albanian dogma the two greatest evils in the world were revisionism and imperialism, personified, respectively, by Yugoslavia and the United States. Toward the end of the 1950s it became apparent to Hoxha and Shehu that they were closer ideologically to Peking than to Moscow, and only the latter's economic aid prevented an open break.

In 1960, as Khrushchev sought to line up Communist parties for a condemnation of Communist China, Albania refused to participate and, by the end of the year, the Soviet-Albanian dispute was made known openly. By the end of 1961 diplomatic relations between the two countries were severed, Soviet aid ceased, and Soviet advisers and technicians left Albania, to be replaced by those of Communist China. Although not formally breaking off diplomatic relations, the other Eastern European Communist countries also halted aid programs and withdrew advisers. Khrushchev then became the object of violent attacks in the Albanian press, being castigated as more of a revisionist than Tito. Khrushchev counterattacked to defend himself but, in addition, used Albania as a proxy for violent propaganda blasts that were obviously directed against the Chinese Communists.

After the final break with the Soviet Union, Albania entered the third stage of its Communist existence—the alliance with Communist China. Stages one and two had been as a satellite, first of Yugoslavia and then of the Soviet Union. In stage three, if not a satellite, it was a client of a powerful sponsor. Albania, throughout the 1960s and into 1970, continued to require the economic support of an outside power. Communist China has provided that support, though apparently on a much reduced scale.

In return for Chinese support the Albanians accept the Chinese view of world affairs and speak for their sponsor in Eastern Europe and in the United Nations. Albania successfully defied Moscow, but its internal and international positions remained weak. In 1968 Hoxha withdrew his country from the Warsaw Pact in protest against the invasion of Czechoslovakia, but this was primarily a symbolic move because Albania had not participated in Warsaw Pact affairs since 1961.

By 1970 Albania was attempting to normalize relations with its Balkan neighbors, but its main propaganda thrusts continued to be against revisionism and imperialism. Overtures toward both Greece and Yugoslavia were made in 1970, which may indicate that the Hoxha regime recognized the futility and danger of an isolationist policy. Official attitudes toward the Soviet Union remained as they had been for ten years—strident and abusive—but better relations were being sought among Eastern European nations as well as with some non-Communist states. Seemingly the regime recognized that Communist China was a distant ally, that the Chinese could not support the Albanian economy, and that, if Albania was to remain a viable national entity, it would have to relate to its European neighbors and, in effect, become a part of Europe.

CHAPTER 7

COMMUNICATIONS AND CULTURAL DEVELOPMENT

Information channels in 1970 were relatively well developed compared with those of the pre-World War II period. The press was the most advanced, although by 1970 a substantial radio network existed. Throughout the 1960s there was only a single experimental television transmitter, at the end of 1969, however, the government reportedly requested the French to install a television system.

The press and radio were indispensable instruments in the efforts of the Albanian Workers' Party (Communist Party) to revolutionize all aspects of life. To supplement the formal channels, there were several thousand Party activists who orally transmitted the Party line to the people on a more personal and informal level.

The various aspects of culture, such as literature, art, music, and drama, were also structured to promote the goals of the Party. They have been used extensively to promote support among the masses for the Party and its principles, to combat religion, and generally to increase the political and social consciousness of the people.

The guidelines set forth by the Party for all writers and artists to follow in their creative endeavors are the principles of socialist realism. The general definition of this approach to art and literature is that the form of creative works must be national, but their content must be socialist. The principle of art for art's sake has been rejected by the Communist leaders. All cultural developments must reflect the efforts to create a socialist society.

The information media are controlled by the Party directly or indirectly through the government and such organizations as labor unions, youth groups, and cultural societies. Private ownership of such media has been prohibited since the Communist regime came to power.

NATURE AND FUNCTIONS OF THE INFORMATION MEDIA

The media are invaluable instruments for the achievement of the goals of the Communist leaders. When the Communist regime came to power in November 1944, it seized control of all such media, although they were not formally nationalized until 1946. From the outset, the press and radio were used to justify and extend Communist rule. In general, the function of the media has been to propagate Marxist-Leninist ideology, as modified to relate to the specific conditions in Albania, and to liquidate the traditional religious, social, and economic beliefs of the people (see ch. 4, The People; ch. 2, Historical Setting).

The functions of the media have remained essentially unchanged throughout the twenty-six years of rule by the Albanian Workers' Party. The leaders have used the media extensively in their efforts to revolutionize all aspects of the national life. In this connection, there are many specific functions performed by the press and radio that generally fall into the categories of education, organization, and control.

The first functional category has two aspects: the press and radio are instruments of political and social indoctrination, and they help to raise the educational and cultural levels of the masses. In practice, however, these two aspects are often combined—that is, in the process of education, Marxist-Leninist ideology is usually interjected. In general, the educational function has been performed by conducting campaigns against illiteracy and ignorance, encouraging maximum utilization of the educational and cultural facilities set up throughout the country, and making literary works accessible to the population (see ch. 5, Social System).

The media, in the final analysis, are used to saturate the population with Marxist-Leninist ideology. The content of the media—whether it is news, music, or literature—is structured to promote the goals of the Party and designed to further the building of a Communist society. In order to facilitate ideological indoctrination, content is devised to appeal to sentiments of Albanian nationalism. The development of communism, for example, is related to the theme of developing the nation and preserving its independence; and Enver Hoxha, the Party leader, is quoted as frequently as are Marx and Lenin.

One of the most important uses of the press and radio, which falls into the category of organization, has been to mobilize the people actively to support, and participate in, the implementation of specific policies, such as the fulfillment of economic plans or antireligious campaigns. Often, in conjunction with mobilization campaigns, the media are used to transmit specific information that is necessary for the implementation of various aspects of the policies. In the economic sphere, for example, discussions of industrial processes or agriculture often appear in the press.

The media are also means of Party control over officials at all levels of the government and the Party hierarchies, as well as over the population in general. This function is performed primarily through exposure of corruption, negligence, and inefficiency on the part of various officials or workers or by issuing warnings against such crimes and behavior. In addition, the press and radio are channels through which the top leaders issue directives or communicate changes in the Party line to the lower level administrators and activists throughout the country.

The importance of the pervasive role of the press was stressed in the following statement by Enver Hoxha that was quoted in the December 1965 issue of *Rruga e Partise* (Party Path): "Without the press there can be no education of the masses; without the press there can be no conscientious mobilization of them, organization, nor solution to the problems of the economic and cultural construction in the new socialist society." Although the article dealt specifically with the press, it can be assumed that the role assigned to it also pertains to the other media of communication.

The functions assigned to the media necessitate strict control over their operation and content by the Party. Although there appears to be no formal institution for censorship, an elaborate system was created whereby the Party leaders could maintain the necessary control either directly or indirectly through the government and mass organizations.

Fragmentary information suggests that the Party leaders have several mechanisms for the maintenance of control over the dissemination of information. Within the Party there is a hierarchical organization that implements decisions made by the Party leaders concerning public information and propaganda activities. It is headed by the Directorate of Agitation and Propaganda, which is directly under the Central Committee of the Party. The directorate is divided into various functional sectors, for example, one dealing with the press. Throughout the Party and government hierarchies, as well as in the mass organizations, there are sections for agitation and propaganda that are directed by the central directorate.

The Political Bureau (Politburo), the highest decision-making body of the Albanian Workers' Party, formulates policy concerning ideological indoctrination and the use of the media of mass communication. The Directorate of Agitation and Propaganda coordinates the implementation of such policy (see ch. 6, Government Structure and Political System).

Perhaps the most effective control mechanism is that which is built into the Party structure and in the Party's relationship to the government and to society in general. The media are formally owned and operated by the government with the exception of the Party press and publications of the mass organizations. Since all government officials are members of the Party or its front organization, the Democratic Front, and since the mass organizations are dominated by Party members, Party supervision of all publications is assured. Radio broadcasters, film directors and editors, administrators and editors of the publishing houses, journalists, and newspaper editors are also Party members.

Thus all individuals who work with the mass media, either directly or indirectly, are subject to Party discipline. Failure to adhere to directives from the Politburo is a crime against the Party, and punishment for such crimes can be severe (see ch. 6, Government Structure and Political System).

To supplement the formal media of communication, there are about 25,000 Party agitators who propagandize among the masses. These agitators work in factories, villages, neighborhoods, and on farms with the objective of bringing the Party line to every individual. Besides explaining the content of the press and radio to the people, the agitators conduct courses, present lectures, and guide discussions on Party history, the oppressiveness of religion, friendship with Communist China, Soviet revisionism, and other such topics. For example, in the weekly meetings held for women, emphasis is placed upon how religion causes discrimination against them.

In the factories the agitators explain the Party line to their coworkers and rally them to compete to outproduce each other, a practice called socialist competition. Agitators in rural areas are usually of peasant origin and consequently are better able to gain the trust of the peasantry. They explain the Party line to them in a manner that is relevant to local conditions and mobilize them to produce their quotas.

The agitators also sponsor cultural and sports activities, such as organizing trips to museums and arranging for athletic events. When new laws are passed, the agitators explain them to the masses in terms that they will understand. Before elections the agitators mobilize the people to go out and vote, even though there is only one candidate on the ballot.

To aid the agitators in their work, the *Agitators' Notebook* is published monthly listing the various points of the Party line which do change from time to time. The agitators also have books, pamphlets, pictures, and films to facilitate the indoctrination of the masses. In addition to the activities of the agitators, the Statutes of the Albanian Workers' Party require that all Party members work to educate the masses in Marxist-Leninist ideology. The same requirement is made of the members of the Union of Albanian Working Youth.

THE PRESS

The press is the most developed of the information media. According to official statistics, in 1967 there were nineteen newspapers and thirty-four periodicals as compared with six and fifteen, respectively, in 1938. Circulation figures per issue for all newspapers and periodicals are not available, but the government statistics indicate that total circulation for newspapers increased by about sixteen times between 1938 and 1967, and the figures for periodicals indicate a sixfold increase for the same period.

Most publications originate in Tirana, although during the 1960s the regime began to establish local newspapers. Information on the press is sparse, and it is difficult to ascertain how many publications were in circulation in 1970; there are indications that new publications were added, while others were consolidated after 1967.

There are three daily newspapers, all of which are published in Tirana (see table 7). *Zeri i Popullit* (The Voice of the People) is published by the Central Committee of the Albanian Workers' Party, and in 1967 it had a daily circulation of 86,000. *Bashkimi* (Union) is published by the Democratic Front and is the mouthpiece of the government. It had a daily circulation of 20,000 in 1967. *Puna* (Work) is the daily newspaper of the Central Council of the United Trade Unions of Albania. In 1967 it reportedly had a circulation of 18,000. *Zeri i Rinise* (The Voice of Youth), a twice weekly newspaper of the Central Committee of the Union of Albanian Working Youth, had a circulation of 36,000 in 1967.

Circulation figures do not necessarily give an accurate picture, however, because many of the subscriptions are held by institutions, libraries, and cultural houses rather than by individuals. Factories, farms, schools, and other institutions have reading rooms with subscriptions to newspapers and magazines. In addition, the Party agitators frequently read articles aloud to groups. Thus there is greater exposure to the press than the circulation figures indicate.

Local newspapers are all published by the local Party committees. Examples of such newspapers are: *Jeta e Re* (New Life), published in Shkoder; *Perpara* (Forward), published in Korce; *Pararoja* (Vanguard), published in Gjirokaster; and *Adriatic*, which is published in Durres. These newspapers have been assigned the function of explaining Party policies in relation to the specific conditions found in the various localities. They also propagandize against religion and such so-called crimes as laziness and indifference. Local newspapers give a great deal of attention to the economic, social, cultural, and political problems that are specific to their districts.

Table 7. Selected Albanian Newspapers, 1967

Newspaper	Frequency	Publisher	Circulation
Zeri i Popullit (The Voice of the People)	daily	Central Committee of the Albanian Workers' Party	86,000
Bashkimi (Union)	daily	Democratic Front	20,000
Puna (Work)	daily	Central Council of Albanian Trade Unions	18,000
Zeri i Rinise (The Voice of the Youth)	twice weekly	Central Committee of the Union of Albanian Working Youth	36,000
Jeta e Re (New Life)	n.a.	Shkoder Party Committee	n.a.
Pararoja (Vanguard)	n.a.	Korce Party Committee	n.a.
Adriatic (Adriatic)	n.a.	Durres Party Committee	n.a.

n.a.—not available.

In addition to the local newspapers there are wall newspapers, or flash bulletins, as they began to be called after the 1966 initiation of the so-called Cultural Revolution in the Party drive to rekindle among the people a Marxist-Leninist revolutionary spirit. These wall newspapers are usually single sheets that are posted on bulletin boards in factories, farms, schools, offices, cultural houses, and other such places. They are usually written by either the Party agitators or members of the youth organization, and they serve the same purposes as the formal press—that is, agitation for increased productivity by workers and peasants, antireligious campaigns, and so on (see ch. 6, Government Structure and Political System).

The periodical press is as important as the newspaper press and is slightly more diversified. The number of periodicals published grew from fifteen in 1938 to thirty-four in 1967. In 1967 there were almost twice as many periodicals published as newspapers. Thus it is possible to design many of the periodicals for consumption by specific audiences.

The Party, many government ministries, and each of the various mass organizations publish periodicals (see table 8). *Rruga e Partise* (Party Path) is the theoretical journal of the Party and is published by its Central Committee. *Ylli* (Star) is the monthly illustrated review that supplements *Zeri i Popullit*. It was first published in 1960.

Table 8. Selected Albanian Periodicals, 1967

Title	Publisher
Arsimi Popullor (People's Education)	Ministry of Education and Culture
Bujqesia Socialite (Socialist Agriculture)	Ministry of Agriculture
Buletin i Shkencave Bujqesore (Bulletin of Agricultural Sciences)	High Agricultural Institute
Drita (Light)	Union of Albanian Artists and Writers
Fatosi (The Brave One)	Central Committee of the Union of Albanian Working Youth
Hosteni (The Goad)	Union of Journalists
Kultura Popullore (People's Culture)	Ministry of Education and Culture
Llaiko Vima (The People's Voice)	Democratic Front (in Greek)
Luftetari (The Warrior)	Ministry of Defense
Mesuesi (The Teacher)	Ministry of Education and Culture
Nendori (November)	Union of Albanian Artists and Writers
Pionieri (The Pioneer)	Central Committee of the Union of Albanian Working Youth
Rruga e partise (Party Path)	Central Committee of the Albanian Workers' Party
Shqiperia e Re	Committee for Foreign Cultural Relations (in

(New Albania)	Albanian, Chinese, English, French and Russian)
Shqiptarja e Re (The New Albanian Woman))	Union of Albanian Women
Sporti Popullor (People's Sport)	General Council of the Union of the Federation of Sports of Albania
Teknika (Technology)	Ministry of Industry
Tregetija Popullore (People's Trade)	Ministry of Commerce
Ylli (Star)	Central Committee of the Albanian Workers' Party

Source: Adapted from *Europa Year Book, 1969*, London, pp. 457-458.

The Albanian Telegraphic Agency (Agjencia Telegrafike Shqipetare) is government controlled and the only source of news, both domestic and foreign. It supplies all national and local newspapers with news items, as well as radio stations and the single television station. The agency has agreements with foreign news agencies for the exchange of news items.

RADIO AND TELEVISION

The radio is another important instrument of political and social indoctrination. It was barely in existence when the Communist regime came to power. In 1945 there were only two radio transmitters in the entire country. Since that time the radio system has been developing rapidly, although it still lags behind the press. In 1969 there were fifty-two radio transmitters, and in 1968 there were 150,000 receivers.

The radio system is under the jurisdiction of the Directorate of Radiobroadcasting, which is under the Council of Ministers. In actuality, however, the Party is in control because the members of the directorate, as well as all personnel involved in radio broadcasting, are Party members.

All but eight of the transmitters are shortwave, which is indicative of the emphasis placed upon transmitting propaganda abroad. Broadcasts from mediumwave transmitters, however, are directed to the countries of Eastern Europe, parts of the Soviet Union, Italy, and some Arab countries.

Shortwave is used for domestic programs in cases where the mountainous topography creates an obstacle to the mediumwaves.

There are only six radio stations in Albania (see table 9). Radio Tirana is the largest, with four mediumwave transmitters and forty-one shortwave transmitters. Radio Gjirokaster and Radio Korce each have only one mediumwave transmitter. Radio Kukes and Radio Shkoder each have one mediumwave and one shortwave transmitter. Radio Stalin has only one shortwave transmitter. Radio Tirana broadcasts all of the programs directed abroad and has the most powerful transmitter (50,000 watts) for domestic programs, whereas local transmitters usually have only 200-watt power. Quite possibly the local stations simply relay programs from Radio Tirana.

The domestic service is on the air 13-1/2 hours daily and 17 hours on Sundays. In 1969 domestic programs were scheduled between 4:30 and 7:00 A.M. and 11:00 A.M. to 10:00 P.M. daily. The Sunday schedule was from 5:00 A.M. to 10:00 P.M. Included in the domestic programs were twelve daily newscasts, children's programs, theatrical presentations, operettas, and other types of cultural programs.

Foreign broadcasting is done in seventeen different languages and on five beams directed to Latin America, North America, Africa, Asia, and Australia. Besides Albanian, the foreign broadcasts are made in Arabic, Bulgarian, Czech, English, French, German, Greek, Hungarian, Indonesian, Italian, Polish, Portuguese, Romanian, Russian, Serbo-Croatian, and Spanish.

Table 9. Albanian Radio Stations, 1969

Station	Total Number of Transmitters	Shortwave	Mediumwave
Radio Gjirokaster	1	-	1
Radio Korce	1	-	1
Radio Kukes	2	1	1
Radio Shkoder	2	1	1
Radio Stalin	1	1	-

| Radio Tirana | 45 | 41 | 4 |

Source: Adapted from Foreign Broadcast Information Service, *Broadcasting Stations of the World*, Part I: Amplitude Modulation Broadcasting Stations According to Country and City, Washington, September 1, 1969.

As late as the end of 1967 the Albanian government reportedly was not jamming broadcasts from abroad. This probably was not because of a relaxed attitude on the part of the ruling elite; rather, it was more likely because of the lack of technology necessary for jamming operations and the expense involved.

In 1964 the Albanian government published statistics on the distribution of radio receivers by social composition. The categories of "workers," "employees," and "peasants" were not explicated; however, it can be assumed that workers refer to blue-collar workers or manual laborers and that employees refer to white-collar workers or office, administrative, and professional personnel. In 1963, out of a total of 70,913 radio receivers, 28,672 were owned by workers, 30,391 were owned by employees, and 6,303 were owned by peasants. Clubs and institutional enterprises held 1,236 receivers, and 4,311 were listed under the heading "other."

The Albanians opened their first television station for experimentation in May 1960. At the end of 1969 they were still experimenting, transmitting programs three times a week. The government had reportedly asked the French to install a television network at the end of 1969. At that time there were about 2,100 television receivers in the country.

BOOK PUBLISHING AND LIBRARIES

There were three book-publishing enterprises in 1970, all of which were located in Tirana. Ndermarja e botimeve ushtarake (Enterprise for Military Publications) was operated by the Ministry of National Defense. N.I.S.H. Shtypshkronjave "Mihal Duri" (State Printer "Mihal Duri") was operated by the Party, and Shtepia Botonjese "Naim Frasheri" (State Publishing House "Naim Frasheri") was directed by the Ministry of Education and Culture. Ndermaja Shteterore Tregetimit te Librit (The Book Selling State Enterprise), located in Tirana, had a monopoly over the distribution of books under the direction of the Ministry of Education and Culture.

According to official Albanian statistics, there were 628 books published in 1967, with a total of 5,605,000 copies printed. This is a great increase over the number published in 1938: 61 books with a total of 183,000 copies printed.

According to the latest statistics available, a total of 502 books were published in 1965, of which 110 were literary works. Another 197 dealt with the social sciences; 42, with philology; 61, with pure science; 47, with the applied sciences; and 24, with geography and history. It was not indicated how many of these titles were first editions or how many were translations. In 1966, 140 translations from abroad were published, of which 72 dealt with the social sciences, 57 were literary works, 10 were pure science books, and 1 dealt with applied science.

Because books are an additional channel for propaganda, foreign works to be translated into Albanian are carefully scrutinized. Literary works must be of the sort that portray the ills and conflicts within capitalist societies. Often, although a literary work might be generally ideologically acceptable, parts of it are unacceptable. In such cases, the book is carefully edited and abridged before publication in the Albanian language is permitted.

Scientific and technical literature from abroad, on the other hand, is actively sought for translation. On December 21, 1967, the Council of Ministers issued a decision "On the Assurance, Publication, Organization, and Massive Utilization of Technical-Scientific Literature" from abroad. In this decision, the Ministry of Foreign Affairs was called upon to devise new ways for obtaining such literature through its embassies and through international organizations. Once the foreign works are obtained, the decision stresses that their translations must be of the best quality. Such translations are done under the direction of the Ministry of Education and Culture.

There are numerous libraries of varying sizes throughout the country. Official sources report that in 1967 there were twenty-nine people's libraries with a total of 1,367,000 volumes, compared with only five such libraries in 1938 with a total of 12,000 volumes. The largest of these libraries is the National Library in Tirana, which in the late 1960s had 450,000 volumes. The second largest library is the University Library, also in Tirana, which in the late 1960s had 321,680 volumes and 19,640 periodicals.

Each district has at least one library. The local libraries are on a much smaller scale than those in Tirana in terms of their total number of volumes. In addition to the district libraries, there are several hundred houses of culture, cultural circles, and clubs that subscribe to the libraries in order to make books more accessible to the population.

CULTURAL DEVELOPMENT

Intellectual and Artistic Expression

In 1944, when the Communist regime came to power, there was little or no heritage in the various areas of cultural activity—literature, music, drama, or painting and sculpture—upon which the Communist leaders could build. Since the end of World War II, however, a consistent effort has been made to foster the growth of an Albanian cultural tradition and to generally raise the cultural level of the people. Writers and artists are supported by the state, and cultural institutions have been established throughout the country to ensure maximum cultural exposure of the masses. In 1967 there were 35 houses of culture in cities, 395 in villages, and 1,266 cultural circles throughout the country. In addition, there were 24 national museums and 25 local museums.

The various cultural institutions sponsor plays, concerts, and literary readings; subscribe to libraries; arrange trips to museums; and direct other such activities. Often courses in the arts, such as music lessons, are conducted. The activities of the houses of culture and the cultural circles are not restricted to cultural recreation, however. They also have been assigned the general task of educating the masses.

Special cadres of culture are trained to direct the cultural institutions. Their preparation extends beyond the realm of culture to Marxism-Leninism, however, and they are generally trained to enable them to become involved in all aspects of the life of the community. The various cultural institutions, while genuinely serving to expose the masses to culture, are also important instruments of political and social indoctrination.

In practice, the principles of socialist realism require that literary and artistic works actively promote the goals of the Party and reflect Communist ideology. Besides generally being "a weapon for the education of the new man with the ideals of socialism and the principles of Communist morality," literature, drama, music, and art must inspire nationalism and allegiance to the Party and stimulate the people to work toward fulfillment of Party plans, whether they are in the economic or the social spheres. The criterion used to evaluate cultural works is the degree to which they further the goals of the Party and socialist development.

In conjunction with the initiation of the Cultural Revolution, Enver Hoxha expounded upon the vital role of the various aspects of culture in a speech to the Fifth Congress of the Albanian Workers' Party in November 1966. The task set by the Party is that "literature and art should become a powerful weapon in the hands of the Party for the education of the working people in the spirit of socialism and communism; that literature and art should stand at the vanguard of the struggle for the education of a new generation ideologically and morally pure; that all artistic creation should be of a high ideological level and be permeated by both the Party's militant revolutionary spirit and a healthy national spirit."

Such demands have been made of authors, artists, and musicians since the inception of the Albanian People's Republic. Since 1966, however, when the Cultural Revolution was initiated, the importance of culture has received greater emphasis and the demands for ideological purity of all creative works have increased. The Cultural Revolution was still in motion as of the early months of 1970.

The dominant themes of Albanian culture under communism have concerned the history of Albania, the struggle of the Communist-led partisans during the War of National Liberation, and the transformation of the backward, superstitious society into one that is modern and governed by progressive, socialist principles. In the mid-1960s, however, the Party called upon writers and artists to go beyond these themes and to portray the contemporary struggles for the creation of socialism. Party guidance stipulates that it is not enough to describe the past struggles and achievements. The ongoing hardships faced by the peasants and workers must be reflected in artistic works. The heroes are to be workers, peasants, and engineers, as well as the partisans.

Throughout the period of the Cultural Revolution, artists and writers have been going to the mountain villages, industrial centers, and agricultural cooperatives to live for varying lengths of time. Living and working with the people provides the writers and artists with insights into the life and problems that the various types of people must face. These experiences are designed to help them create themes that reflect the contemporary developments more accurately and to make cultural works more relevant to the masses.

Given the influential role of culture in society, it was imperative that the Party establish strict control over all creative activities. Authors, dramatists, musicians, and artists must belong to the Union of Artists and Writers. This organization is nominally independent of the Party, but in reality it is firmly under Party control. Another source of control is the Ministry of Education and Culture, which has close ties with the Directorate of Education and Culture under the Politburo of the Party. Furthermore, all individuals involved in cultural pursuits are dependent upon the state for their income as well as for the financing of their various projects.

The twofold task of the Party leaders in the cultural field—that of fostering cultural development while maintaining control over the content of the cultural works—was difficult in many respects and easy in others. The lack of a firmly established tradition in many cultural fields, as well as the lack of a substantial cultural community, facilitated the establishment of Party control. Writers and artists who received their training under the Party's tutelage know only the socialist realist approach. On the other hand, the lack of experience and personnel in many fields, such as drama, meant that the developments in these areas would be slow. Furthermore, the leaders were dependent first upon the Yugoslavs and, after 1948, on the Soviets to train people in the areas that were totally lacking in Albania's cultural heritage.

The paucity of artistic and intellectual achievements, compared with those of other nations throughout the world, was basically the result of Albania's long history of foreign domination and of the rugged topography of the country, which facilitated the isolation of many communities for centuries. During the several centuries of Turkish rule, the Albanians were forbidden to develop a written language. Furthermore, there were no schools that conducted classes in the Albanian language; there were only Turkish schools for the Muslim population and Greek schools for the Orthodox population. To compound these difficulties, there are two major dialects of Albanian—Geg, spoken in the north, and Tosk, in the south. Albania did not have a uniform alphabet until November 1908, when a congress of intellectuals agreed upon the use of the Latin alphabet. It was not until the Communist regime came to power that it was decided that Tosk would be the official literary dialect (see ch. 2, Historical Setting; ch. 3, Physical Environment; ch. 4, The People).

An additional obstacle to the development of a substantial intellectual and artistic community and tradition was the fact that until 1957 there were no universities in the country. The State University of Tirana, Albania's only university, was not established until that year. Before World War II Albanian students went abroad, primarily to Western Europe, in the pursuit of higher education. After World War II students were usually sent to the Soviet Union or other Eastern European countries to attend universities and other institutions of higher learning (see ch. 5, Social System).

In 1970 there was still evidence that the Communist leaders were not entirely satisfied with the cultural works produced in the past twenty-six years. There were also indications that many creative works were not ideologically pure. Few cultural works produced during the Communist period are known in the West owing to Albania's virtual isolation. Evaluation of literature, drama, music, and art can only be made on the basis of criticism and praise of such works that appear in the press.

Literature

Albania has a strong tradition of folklore, which had been transmitted orally for several centuries. At the end of the nineteenth century and in the early twentieth century, much of this lore was written down in anthologies and collections. The folklore consists of heroic songs, lyrics, tales, and proverbs. The predominant themes are the heroic feats of the mountain tribes in the north against the Slavs across the border, the important role of the Albanians in the Ottoman Empire, and the glorious resistance led by the country's national hero, Gjergi Skanderbeg, against the Turks in the fifteenth century. There are also a large number of love songs and wedding songs found in the folk tradition.

An oral tradition was also developed by the Albanians who had left their homeland in the second half of the fifteenth century, during and immediately after the wars against the Turks led by Skanderbeg. The songs and poetry of the Italo-Albanians reflect fifteenth-century Albanian society. The most important theme is the heroic resistance against the Turks. There are also lyric songs that portray love for one's mother and wife. Lyric songs were also developed in the Albanian settlements in Greece, although less is known about them. There were no heroic songs from this area until the nineteenth century when the Albanian communities fought to preserve their independence and Orthodox Christianity against Muslim incursions.

The first written literature found in Albania dates back to the fifteenth century. Until the nineteenth century such literature was of a religious nature. Nationalist literature was not developed until the nineteenth century and, because of the restrictions imposed by the Turks, such literature first appeared in the Albanian settlements abroad. The most outstanding writer of the nineteenth century was Naim Frasheri, who played an important role in the awakening of Albanian nationalism.

The literature of the early twentieth century also was produced outside Albania. The writers were instrumental in the development of the movement for Albanian independence, and their works were increasingly nationalistic. After independence was achieved in 1912, Albanian writers were able to return to their country to work. Several volumes of lyric poetry were produced by such people as P. Vincenc Prennushi, Dom Ndre Mjeda, and Asdreni. Bishop Fan S. Noli lived in the United States most of his life but made important contributions to Albanian literature. In 1907 he published a three-act play entitled *Israelites and Philistines*, and he later translated several world renowned literary works into Albanian, including Shakespeare's *Macbeth*, *Hamlet*, and *Othello*; Ibsen's *Inger of Ostrat*; and Cervantes' *Don Quixote*.

In the 1920s and 1930s Albanian literary and philosophic periodicals appeared both at home and abroad. The journal *Djaleria* (Youth) was published in Vienna by Albanian students. It was in this journal that the poetry of Lasgush Poradeci first appeared, and his works made a tremendous impact on Albanian youth. Two periodicals appeared in the 1930s, *Illyria* and *Perpjekia Shqiptare* (The Albanian Effort), which reflected the intellectual fervor of the decade. New ideas were spread throughout the country by students who returned from universities in Italy, France, and Austria. The depression and Italian penetration of Albania also incited intellectual ferment.

During World War II the Balli Kombetar (National Front), a democratic resistance movement, was founded by Midhat Frasheri, a prominent nationalist writer. The first resistance literature to be openly published, however, was found in the periodical *Hylli i Drites* (The Star of Light), published by the Franciscan Brothers in Shkoder. The Fascist occupation forced the publication of this review to cease in 1941. Beginning in 1942, clandestine resistance literature began to increase in volume. It was published by the Balli Kombetar and by the National Liberation Movement (Communist front organization).

After World War II literature came under the control of the Communist regime and, consequently, all literary works were made to conform to the principles of socialist realism. The predominant theme of literary works in the early postwar period was the War of National Liberation. A few works also dealt with the reconstruction after the years of ravaging war. Among the writers of the early Communist period were the poets Mark Ndoja, Llazar Siliqi, Gjergi Kominino, Ziza Cikuli, and Vehbi Skenderi. Zihni Sako, Fatmir Gjata, and Jakov Xoxe wrote short stories.

During the 1944-48 period translations of Serbo-Croatian works were published, and several books were translated from Russian. At the end of 1949 the Soviet Union and Stalin, in particular, became additional themes for Albanian literature; after 1960 the Chinese were substituted for Soviet heroes.

Theater and Cinema

There were no professional theaters before 1945. Sokrat Mijo, an Albanian who had studied drama in Paris, tried to set up a professional theater in the 1930s but was unable to generate interest in the project. Occasionally, amateur groups performed plays, but that was the extent of theatrical experience before the Communist era. The people objected to the presence of women on the stage, and in most amateur performances men played the feminine parts. The plays performed by the amateur groups were primarily of a romantically patriotic nature.

The absence of repertory theaters did not inhibit the emergence of Albanian playwrights and, although their works were rarely performed, they did have readers. The first playwright to appear on Albanian territory was Pasko Vasa Pasha, who wrote *The Jew's Son*. Pasha was able to write in his native land because he lived in the city of Shkoder, which was the only area to enjoy some immunity from the rigid restrictions imposed by the Turks against cultural activity in Albania. His play was produced in 1879 by an amateur group at Xaverian College.

Several playwrights emerged in the Albanian settlements abroad, and a few within Albania, but their works had to be published abroad before 1912. Two of the most prominent of these writers were Sami Frasheri, who wrote *Besa* (The Pledge), and Kristo Floqi, who wrote *Religion and Nationality*. Ernest Koliqi made significant contributions to Albanian dramatic literature after independence was won.

The potential of the theater as an instrument of political and social indoctrination was recognized by the Communist leaders, and in 1945 they invited the president of the Society of Yugoslav Actors to come to Albania to establish a professional theatrical group. With the aid of Sokrat Mijo, who had become the director of the school of drama in Tirana, such a group was formed. Their first performance, in September 1945, was a presentation of *The Lover*, which was adapted from a play written by Yugoslav playwrights.

In 1949 a professional theater was created in Shkoder, and in 1950 another theater was founded in Korce. Since then numerous professional and amateur groups have sprung up throughout the country. They perform serious drama, comedies, variety shows, and puppet shows, the themes of which must conform to the principles of socialist realism. In 1964 it was reported that there were twenty-two professional drama and variety theaters.

There is evidence that the lack of experience in the theatrical field created problems for the political leaders' efforts to foster its development. Periodically, articles appear in the press that criticize various shortcomings in the production of drama and variety shows. The targets of criticism range from content to the skills of the performers to the management of the stage and theater.

Cinematography is another field that was not developed until after World War II. There had been a joint Italian-Albanian company established in Tirana during the Italian occupation that produced mostly documentary films, but the film industry did not actually begin to develop until 1949 and 1950. The Soviet Union was instrumental in the foundation of this industry, and it initially provided the Albanians with the necessary equipment. Since that time great efforts have been made to increase the number of films produced and to expand facilities for showing them to the public.

A few full-length, artistic films are produced each year, and a greater number of short films and documentaries are completed annually. Often literary works are made into art films. Figures are not available as to the exact number of each type of film produced. Films are also imported, under the direction of the Ministry of Education and Culture, mostly from Communist countries, although a few Western films are shown after careful editing. The foreign films are usually dubbed into Albanian. Few, if any, Albanian productions have been seen in the West.

The film industry has been nationalized since its inception. The Ministry of Education and Culture controls the exhibition and distribution of motion pictures. In 1967 there were 50,000 performances, which were attended by about 8.25 million people.

Music

Albania has a rich tradition in folk music. Heroic and lyric songs, usually accompanied by folk instruments, were passed down from generation to generation over the centuries. In the mountains of the north the *lahute* (lute), which is a stringed instrument, is popular. Other Albanian folk instruments are the *roja*, which is a bagpipe, and the *tupan*, which is similar to a tambourine. Orchestras, called *saze*, are found in many towns in the southern part of Albania. These are usually composed of about five instruments and often provide music for folk dances at weddings and on other special occasions.

Western music was first spread throughout the country in the 1920s by an Albanian brass band that had received training in the United States. After touring the larger towns, it established itself in Korce, giving regular popular and classical concerts. The Royal Band was later established in Tirana, whose repertoire consisted of Western music but, generally, indigenous music predominated and Western music made little impact.

Western-trained Albanian singers appeared in the mid-1930s. Tefta Tashko, Gjorgjija Filce, and Maria Paluca were well-known sopranos who sang both operatic music and folk tunes. Kristaq Antoniu began his career as a tenor before World War II and continued it under the Communist regime. Filce and Paluca also remained musical stars after World War II.

Kristro Kono was the only composer of significance in pre-World War II Albania. He remains a highly rated composer under the Communist regime. In the 1950s he wrote several songs, some of which were dedicated to Enver Hoxha and Stalin. Some of his orchestral pieces are "Fantazi Shqiptare" (Albanian Fantasies) and "Agimi" (The Dawn). Konstantine Trako is another popular composer of the Communist period.

The predominant musical creations are songs with lyrics because they are effective means of inspiring patriotism and pro-Communist sentiments. All activity in the musical field is controlled and supported by the Party, primarily through the Union of Artists and Writers and the Ministry of Education and Culture. There are state-supported music academies and institutions for training in this field. Besides the many local musical groups, there are the state-supported Opera and Ballet Theater of Tirana and the Song and Dance Ensemble of Tirana (see ch. 5, Social System).

Fine Arts

The first art school was established in Tirana in the 1930s. The curriculum of this school did not go beyond the fundamentals of art and, consequently, talented students had to go abroad. Vangjush Mijo and Androniqi Zengo were the first to introduce modern art to Albania in the form of impressionism. Mijo had studied in Italy and Zengo in Greece. Odhise Paskal was the only notable sculptor of prewar Albania. He had received his training in Florence. His creations include the Skanderbeg monument in Tirana and the National Warrior monument in Korce. Paskal and Zengo continued to work under the Communist regime.

Courses in the fine arts have increased since the end of World War II. Artists and sculptors are supported by the state, and the main themes of their creations are workers, peasants, partisan heroes, youth working on agricultural and industrial projects, soldiers, and liberated women in their various activities. Examples of artistic creations praised in the Albanian press are: "High Revolutionary Spirit" by M. Dhrami, "The Adult of the Republic" by K. Rama, and "The Partisans of the Revenge Battalion" by S. Shijaku. Besides Paskal, J. Paco and A. Mana have been cited as distinguished sculptors.

CHAPTER 8

ECONOMIC SYSTEM

In mid-1970 the economy, which is wholly controlled by the Albanian Workers' Party, approached the conclusion of the Fourth Five-Year Plan, during which it made a further advance along the road of industrialization, in line with the totalitarian leadership's goal of transforming the economy from the stage referred to as agricultural-industrial to a more advanced industrial-agricultural level. The Fourth Five-Year Plan (1966-70) actually called for a more rapid growth of agriculture than that of industry and for an increase in the share of agriculture in the national product by 1970. This departure from proclaimed policy was dictated by the failure of agriculture to meet the goals of the Third Five-Year Plan (1961-65) and by an overriding need to increase farm production in order to reduce to the maximum extent possible the perennial food deficit.

Despite government efforts, the five-year plan goals for agriculture are not being achieved, even though substantial advances in production have been made. The agricultural output target set by the annual plan for 1970 is significantly below the five-year plan figure for that year. By contrast, the five-year plan goal for industrial output was reported to have been surpassed in 1969 and to have been raised in the annual plan for 1970 substantially above the original level.

The basic reasons for the failure to attain the planned farm output targets, apart from their magnitude, lie in the difficulty of inducing peasants to relinquish age-old traditions in favor of modern scientific farming methods and of motivating them to work industriously in a collective farm system that they strongly reject. Although problems of adaptation and motivation are also present in industry, the much smaller size of the industrial labor force and the presence of foreign technicians in key areas mitigate the difficulties and make possible a somewhat more rapid rate of growth.

Reliable information on Albania is scarce. Few foreigners capable of observing and evaluating conditions objectively have been able to visit the country in the past twenty-five years. Articles from official journals or newspapers available in English translation, which constitute the major source of data, provide only a partial coverage and must be used with caution because of a lack of means for verification. Published statistics, available in detail to 1964 and nonexistent after 1967, leave many important gaps. Because of apparent shortcomings in the underlying statistical methods, only data in physical terms can be accepted with some degree of assurance as to their accuracy.

The economy is administered through a small number of specialized ministries, and most information about it comes from Communist sources. Control over labor is maintained through trade unions, which constitute a political arm of the Party (see ch. 6, Government Structure and Political System). Economic activity is governed by a series of five-year and annual plans prepared by the State Planning Commission in accordance with Party directives.

Agriculture is organized into state and collective farms, which are dependent upon machine-tractor stations for the performance of mechanized farm operations. Industry is poorly balanced with regard to the country's domestic needs and is heavily oriented toward exports. Foreign trade primarily serves the purpose of obtaining needed resources for the development of production. Limited domestic resources are only partially developed, and the economy depends heavily on foreign economic and technical assistance. The country's political orientation has restricted the sources of such aid to other Communist states, and its alignment with Communist China in the Sino-Soviet dispute brought about the loss of Soviet support with severe repercussions to the economy.

After twenty-five years of forced draft economic development, the country in 1967 was described by a correspondent of a European journal as a mixture of the fourteenth and twentieth centuries, where oxen and buffaloes were to be seen side by side with modern foreign-made tractors, and where a policeman directed traffic in the main square of the capital city like a conductor waving his baton at a nonexistent orchestra.

After a visit in the fall of 1969, a specialist on Balkan affairs reported that austerity and regimentation were still the rule despite a substantial measure of economic progress achieved during the period of independence. He also expressed the view that Albania undoubtedly remained the poorest country in Europe but that the economic and social advances attained could be envied by the countries of the Near East.

LABOR

Although economic development is still in its infancy, growing concern has been officially expressed about the adequacy of the labor force to meet the needs of industrialization and of expanding social services without adversely affecting agricultural production. The main cause of the incipient labor shortage is low productivity owing to a lack of industrial experience, a low level of mechanization, and the survival of backward traditional methods in agriculture. Officially, low productivity has been ascribed to poor labor discipline and inefficient management arising from an inadequately developed sense of political and social responsibility. It has also been blamed on a failure of manpower planning and on the relaxation of central controls over enterprise funds.

At the end of 1969 the Central Committee of the Party adopted a decision on means for correcting this situation. An important element of the program is the education and political indoctrination of the workers. This task is a major function of the trade unions, which are primarily a political arm of the Party for the control of labor, without any significant responsibilities in the field of labor relations (see ch. 6, Government Structure and Political System).

In 1967, the last year for which official employment data are available, the working-age population comprised 932,000 persons, 739,200 of whom were actually employed. The number of employed did not include roughly 6,000 peasants working on the private holdings still remaining in that year. Including these peasants, the participation rate in the labor force was 80 percent.

Two-thirds of the labor force was employed in agriculture, the remainder in a variety of nonagricultural pursuits, chief among which were industry, construction, trade, and education. Apart from the peasants working their own land, farm labor included about 427,000 persons on collective farms and 64,000 on state farms. The industrial labor force of 105,300 accounted for 14.1 percent of total employment, and 40,000 construction workers, for 5.4 percent. The nearly 32,000 workers in trade and 25,000 workers in education constituted, respectively, 4.2 and 3.4 percent of the employed manpower.

The officially reported labor force, which comprises nonagricultural labor and state farm workers only, increased by 53 percent between 1960 and 1967, from 203,800 to 312,400 persons. The increase represents an annual growth rate of 6.3 percent. At this rate, the labor force in 1970 would be about 375,000 persons. It has been informally reported as 400,000. Collective farm employment rose, in round numbers, from 282,000 in 1960 to 336,000 in 1966 and to 427,000 in 1967. The unusually large increase in 1967 resulted from an intensive drive to collectivize the remaining privately owned farms and also from a government policy of reversing the population flow from the farms to the cities. With the major reservoir of individual farms exhausted, the number of collective farm workers could increase up to 1970 by roughly 45,000 to 50,000 through natural population growth. Absence of data on rural-urban population shifts precludes any firm estimate of the size of the collective farm labor force in 1970.

According to preliminary estimates by the planning authorities, an increase of between 120,000 and 130,000 workers outside the collective farm sector would be needed to implement the industrial and social programs of the five-year plan for the 1971-75 period if productivity remained at the level of the 1965-69 period. The natural growth of the able-bodied urban population during this period was estimated not to exceed 29,000 persons. An outflow of up to 100,000 persons from the rural areas would therefore be necessary to meet the estimated manpower needs. Such a contingency could not be countenanced because of the severe damage it would inflict on the rural economy. Attainment of a higher rate of participation in the labor force and of a substantial increase in labor productivity has therefore been considered by the Party leadership of utmost urgency to ensure sustained economic development.

The latest evidence of the leadership's profound concern about these basic labor problems was provided by the Party's Central Committee plenum held at the end of December 1969, devoted to a discussion of means for raising productivity and tightening labor discipline. In its report delivered to the plenum, the Political Bureau (Politburo) of the Central Committee expressed strong dissatisfaction with what it considered an unsatisfactory rate of participation in employment by the collective farm population. It placed the blame for this situation on local government organs, which had become reconciled to the backward traditional concepts that keep homemakers and some young girls in the home and that require a member of the family to look after the family's privately owned livestock and thus be unable to seek outside work.

The Party's report also called attention to the prevalence of a petty bourgeois attitude among many families of workers, employees, and servicemen that keeps their members from accepting employment. To facilitate the employment of women, the Party urged more widespread provision of amenities, such as nurseries and dining halls, that would free them from household duties.

Meaningful information on labor productivity is not available because statistics on this subject have not been published and because essential details of the methods used in calculating the percentage rates of increase in productivity that appear from time to time in official public statements are not sufficiently known. Based on physical output and labor data, Western observers believe that the published data overstate the actual advance achieved.

According to the Politburo report, productivity in industry rose 2.2 times between 1950 and 1968, and this growth accounted for 60 percent of the increase in industrial production during that period. In agriculture 67 percent of the increase in output during those years was attributed to the growth of productivity. These figures indicate a slightly faster advance in agricultural productivity, but in absolute terms productivity in agriculture has been very much lower than in industry.

During the Third Five-Year Plan (1961-65) labor productivity reportedly rose by an annual average of 2.1 percent in industry, 4.6 percent in construction, and 2.7 percent in automotive transport. Data for the years after 1965 had not been published by mid-1970 except for official statements that the planned levels had not been reached.

The lag of productivity has been attributed by the Central Committee to a pronounced shortage of skilled manpower and to various manifestations of poor labor discipline and faulty management. Chief among the cited shortcomings in the field of labor are excessive absenteeism, resulting in part from inadequate medical and public dining facilities; loafing on the job; and a generally negligent attitude toward work that entails a loss of time and a low quality of the product. On the management side, the main shortcomings include poor organization of production, acceptance of unjustifiably low work output norms, and labor hoarding.

Both workers and managers have been accused of a reluctance to adopt progressive production techniques and of frequently putting their own personal interest or that of their enterprise ahead of the public good. A disorganization of the material supply arising from frequent noncompletion of production assignments and poor coordination among plants and industry branches has also been cited as an important factor responsible for substantial losses of worktime and, consequently, of reduced productivity.

Enterprise managers have been repeatedly accused of irresponsibility in the use of resources, which has entailed a wasteful use of machinery and labor. Inadequate planning of production schedules and poor maintenance are said to cause an inordinate loss of machine time. Managers have also been charged with abusing the legal provision that allows them to employ up to 2 percent more workers (presumably to meet emergencies or to increase output) than are called for by the enterprise plan. Such abuse has been facilitated by the elimination sometime in the middle or late 1960s of the control by banks over enterprise funds allotted for the payment of wages.

A change in the method of productivity planning, which involved a redefinition of productivity as a calculated index, is reported to have been widely misinterpreted as downgrading the importance of productivity. This misconception has been reinforced by the circumstance that productivity levels are planned for only about 70 percent of the nonagricultural workers.

In many enterprises labor norms—that is, the minimum amount of work a worker in any given job is required to perform per unit of time—are officially said to be inordinately low. There are reported to be many enterprises in which the established norms are substantially overfulfilled despite the fact that the effective workday does not exceed 6 to 7 hours. These norms, it is said, require only about 5-1/2 to 6 hours of work per day and are thus responsible for a 25- to 35-percent loss of output or, conversely, of labor wastage. Yet, despite the low norms, about 14 percent of the workers fail to complete their assigned tasks. Although a Politburo decision in April 1967 called the attention of Party, government, and economic organs to the importance of correct labor norms, this matter has been generally neglected and little has been accomplished. Many of the existing norms have become obsolete.

The Politburo's program that was adopted toward the end of 1969 for raising productivity is based essentially on an appeal to the social consciousness of all participants in the economic process and calls for improved performance in all aspects and at all levels of production through greater self-discipline and more stringent controls. A practical difficulty faced by the leadership in the execution of its program is the lack of a precise concept of productivity and of an effective methodology for establishing sound productivity targets or for measuring actual performance. The problem is particularly pronounced in agriculture. Experimentation with new concepts and methods has been underway for some time under the joint guidance of the State Planning Commission, the Ministry of Industry and Mining, and the Ministry of Construction. Results of the experimentation are to serve as a basis for further decisions by the Council of Ministers in 1970.

A distinctive feature of the country's labor scene is the practice of mobilizing large numbers of the population for so-called voluntary work on various types of construction and agricultural projects, including the building of railroads, housing, and irrigation canals; land improvement; harvesting; and the planting of trees. Thousands and, at times, tens of thousands of individuals from all walks of life, including members of the armed forces, are assembled by the government to carry out specific jobs with simple tools or with their bare hands.

Party dogma holds that these projects, which use vast numbers of people, reflect the Party's strength, the might of the masses, and the great reserves to be found in their midst. The projects are considered to be not only of great economic and social importance but also of great ideological, political, and educational significance because, among other things, they reflect the determination and readiness of the broad working masses to implement the Party's line. Official complaints about flagging enthusiasm for housing construction in 1968 suggest a less favorable public acceptance of this practice than that proclaimed by the Party dogma.

AGRICULTURE

Agriculture is organized on the Stalinist Soviet model: all activity is centrally planned, and farm operations are carried out by state and collective farms. Government policy has accorded a high priority to the expansion and modernization of agricultural production as a means of attaining self-sufficiency in foods. In an effort to obviate the historical dependence on grain imports, the government has placed special emphasis on increasing the output of bread grains, which furnish the bulk of the people's diet, and on a rapid rise in the production of potatoes as a substitute for bread.

Great importance is attached to the expansion of industrial crops, such as cotton, tobacco, sugar beets, and sunflowers, in order to provide raw materials for the growing domestic industries, in addition to maintaining traditional exports. Expansion of grape vineyards, olive groves, and other fruit and vegetable growing has also been promoted to develop larger exportable surpluses. According to official data, farm output increased half again as fast as the population between 1950 and 1967, but it is still inadequate to supply the country's minimum needs for bread and livestock products.

The government's ambitious farm modernization program has been imposed on tradition-bound peasants averse to rapid change. A large part of the land improvement and irrigation work has been accomplished through mass mobilization of peasants and of the urban population for so-called voluntary work on the model of the Chinese coolie system. Socialization of the land has had a deleterious effect on work incentives, with a consequent lag in the planned growth of agricultural production. Measures adopted by the government to ensure better work performance on the collective farms did not prove sufficiently effective, and a scaling down of the five-year plan target for agricultural production could therefore not be avoided.

To provide the additional acreage needed for crop expansion, large-scale programs of land reclamation and melioration have been executed. At the same time, heavy stress has been laid on the improvement of farm techniques and on mechanization as means for increasing yields and production. A planned expansion of livestock herds and of the output of livestock products has been hampered by inadequate incentives for peasants and by a shortage of fodder. The agricultural potential is limited by the predominance of rugged mountain terrain and by frequent spring droughts that cause extensive damage to crops. To minimize the adverse effects of the droughts, an extensive irrigation system is being developed.

In 1967 the area of land in agricultural use, excluding forests, roads, and homesites, amounted to about 3.0 million acres, or 43 percent of the country's total area. More than half of the agricultural land was in unimproved natural pastures, with an additional small acreage in natural meadows. Cultivated land bearing field and tree crops totaled about 1.4 million acres, of which about 1.1 million acres were arable land, equivalent to about two-thirds of an acre per capita. Almost half of the cultivated land was located in hilly and mountainous zones, which are less productive than the coastal plains. The agricultural acreage was expanded by 3 percent between 1950 and 1967, but a significant further expansion is precluded by the country's rugged terrain.

A high priority has been placed by the leadership on expanding the cultivated area and raising its productivity through land reclamation, soil improvement, and irrigation. Most of this work has been accomplished manually, through mobilization of large numbers of people for massive projects and with the participation by members of the armed forces. Between 1950 and 1969 the area of cultivated land rose by almost one-half to a total of more than 1.4 million acres, at least 185,000 acres of which have been reclaimed since 1965. The bulk of the increase in cultivated land was achieved at the expense of natural pastures and meadows, the area of which has declined by about 265,000 and 50,000 acres, respectively, since 1950. About 70 percent of the increase in cultivated land was added to arable acreage.

By the end of 1969, however, the reclamation work had fallen behind the five-year plan schedule. In early 1970 the government therefore took special measures to ensure that the entire 285,000-acre reclamation program would be completed as planned, bringing the total cultivated acreage to about 1.5 million acres. Very substantial progress in this endeavor was reported to have been achieved by the end of March, largely through the mobilization for this task of about 200,000 persons from urban and rural areas.

Expansion of the irrigation network has proceeded somewhat more slowly than planned, with the use of the same mass construction methods. As reported by the State Planning Commission to the People's Assembly in mid-February of 1970, about 140,000 acres had been brought under irrigation during the 1966-69 period, and approximately 55,000 more acres were to be added in 1970. These figures imply a total irrigated area of about 645,000 acres in 1969 and about 700,000 acres planned for 1970—an increase of 2,470 acres over the original five-year plan target. Attainment of this goal would require a construction volume in 1970 equal to the total achieved during the first two years of the five-year period and almost half again as large as the volume in 1968. About half the arable acreage was irrigable in 1969.

The agricultural organization consists of two types of farms: state farms, operated under the direction of either the central or the local government, and collective farms. State farms, modeled after the *sovkhozes* of the Soviet Union, were established beginning in 1945 on lands confiscated from large landowners and foreign concessionaires and contain some of the most productive land in the country. Managers and workers of state farms are salaried government employees, who may receive special bonuses for superior production achievements.

Collective farms were organized through the forcible consolidation of private holdings. Begun in 1946 against strong peasant resistance, collectivization did not assume major proportions until 1955 and was virtually completed only in 1968 with the consolidation of remote mountain villages. The basic features of the collective farm are: complete government control; collective use of the land and other principal means of production; obligatory common work by the members, based on established minimum work norms and enforced through economic and other sanctions; and distribution of the net income to members on the basis of the quantity and quality of work performed.

With regard to income distribution, collective farm members are residual claimants entitled to share whatever remains after completion of compulsory deliveries to the state; provision of prescribed investment and operating funds for the farm; payment for irrigation water, machine-tractor station services, and other outstanding obligations; and setting aside 2 percent of the income for social assistance to members. Information on farm income levels is not available. Nominally, the General Assembly of all the members is the highest ruling organ of the collective farm, but actual control rests with the farm's basic Party organization (see ch. 6, Government Structure and Political System).

An important feature of the state and collective farms is the small private plot allotted to a member family for its own personal use. Since 1967, when these allotments were reduced in size, the maximum legal size of the private plots, including the land under all farm buildings other than the family dwelling, has ranged from 1,000 to 1,500 square meters (about 10,750 to 16,150 square feet, or one-quarter to three-eighths of an acre), depending upon the location and availability of irrigation. The collective farm statute also entitles each family to maintain a few domestic animals privately. Only one cow or one pig is authorized, but up to ten or twenty sheep and goats may be allowed. In typical cases a family may have a cow or pig and a few sheep or goats. More liberal allowances for poor mountain farms may include both a cow and pig as well as the maximum number of sheep and goats.

In 1964 there were thirty-eight large, centrally controlled state farms with an average of about 7,700 acres of farmland, including about 4,800 acres of cultivated land. In 1968 the average size of the state farms, the number of which had remained stable, was reported to be about 7,350 acres, a reduction of almost 600 acres since 1964. This decline in acreage was brought about by a transfer of some state farmlands to small collective farms as a means of increasing their viability. In 1964, 250 locally administered state farms were reported to average about 380 acres and have probably continued unchanged. In 1970 state farms cultivated 20 percent of the total acreage under cultivation, and collective farms worked 80 percent.

The number and average size of collective farms have varied widely as a result of the continuing creation of new farms and the consolidation of existing units. In the fall of 1969 there were 805 collective farms, compared with 1,208 in 1967. The consolidated farms included 568 units consisting of two to three villages each, eighty farms of six to ten villages, and another five farms of eleven villages each. Eighty-seven percent of all collective farms had less than 2,470 acres of cultivated land each, and only nine percent had more than about 6,200 acres.

Highland farms were among the smallest, many being smaller than 750 acres. In 1968 the average size of all collective farms was reported to be about 1,400 acres of cultivated land. In 1967, before collectivization was completed, the population on collective farms consisted of 184,400 families—an average of about 150 families per farm—which provided about 427,000 farmworkers. As a result of further consolidation, the number of families per farm increased significantly.

Although available statistics are inadequate for a comprehensive review of the crop and livestock situation, five-year plan data and fragmentary information contained in annual official reports on economic plan fulfillment provide a reasonable approximation of the production volume of major crops but only a rough approximation of the size of the livestock herds (see tables 10 and 11).

Published data on total agricultural production claim a virtual doubling of output between 1960 and 1969. During this period the share of field crops in total output is reported to have increased at the expense of livestock production—a direct result of the government's emphasis on bread grains. The share of field crops is reported to have risen from 44 percent in 1960 to 59 percent in 1967, whereas the share of livestock output declined from 43 to 29.5 percent. Fruit production contributed about 10 percent of total output during the period, and collection of wild medicinal plants, another 1 to 4 percent.

Bread-grain production, including wheat, rye, and corn, increased by 80 percent in the 1966-69 period, but attainment of the five-year plan target requires a reversal of the downward trend in annual output increases since 1966 and a tonnage increase in 1970 from 20 to 38 percent greater than those obtained in the 1967-69 period. The output of potatoes in 1969 was eleven times larger than production in 1965 yet was only half the volume planned for 1970. The required doubling of the output to meet the five-year plan target is roughly equivalent to the increase in production achieved during the preceding three-year period. Nevertheless, the substantial rise in the output of bread grains and potatoes achieved during the first four years of the five-year plan significantly, although not entirely, reduced the need for grain imports, which amounted to about 110,000 tons of wheat and 20,000 tons of corn in 1963 and 1964.

Production of rice, cotton, and tobacco was reported to have lagged through 1969, and the output of cotton actually declined in 1967 and 1968. This and other reported information about these crops indicate that the possibility of attaining the 1970 target is precluded for rice and is questionable for cotton. In the case of tobacco, however, reported production in 1969 was already about 1,000 tons above the five-year plan goal, in spite of the reported lag. As early as 1967 the output of sugar beets approached the volume planned for 1970, but subsequent developments regarding this crop have been cloaked in official silence. According to officially reported data, the production of vegetables in 1969 surpassed the 1970 target by some 60,000 tons, or nearly 27 percent, yet no mention of this fact was contained in the report on plan fulfillment for that year.

Table 10. Production of Field Crops and Fruits in Albania, 1960 and 1965-70 (in thousands of metric tons)

	1960	1965	1966	1967	1968	1969	Plan 1970
Grains	216.7	324.6	n.a.	n.a.	n.a.	n.a.	659.0*

Breadgrains**	(197.1)	(296.6)	(389.3)	(445.0)	(494.0)	(533.4)	(593.0)
Potatoes	23.4	21.2	108.0	115.9	166.0	238.8	475.0
Rice	4.6	10.2	10.5	11.3	n a.	n.a.	24.0
Cotton	16.1	24.6	24.7	21.9	18.5	25.0	34.0
Tobacco	8.1	13.3	13.7	13.1	14.9	17.1	16.0
Sugar beets	72.7	90.2	132.9	138.5	n.a.	n.a.	140.0
Vegetables	71.3	140.9	156.5	172.2	180.8	283.8	224.0
Fruits, deciduous	25.3	39.7	47.8	40.7	58.6	n.a.	69.5
Fruits, citrus	1.7	2.0	2.2	2.6	n.a.	n.a.	5.6
Grapes	22.3	42.9	54.1	48.5	61.1	n.a.	94.4

n.a.—not available

* Except for the data on fruits, all figures in this column are rounded to the nearest thousand tons.

** Wheat, rye, and corn.

+ The Fourth Five-Year Plan (1966-70) calls for more than this amount.

In the absence of information on the planting of fruit trees and vines, the fruit production trends of recent years provide the only indication of the extent to which the fruit production program of the five-year plan may be realized. Available data through 1968 for deciduous fruits and grapes and through 1967 for citrus fruits indicate that the 1970 goals for grapes and citrus fruits may not be reached. Production of citrus fruits would have to more than double in three years, whereas an increase of only 53 percent was achieved in the 1961-67 period. Similarly, grape output would have to rise by 54 percent in two years, compared with an increase of 42 percent in the preceding three years. The outlook for deciduous fruits is more favorable. The needed output increase of 20 percent over two years is well within previously attained limits.

Table 11. Livestock in Albania, 1960, 1964-66, and 1970 Plan (in thousands)

	1960	1964	1965	1966	Plan* 1977
Horses	49	44	44	44	n.a.
Mules	17	20	20	21	n.a.
Donkeys	57	60	60	60	n.a.
Cattle	420	427	424	27	475
Cows	146	157	156	158	n.a.
Oxen	100	87	n.a.	n.a.	139
Buffalo	7	5	5	5	n.a.
Sheep	1,546	1,682	1,637	1,670	1,800
Goats	1,104	1,199	1,175	1,200	1,400
Hogs	130	147	141	142	n.a.
Poultry	1,580	1,671	1,722	1,746	3.000

n.a.—not available.

* Fourth Five-Year Plan (1965-70).

Information on livestock numbers is much more sketchy. The dearth of published data and repeated official pronouncements indicate unsatisfactory progress in this farm sector, particularly with regard to the high-priority target for cattle raising. An important cause of this lag has been an acknowledged shortage of fodder. Another major reason has been an officially induced transfer of livestock from individual peasant ownership to the collective and state farms, where it is subject to the much-criticized negligent attitude of the peasants toward state and communal property. About 60 percent of the cattle and sheep and 85 percent of the hogs were kept on state and collective farms in 1969, as against only about 36 and 64 percent, respectively, in 1964.

Collective farm managers and local government officials have blamed the fodder shortage on the diversion of pastures and meadows to the production of bread grains. Statistical evidence indicates that the output of feed grains declined by about 40 percent from the mid-1950s to the mid-

1960s but that the loss of fodder from grazing lands and meadows was compensated fourfold through increased production of forage crops. The validity of the explanation offered by the farm and village officials was vigorously denied in the theoretical monthly journal of the Party's Central Committee, which attributed the fodder shortage to a failure by collective farmers to adopt improved methods of crop production and to exploit all available fodder resources. In January 1970 all basic Party organizations in farming areas were urged to eliminate distrust and every conservative idea and harmful tendency that stood in the way of the rapid development of cattle raising and to see to it that the existing gap between the collective farms and private plots was gradually eliminated.

Government efforts to improve livestock breeds and yields through selective breeding, artificial insemination, and better management practices have also been impeded by peasant apathy. Although yields of up to 5,500 pounds of milk per cow were obtained on some state farms in 1966 and yields of about 3,300 pounds to 3,950 pounds on the more efficient lowland collective farms, the average yield of milk per cow on all lowland collective farms in that year was only about 1,750 to 2,200 pounds, and a large number of upland farms obtained even less.

The latest available official Albanian livestock statistics are for the year 1964. Data for 1965 and 1966 have been published by the Food and Agriculture Organization (FAO) of the United Nations. The Fourth Five-Year Plan indicates the numbers planned for some of the livestock categories in 1970 through percentage increases expected to be attained over the numbers in 1965. In the case of cattle, the largest increase by far has been planned for draft oxen—60 percent as against only 12 percent for all cattle—in an effort to reduce a draft power shortage. This increase would inevitably be at the expense of the growth in the numbers of cows and young stock.

The growth of productive livestock herds, excluding draft animals, lagged very substantially in relation to the increase in population, at least through 1966. This has entailed a significant worsening of the initially very meager supply of livestock products. According to estimates published by the FAO, total annual meat production, including all types of meat in terms of carcass weight but excluding edible offals, increased from an average of 40,000 tons in the 1952-56 period to 50,000 tons in 1967. The output in 1967 implies a per capita daily meat availability of only about 2.5 ounces, including bones. A similar situation prevailed with regard to dairy and poultry products because there were only about 75 low-production cows per 1,000 population and one head of inferior poultry per capita.

Total agricultural production, which was planned to increase at an average annual rate of 11.5 percent or from 71 to 76 percent for the five-year plan period as a whole, consistently fell short of the targets in the 1966-69 period and was not likely to attain the 17-percent increase planned for 1970. Thus, for instance, the actual output increase achieved in 1969 was only about 10 percent as against a planned rise of 22.1 percent and in 1968, similarly, about 1.6 as against 12 percent.

This persistent lag in farm output has been extensively and publicly discussed by the leadership, which is intent on raising the general level of performance in agriculture and ensuring an adequate domestic supply of food products. Although some blame has been attached to unfavorable weather conditions, the lag has been ascribed primarily to the reluctance of peasants to adopt modern production techniques, poor farm management, insufficient effort to use available resources to best advantage, widespread indifference and negligence, and an excessive preoccupation with personal interests leading to an irresponsible attitude toward work in the collective sector. These shortcomings were said to exist not only among the peasantry at large but also among Communists, who should be serving as models of responsible behavior. The basic reason that clearly emerges from public discussion is a widespread opposition of peasants to the collectivization of farms and an associated tendency to devote their best efforts to the cultivation of their own private plots.

Impressive evidence on this point is provided by official production statistics for 1964, the latest available on this subject. These data show that output per acre on the small private plots of collective farmers and state farm workers was four times larger than output on state farms and six times larger than that on collective farms. Constituting only 6 percent of the cultivated land, the private plots produced 23 percent of the total farm output. Nevertheless, the leadership has publicly credited the advance in agricultural production to the collectivization of farms.

In 1967 the government proceeded to reduce the size of the private plots, with a view to their eventual elimination, both for ideological reasons and as a means of forcing peasants to devote greater efforts to work on collectivized land. Subsequent steps were taken to transfer to collective ownership some of the livestock allotted to the farm families by the collective farm statute.

This action did not measurably improve agricultural performance. Shortfalls in the production of several important crops, including cotton, tobacco, and rice, were admitted to have occurred both in 1968 and 1969, and the situation in the livestock sector continued to be unsatisfactory. A scaling down of the original production goal for 1970 could therefore not be avoided. The farm output target set by the annual plan for 1970 was 12.5 percent below the minimum and 15 percent below the maximum five-year plan figures for the same year.

INDUSTRY

A few primitive plants producing consumer goods had been built before World War II, but industrial development began only in 1949, when construction was undertaken of a 50,000-kilowatt hydroelectric power station, a textile mill capable of producing 22 million yards of cloth per year, and a sugar mill with an annual capacity of 10,000 tons of sugar. Industrial construction continued under the first and second five-year plans (1951-55 and 1956-60, respectively) during the 1950s, with substantial financial and technical assistance from the Soviet Union. This development was temporarily interrupted in the wake of the political break with the Soviet Union in 1961 but was soon resumed with aid from Communist China (see ch. 6, Government Structure and Political System). The interruption was said by the Albanian leadership to have retarded industrial growth by three years. Disinterested foreign observers, however, reported that the equipment acquired with the aid of Communist China was better suited to the needs of the country and of better quality than that supplied by the Soviet Union.

Among the major industrial projects completed or under construction in 1970 with the assistance of Communist Chinese technicians were: copper, chromium, and iron-nickel mines; an oil refinery at Fier with an annual capacity of 500,000 tons of crude oil, a 225,000-kilowatt hydroelectric power station at Vau i Dejes on the Drin River; a 100,000-kilowatt capacity of 500,000 tons of crude oil; a 225,000-kilowatt/thermal power-plant at Fier; a copper-ore dressing installation and a copper-wire drawing mill; a steel-rolling mill at Elbasan; cement mills at Elbasan and Kruje; large textile combines at Tirana and Berat; and a knit goods factory at Korce.

Of special benefit to agriculture was the construction of a nitrate fertilizer plant at Fier, a superphosphate plant at Lac, and a plant for the manufacture of tractor spare parts at Tirana. A variety of smaller plants were also built for the production of such items as caustic soda, sulfuric acid, rubber products, electrical equipment and light bulbs, footwear, and vegetable oils.

Along with the construction of technologically up-to-date plants, others were built with outdated technology through the lack of construction experience or knowledge of more advanced methods. At the same time, obsolete plants and workshops remained in use. In 1969 these technologically backward plants produced less than half the total output but employed more than half the industrial labor force.

Available information on the structure of industry is ambiguous because of uncertainties regarding the pricing methods underlying the relevant data. According to the official figures for 1967 based on 1966 prices, the food industry accounted for nearly one-third and light industry for almost one-fourth of the total industrial output. The balance of 44 percent was produced by some fourteen or more industry branches, the relative shares of which ranged from 8.0 percent for metalworking and for timber and wood processing to 0.3 percent for the bitumen industry. As a group, six industry branches engaged in oil production and mining contributed about 15 percent of the output. The building materials industry accounted for 5 percent and electric power production, for not quite 4 percent.

The relationship between the output of capital goods and that of consumer goods is equally ambiguous. The share of capital goods in the output of 1968 was officially reported as 55.5 percent, as against 44.5 percent for consumer goods. The apparent discrepancy between the reported shares in total output of consumer goods as compared with the production of the light and food industries may be explained, in part, by the fact that a portion of these industries' output is usually included among capital goods as, for instance, textiles used by the clothing industry and leather used by the shoe industry.

Foreign observers have reported the country's industry to be poorly balanced not only in a technical sense but also in terms of essential domestic needs and the availability of foreign outlets for its products. The metalworking industry, for example, which is limited to the production of automotive and industrial spare parts, apart from a few types of simple agricultural equipment and household utensils, cannot even ensure the maintenance of the existing machinery inventory because it is able to supply only about 60 to 70 percent of the country's needs. Industrial production is substantially oriented toward capital goods and exports, whereas the manufacture of products for domestic consumption continues to be severely restricted.

The leadership is aware of industry's structural shortcomings and is intent on overcoming them through a program involving the reconstruction and modernization of old plants and the concentration of small shops into larger, more efficient specialized units. Progress in this direction, however, has been hampered by inadequate investment resources and by a reluctance of managers and workers to cooperate with this program. It has also been handicapped by a lack of effective planning and by an inability to organize comprehensive studies that would provide a basis for both overall and detailed plans.

Nevertheless, a few plants for the manufacture of machine spare parts and of simple equipment were formed through the concentration of milling machines previously installed in maintenance shops of various enterprises, and a step toward the consolidation of small artisan shops was taken in May 1969 by transforming artisans' cooperatives into state enterprises.

Owing to the lack of prior industrial experience by both managers and labor, industry also suffers from poor organization of production and of the material supply, low labor productivity, and generally inferior quality of product. Extensive discussion of these problems in the official press indicates that government efforts toward reducing the magnitude of these problems are slow in bearing fruit, despite programs for vocational training and intensive campaigns of political indoctrination aimed at generating productive enthusiasm and innovative initiative among workers and managers. A major campaign is being waged to eradicate artisan traditions and to replace them with industrial production line methods. The basic difficulty in achieving greater efficiency lies in the continuing severe shortage of skilled manpower and of personnel with adequate training in the economics and mechanics of industrial production.

Because of the underlying pricing methods, officially reported data on total industrial production in value terms overstate the actual rate of growth attained. Substantial industrial progress is, nevertheless, indicated by physical production data for a number of commodities (see table 12). Since production had started from nothing or from very low levels in the early post-World War II years, the rates of growth in output were substantially higher during the 1950s than in the following decade.

The highest rates of increase during the 1960s, ranging from five to three times the initial volume, were achieved in the production of copper, electric power, and cement. Increases of from 69 to 80 percent were attained for coal, oil, and iron-nickel ore. Production of textiles and footwear grew by more than half, and that of knitwear more than doubled. A substantial advance was also made by the food-processing industry. Least progress was made in the production of cigarettes and bricks—only about 6 to 7 percent—and the output of timber actually declined from 6 million to 5 million cubic feet. Most of the mining output and a substantial share of the food industry production are exported.

Rapid electrification of the country has been a major goal of the leadership. Electrification is intended to meet the needs of industrial development and help attain a higher standard of living in rural areas. A crash program has been underway to bring electric power to every village, even in the remotest areas. This project was originally scheduled to be completed in 1985, but the date has been advanced to November 8, 1971, the thirtieth anniversary of the founding of the ruling Albanian Workers' Party. The program is being carried out by the prevailing method of mass mobilization for voluntary work.

Installed capacity in 1969 was reported to be 210,000 kilowatts, of which 128,000 kilowatts were in thermal powerplants and 82,000 kilowatts in hydroelectric power stations. This capacity reflected a fourfold increase since 1960, a large part of which was accounted for by a single thermal plant of 100,000-kilowatt capacity put into operation in late 1969. The country's hydroelectric power potential has been estimated by Albanian technicians as roughly 3 billion kilowatt-hours per year, half of which is represented by the Drin River. Development of this potential has barely begun. The first major plant on the Drin with a capacity of 225,000 kilowatts is scheduled for completion at Vau i Dejes in 1971, and a second station on that river with a capacity of 400,000 kilowatts is to be built at Fierze during the Fifth Five-Year Plan (1971-75).

Table 12. Industrial Production in Albania, 1960 and 1964-69

Commodity	Units	1960	1964	1965	1966	1967	1968	1969
Electric power	million kilowatt-hours	194	288	322	433	589	712	n.a.
Crude oil	thousand metric tons	728	764	822	887	984	1,137	1,310
Petroleum products	thousand metric tons	369	476	509	590	692	n.a.	n.a.
Coal	thousand metric tons	291	292	331	393	434	491	n.a.
Chrome ore	thousand metric tons	289	307	311	302	327	369	n.a.
Copper ore	thousand	82	145	219	228	267	304	326

	metric tons							
Blister copper	thousand metric tons	1	2	4	5	5	n.a.	n.a.
Iron-nickel ore	thousand metric tons	255	351	395	395	403	440	n.a.
Cement	thousand metric tons	73	127	134	139	221	n.a.	n.a.
Bricks	million units	130	121	1112	106	139	n.a.	n.a.
Ginned cotton	thousand metric tons	7	9	8	9	9	n.a.	n.a.
Textiles	million yards	28	33	33	37	44	n.a.	n.a.
Cotton	million yards	27	31	-	-	-	n.a.	n.a.
Knitwear	million units	1	2	2	3	3	n.a.	n.a.
Leather	thousand square yards	109	126	124	161	158	n.a.	n.a.
Footwear (other than rubber)	thousand pairs	1,365	1,835	2,103	2,259	2,103	n.a.	n.a.
Shoes and sandals	thousand pairs	831	955	n.a.	n.a.	n.a.	n.a.	n.a.
Rubber boots	thousand pairs	155	201	191	211	248	n.a.	n.a.

Flour	thousand metric tons	125	145	152	1661	157	n.a.	n.a.
Cigarettes	million units	3,436	3,990	4,390	3,310	3,620	n.a.	n.a.

n.a.—not available.

Electric power production is reported to have attained in 1968 the level planned for 1970. Output of power rose from 194 million kilowatt-hours in 1960 to 324 million kilowatt-hours in 1965 and almost 800,000 million kilowatt-hours in 1969. The distribution system has also been rapidly extended and in 1969 included about 800 miles of high-tension transmission lines of 35 and 110 kilovolts. Distribution and use of electric power were reported to be very wasteful, with losses as high as 115 million kilowatt-hours in 1969—almost 15 percent of total output. Information on the pattern of electric power consumption has not been published.

FINANCE

Financial operations have been shrouded in secrecy, and little information can be gleaned from the limited published data. These data, nevertheless, reflect some of the leadership's basic economic policies, such as its emphasis on rapidly increasing production while restraining a rise in consumption, its preference for industrial development as against agricultural growth, and its drive to mobilize domestic resources for economic development.

The Budget

Information on budgetary practices is not available, and statistics relating to the budget are incomplete. The relation between three different budgets approved annually by the People's Assembly on recommendation of the Council of Ministers is therefore unclear. There is a state and a national budget and a budget for local government. The budget for local government has been growing slowly in relation to the state-budget—from 16 percent in 1955 to 17 percent in 1960 and 20 percent in 1969 and 1970.

Only about one-fourth of local budgetary revenue is derived from local taxation, which implies a substantial subsidy from the central government budget. The amount of this subsidy is roughly double the usual 7- to 8-percent difference between the state and the smaller national budget. A surmise that the state budget represents an overall budget and that the national budget serves to finance central government activities only is therefore not warranted.

Except for a slight decline in revenues in 1961 and 1963, coincident with the country's political and economic break with the Soviet Union, the annual state budget has been rising steadily to a level of 5.21 billion leks (5 leks equal US$1—see Glossary) in revenues and 5.11 billion leks in expenditures for 1970. By comparison with the budget for 1960, revenues increased by 85 percent and expenditures by 102 percent, with a corresponding decline of 65 percent in the budgetary surplus. On a five-year basis, comparing the Fourth Five-Year Plan with the Third Five-Year Plan, both revenues and expenditures rose by about 40 percent, with a slightly higher increase in revenues.

A relatively greater stringency of funds for budgetary purposes after the break with the Soviet Union is reflected in the planned annual budgetary surplus, a permanent feature since 1946 and a matter of great pride for the leadership. From a level of almost 24 percent in 1950, 15 percent in 1955, and 10 percent in 1960, the surplus dropped to 1.1 percent in 1962 and 1.5 percent in 1963. Despite a slight recovery in subsequent years, except for 1968 when it declined to only 1 percent of revenues, the planned surplus did not again approach its earlier size.

Partial information on sources of revenue is available to 1967. Published statistics listed a turnover tax on all goods produced, deductions from enterprise profits, direct taxes on the population (primarily income taxes), and social insurance premiums. These sources yielded, on an average, 60 percent of the total revenue in the 1960-65 period, and their share rose steeply to 74 percent in 1967. The balance of the revenue, omitted from official statistics, consisted primarily of income from agriculture in the form of compulsory deliveries, proceeds from state farm operations, payments to machine-tractor stations, and taxes.

The most important among the listed revenue sources were the turnover tax and deductions from profits. Together their yields ranged from 50 percent of total revenue in 1960 to almost 69 percent in 1967, but their relative weights changed markedly during this period. In 1960 the turnover tax yielded 40 percent and profit deductions 10 percent of revenue; by 1967 their respective shares were 43 and 26 percent. Social insurance premiums contributed between 3.2 and 4.5 percent, while the yield from direct taxes on the population declined from 2.7 percent in 1960 to less than 1 percent in 1967. In 1969 income taxation was abolished for individuals and for some poor collective farms in hilly and mountainous areas.

The leadership has claimed that the abolition of direct taxes on the population with the concomitant improvement in public welfare was made possible by the country's economic advance based on the Party's correct revolutionary policy, and it contrasted the progressive nature of this measure with an alleged intensification of exploitation and misery of workers in what are officially called imperialist and modern-revisionist countries. This comparison ignores the existence of the turnover tax, which is particularly heavy on consumer goods, and of the enterprise profits deduction, both of which are reflected in the sales price of commodities and, consequently, represent a hidden form of sales taxes. This method of taxation is known to be regressive, in that it takes no account of differences in income and places the heaviest burden on those least able to pay.

The published budget laws usually specify the amount of revenue to be derived from the socialized economy, including collective farms and cooperative enterprises. The proportion of this revenue was reported to have been 85.5 percent in 1960 and from 88 to 89 percent in the 1968-70 period. This information cannot be reconciled with the published revenue statistics, particularly with the data concerning the taxation of noncollectivized farm enterprises, the proceeds from which were reported to be less than 0.5 percent in 1964. The revenue from the nonsocialized sector consists mostly of taxes imposed on the output from personal farm plots of collective and state farm workers and, to a lesser extent, of taxes on some private artisan and other activities still tolerated by the government within narrowly prescribed limits.

Information on budgetary expenditures is also incomplete. Published statistics failed to specify the use of 17.5 percent of the total outlays in the 1960-65 period, and no explanation is readily at hand for the decline of the unallocated residue from that level to between 3 and 4 percent in 1968-70. The published data included outlays for the national economy, social and cultural needs, defense, and administration.

The proportion of total expenditures devoted to social and cultural needs and to defense remained remarkably stable between 1960 and 1970. Annual outlays for these two categories fluctuated, respectively, only from 22.6 to 25.1 percent and from 7.6 to 9.9 percent of total expenditures. The share of administrative expenditures declined steadily during this period from 2.7 to 1.7 percent. Outlays for the national economy were also shown by the published statistics to have been quite stable in the 1960-65 period, with an annual variation of only 2.6 percent. Coincident with the decline and virtual disappearance of the unreported expenditure residue after 1965, however, the share of industry rose sharply from 46 percent in 1965 to more than 64 percent in 1968 and remained above 61 percent through

1970. The reasons for, and the implications of, this change in reporting practice are not known.

An average of 47 percent of the budgetary expenditures in the 1960-67 period was devoted to investment, with annual fluctuations of this category between 39 and 55 percent. The lowest rates of investment occurred in 1962 and 1963 as an aftermath of the abrupt cessation of Soviet aid deliveries. In absolute terms the volume of investment increased from 1.1 billion leks in 1960 to 1.8 billion leks in 1967. Total investment for the years 1966-70 was planned at 6.5 billion leks, an increase of 34 percent over investments in the preceding five-year period. Actual investment in the years 1966-69 was reported to have exceeded the plan for those years by 12 percent. In line with the Party's policy of promoting a rapid growth of the country's productive capacity, from 80 to 82 percent of the investment has been devoted to the construction of facilities for material production.

Industry has received the largest share of investment—48 percent in the 1961-65 period and 50 percent under the plan for 1966-70. On an annual basis, industry's share ranged from a low of 36 percent in 1962 to a high of 61 percent in 1965. The proportion of agricultural investment was much lower—only 15 percent of the total in 1961-65 and less than 19 percent of the total planned for 1966-70. During the first two years of the 1966-70 period, actual investment in agriculture lagged substantially and amounted to only 11.7 and 16.2 percent, respectively. The lack of adequate investments has been a contributing cause of poor agricultural performance. There has been no consistency in the pattern of industrial and agricultural investment. The respective shares of these two sectors in total investment fluctuated widely from year to year in the 1960-67 period. An adequate explanation of the reasons for this fluctuation has not been found.

Investment in housing and for social and cultural purposes has been minimal—8.1 and 3.7 percent, respectively, in the 1961-65 period and 6.1 and 8.1 percent, respectively, under the plan for 1966-70. As in the case of agriculture, actual investment in 1966-67 was substantially below the planned levels and amounted to less than 5 percent for housing and 2 percent for social and cultural needs. This capital starvation has been largely responsible for the dismal housing situation and for the inadequacy of other essential amenities.

Money and Banking

The lek, divided into 100 quintars, is a nonconvertible paper currency with multiple official exchange rates. The basic official rate since August 10, 1965, has been 5 leks for 1 United States dollar, a rate that has no applicability in practice. Up to 1965 the exchange value had been 50 leks per US$1. The change in par value had no economic significance because prices, wages, and all other monetary values were reduced by the same ratio.

There are two types of so-called tourist or support leks. A rate of 12.50 leks per US$1 applies to the official exchange of Western currencies by nonresidents and to support payments received by residents from Western sources. A rate of 7.55 leks per US$1 applies to the exchange by Communist country residents of their national currencies and to support and other noncommercial payments transferred by them from Albania to Communist states. A third variety of official exchange rates consists of the rates used to balance clearing accounts under special trade and payments agreements with Communist countries. An illegal black market rate of about 60 leks per US$1 from early 1968 through early 1969 was reported by reliable sources.

All currency matters are administered by the National Bank jointly with the ministries of finance and trade. Albania is not a member of the International Bank for Reconstruction and Development or of the International Monetary Fund.

Adequate information is not available on the nature of the relationship between the State Bank and the Ministry of Finance or on the bank's financial operations beyond some outdated statistics on credits and savings deposits. As the principal financial institution, the State Bank carries out the financial policies of the Party and government. It issues currency, provides credit to all economic sectors, accepts savings deposits, and serves as the country's treasury. In addition to these functions, the State Bank helps prepare the financial plans for the economy, is called upon to assist enterprises in completing their planned assignments, and is responsible for controlling all economic activities through the use of its financial levers.

In mid-1969 the State Bank was severely criticized for poor performance, particularly its failure to exercise adequate control over unauthorized use of funds and waste of materials by the enterprises it helped to finance. The bank's failure was largely precipitated by uncertainties created through a decentralization of economic authority, decreed by the Party, and a dilution of the bank's control function.

A specialized system of state savings and securities banks was established within the Ministry of Finance in November 1968, for the purpose of mobilizing the population's savings for investment through loans to the state and the sale of its securities. The text of the law that created this institution contained no provision concerning the relation of these new savings and securities banks to the State Bank. Further information on the new banks was not available in mid-1970.

The only available information on the State Bank's financial operations consists of partial data on loans to agriculture and for housing and on the number and amount of savings deposits. The total volume of farm credits, exclusive of credits to state farms for which statistics have not been published, increased from 95 million leks in 1960 to 252 million leks in 1964, including long-term loans of 38 million and 44 million leks, respectively. By 1967 long-term loans had increased to 56 million leks. The statistics do not indicate whether the published data refer to the annual volume of loans granted or to the total amount of outstanding loans. A small fraction of the loans after 1960 was granted to individual peasants for the purchase of livestock.

Loans for housing construction and repair declined drastically from 17 million leks in 1960 to only 7 million leks in 1964. The distribution of the loans between urban and rural areas fluctuated widely, but urban loans predominated by a large margin and constituted from 69 to 93 percent of the total. The number of savings accounts increased from 235,400 in 1960 to 445,000 in 1968, and the volume of deposits rose from 119 million to 247 million leks. Interest paid on these amounts totaled 3.6 million and 4.8 million leks in the respective years, which implies a reduction of the interest rate from about 3.0 to 2.5 percent.

FOREIGN ECONOMIC RELATIONS

Foreign Aid

The country's foreign economic relations have been conditioned by its leadership's economic goals and political persuasion. As a poor, undeveloped country intent on modernizing and expanding its economy at a rapid pace, Albania has had to rely heavily on foreign economic and technical assistance during the post-World War II period. The leadership's extreme Marxist orientation and hostility toward the Western nations have precluded a recourse to non-Communist sources of aid and have made the country entirely dependent upon contributions by other Communist states. But even within the Communist sphere political disagreements have had a disruptive effect on aid arrangements (see ch. 6, Government Structure and Political System).

From 1945 to 1948 economic and technical assistance was received from Yugoslavia. After the political break between that country and Albania, the Soviet Union assumed the role of major aid donor, and smaller contributions were made by some of the East European Communist states.

Since 1961, when the substantial support of the Soviet Union was lost in the wake of the political schism within the Communist world engendered by the Sino-Soviet dispute, Albania has been able to obtain assistance only from the People's Republic of China (Communist China). The readjustment necessitated by the abrupt withdrawal of all Soviet aid and technical advisers was said by Albanian leaders to have retarded economic development by three years.

The extent of aid received in the form of long-term loans, some of which became grants through debt cancellations, is only partially known. The amount of total loan commitments by the Soviet Union in United States dollar equivalents for the period of 1945 through 1961 was estimated by one Western source at US$246 million. Another Western source reported the amount of loans promised by the Soviet Union and the East European Communist states for the 1961-65 period to have been in excess of US$132.5 million. These loans were cancelled in their entirety in the spring of 1961. A partial list of Soviet loan commitments, compiled by a Western student from Soviet economic literature, totaled US$172 million for 1957-61. The actual amount disbursed, however, was much smaller.

Aid deliveries, as reflected in official Soviet statistics, totaled only US$39.4 million for the years 1955-61. Similar information on aid deliveries from 1949 to 1954 was not readily available. Western observers believe that the economic crisis created by the Soviet withdrawal of aid forced Albania to default on the outstanding loans.

Loans granted by East European Communist states and outstanding in 1965 (in terms of United States dollar equivalents) were given by a Soviet source as follows: Bulgaria, US$11 million; Czechoslovakia, US$25 million; East Germany, US$15 million; and Romania, US$7.5 million. Information about repayments of these loans was not available. Only a fraction of the outstanding amounts could have been liquidated through Albania's trade surplus with these countries. Some Western estimates placed the debt to the Soviet Union and East European Communist states at the end of 1968 at a minimum of the equivalent of US$500 to US$600 million.

Economic aid by Communist China dates back at least to late 1954. Stated in United States dollar equivalents, Albania received in that year a grant-in-aid of US$2.5 million and a loan of US$12.5 million. An additional credit of US$13.75 million was made available in early 1959, and a loan of US$123 million for the purchase of industrial equipment during the Third Five-Year Plan (1960-65) was extended in early 1961, after Albania's break with the Soviet Union. Two more loans, for undisclosed amounts, were negotiated in June 1965 and November 1968 to finance the fourth and fifth five-year plans, respectively. In public references to the 1968 loan, Party and government officials gave the impression that it was substantially higher than the loan of US$123-million obtained in 1961. Aid has been provided by Communist China free of interest.

A Western scholar reported unidentified sources to have suggested that the 1965 loan amounted to about US$214 million, a sum substantially in excess of the credits granted up to that time. Another Western source estimated total direct credits for the 1960-68 period to have been more than US$450 million, exclusive of substantial grants. Yet, other Western sources thought at the time, and also in 1970, they had discerned evidence of disappointment on the part of the leadership with the extent of the financial assistance, delays in the supply of machinery, and an unwillingness or inability to supply much-needed consumer goods. The leadership's awareness of the inadequacy of foreign aid in relation to the planned development program has been evidenced, in its appeals for greater productivity, by the high frequency of references to the Party's principle of reliance on the country's own efforts and in its continuing campaign for the utmost economy of resources.

The country's cumulative clearing debt to Communist China on the commodity trading account at the end of 1968 was estimated at roughly US$300 million. This amount did not include the substantial additional costs of assistance in the form of technical advisers who have guided the construction and operation of major industrial projects. Estimates of these costs or of the number of aid technicians in the country were not available.

Foreign Trade

Because of the dearth of domestic resources in relation to the needs for economic development and consumption, foreign trade has consistently shown a negative balance. A marked improvement in this respect has taken place since 1955, even though the absolute deficit has been growing with the rising trade volume. In the 1960s exports covered 60 percent or more of imports, compared with 47 percent in the 1956-60 period and 31 percent in the preceding eleven post-World War II years. This improvement in the trade balance has been achieved through a consistent policy of diversifying domestic production with a view to import substitution, developing all possible resources for the production of exportable goods, improving product quality, and severely restricting domestic consumption. The annual trade deficit in 1967 and 1968 was about 200 million leks.

The volume of trade has been rising quite steadily from 140 million leks in 1950 to 950 million leks in 1968. During this period imports increased from 110 million to 580 million leks, and exports rose from 30 million to 370 million leks. The Fourth Five-Year Plan calls for an increase of 31 percent in total trade over the volume of the preceding five years, including an increase of 36 percent in exports and 28 percent in imports. These figures imply a planned average annual trade volume in the 1966-70 period of 885 million leks, of which 355 million leks were exports and 530 million leks imports. Although the rate of trade expansion during 1966-68 exceeded the target, the export-import ratio was not as favorable as that called for by the plan.

The directional pattern of the country's foreign trade has conformed to the general observation that trade follows aid. The assumption by Communist China in 1961 of the major aid donor position previously held by the Soviet Union had an immediate and pronounced impact on the direction of trade. In 1960 Communist China accounted for only 7 percent of the total trade volume, as against 54 percent for the Soviet Union. By 1962 trade with Communist China had grown to 51 percent of a somewhat smaller total volume, whereas trade with the Soviets had ceased altogether by 1963. In 1964 Communist China's share of the trade was equal to that of the Soviet Union in 1960, and the actual volume represented by that share was 23 percent larger. During the 1962-68 period trade with Communist China amounted to about half the total trade volume, but the share of Communist China declined below that level toward the end of this period. This decline was the result of a successful effort by the leadership to expand the country's trade with both Communist Eastern Europe and the non-Communist West.

Trade with the Communist countries of Eastern Europe, other than Yugoslavia, continued after the break with the Soviet Union and increased by 66 percent from 226 million leks in 1960 to about 375 million leks in 1968. The share of this group in total trade rose during this period from 35 to 40 percent, almost entirely after 1964. Albania's most important trade partner in this group has been Czechoslovakia, second only to Communist China with a volume of 118 million leks in 1968, equivalent to about 12 percent of Albania's total trade volume in that year. Following Czechoslovakia in order of importance were Poland, East Germany, and Bulgaria, with trade volumes ranging from 69 million to 53 million leks. Trade with Hungary and Romania amounted to about 40 million leks and 32 million leks, respectively. With the exception of Poland and Romania, Albania's trade balance with the countries of Eastern Europe was positive between 1960 and 1968. The excess of exports over imports during this period totaled about 65 million leks.

During the early years of the country's dependence upon Soviet aid, trade with non-Communist countries and with Yugoslavia had been discontinued, but it was resumed on a very small scale by 1955. In 1964 this trade amounted to only 65 million leks (equivalent to US$13 million at the official rate of exchange), or 8 percent of the total trade turnover. Fully two-thirds of this trade was accounted for by Italy and France. During the following four years trade with the West and Yugoslavia increased 2-1/2 times to 160 million leks in 1968, and the share of this trade in the total turnover doubled.

Italy continued to be the major Western trade partner, with a turnover of 66 million leks in 1968, but the largest advance was made in the trade with Yugoslavia. The total trade turnover with that country rose fiftyfold in one year, from 400,000 leks in 1965 to more than 20 million leks in 1966. Under the 1970 trade agreement the trade volume is scheduled to reach 50 million leks. In 1968 Italy and Yugoslavia together absorbed four-fifths of the combined exports to the West and Yugoslavia and supplied more than half the imports from that area.

Another striking example of the country's trade expansion effort is the agreement with Greece, a country with which Albania has had no political or economic relations for thirty years. Signed by the chambers of commerce of both countries in January 1970 and effective for one year, this agreement provided for an initial turnover of 7.5 million leks, of which 4 million leks were in imports and 3.5 million leks in exports. Commercial orders worth about 1.5 million leks on both sides were reported to have been placed by mid-1970.

In 1969 trade relations were officially reported to have been maintained with forty different countries. Relations with thirteen of these countries, both Communist and non-Communist, were formalized by trade agreements.

Imports have overwhelmingly served the needs of production and industrial expansion. Almost 50 percent of the imports in 1964 consisted of machinery, equipment, and spare parts. More than 23 percent was accounted for by minerals and metals, chemical and rubber products, and construction materials. Another 16 percent was made up of agricultural raw materials, about two-thirds of which was destined for the food-processing industry. Only 11 percent of the imports consisted of finished consumer goods and ready-to-eat foods. Continuing Party and government emphasis on increasing production and the improved domestic output of foods suggests that the production-oriented nature of imports did not change significantly by 1970.

Exports have consisted predominantly of minerals and mineral products but have also included significant amounts of agricultural products and manufactured consumer goods. In 1969 petroleum and natural bitumen, chromium and ferronickel ores, and copper (including copper wire), constituted 55 percent of exports. Another 25 percent comprised processed foods, such as canned fish and vegetables and preserved fruits; light industry products, including cotton and linen textiles and some readymade clothes; and a few chemicals. The balance of 20 percent was represented by fresh fruits and vegetables and by agricultural raw materials, such as hides and skins, tannins, and medicinal plants. Exports of fruits and vegetables to central and northern Europe have been growing rapidly.

The share of manufactured and semiprocessed products in exports was also officially reported to be increasing and to have constituted 51 percent of the export volume in 1968. Students of Albanian affairs have reported that some of the country's exports are not competitive in world markets and that Communist China has been willing to absorb them at a good price only for political reasons, as did the Soviet Union before 1961.

CHAPTER 9

INTERNAL AND EXTERNAL SECURITY

The armed forces in 1970 were under the Ministry of People's Defense, and all elements were included within the People's Army. Total personnel strength was about 40,000. Most troops were acquired by conscription, and about one-half of the eligible young men were drafted, usually at age nineteen. All of the tanks, aircraft, and vehicles used by the armed forces were of Soviet design, but since 1961 all external assistance has been provided by the Communist Chinese. Military ranks were abolished in 1966, but the force organization at lower levels in all service components was conventional.

The modern armed forces grew out of the partisan units of World War II, during which they fought against the Italians, the Germans, and each other. By the time of the German evacuation of Albania in November 1944, the Communist-led National Liberation Front held the dominant position among the partisans and was able to assume control of the country without fighting any major battles.

The Albanian Workers' Party (Communist Party) had an active organization within the services. All or nearly all officers in the regular services were Party members in 1970. All cadets over eighteen years of age in the officer candidate military schools were also Party members. Younger cadets were members of the Union of Albanian Working Youth. Probably only a very few of the conscripts were Party members, but nearly all were members of the youth organization. In addition to the influence exerted by Party cells, political commissars throughout the armed forces structure enforced ideological conformity.

The Albanian fighting man has had an excellent reputation for 2,000 years but, with the exception of Skanderbeg, the fifteenth-century national hero—he was born Gjergi Kastrioti and renamed Skanderbeg after Alexander the Great—the military forces of the country have disclaimed any heritage antedating the partisan activities of World War II. Skanderbeg gained brief independence for the country during his opposition to the Turkish invaders, but his exploits in support of nationalism stood almost alone over the entire period between Roman times and the twentieth century.

Moreover, national independence in 1912 did not result from a major military victory. National feelings, aroused late in the nineteenth century, became more intense during the early 1900s but, although there were clashes between fairly sizable armed groups of Turks and Albanians, freedom was not attained from armed struggle involving organized military forces. Rather, in the interests of the balance of power the greater European powers recognized the declared independence of Albania (see ch. 2, Historical Setting).

Police and security forces were under the control of the Ministry of the Interior. They were organized into three directorates: the Directorate of State Security, Frontier Guards, and the People's Police. Except for the fact that they were subject to the same system of military justice, they were entirely separate from the armed forces of the Ministry of People's Defense. The Albanian security police in 1970 were believed to exert more rigid controls over the population than was exercised by similar forces in any other East European Communist country or in the Soviet Union.

The Directorate of State Security contained the internal security police. Organized to protect the Party and governmental system, they were responsible for suppressing resistance to, and deviation from, Party ideology, and for combating crimes that had a national character. Frontier Guards, as their name implies, accomplished border security. The People's Police were the local or municipal police, with the typical routines and local interests of such forces.

It is difficult to ascertain the overall effectiveness of the various police and security forces in the maintenance of public order because no official crime statistics are published. Official statements in the press provide little or no information on the extent of crime other than the inordinate coverage of those crimes that are political in nature and considered threatening to the Party or the state. Statements by the rare Western visitors to the country concerning the police state atmosphere have led to the assumption that public order is rigidly maintained.

Although military and security forces were small in proportion to the size of the military age male population, they were nearly double the per capita average maintained by the North Atlantic Treaty Organization (NATO) or by Warsaw Pact nations. Whether or not the people recognized the armed forces as a burden, the country has never had the industrial or economic base to maintain them. Since World War II it has relied, in turn, on Yugoslavia, the Soviet Union, and Communist China for aid. Chinese assistance since 1961 has been sufficient to maintain equipment previously furnished by the Soviet Union and to replace some of the older weapons as they became obsolete.

HISTORICAL BACKGROUND

The free-spirited and hardy Albanian mountaineers have had excellent reputations as individual fighters. The Romans recruited some of their best soldiers from the regions that later became Albania. In succeeding periods many Albanians became famous in the military service of the Ottomans.

Nationalism was rarely necessary to motivate these men. Before 1912 the country had independence for only one brief period. It was gained then by the national hero, Skanderbeg, and freedom evaporated almost immediately upon his death in 1468. The history and legends attached to him make up a large part of the national military tradition. Other than in his day, freedom was rarely fought for except in the context of defense of tribal areas against the incursions of marauding neighbors. There were few occasions when Albanians rose up against occupying foreign powers. Conquerors generally left the people alone in their isolated mountain homelands and, as a feudal tribal society persisted, there was little if any feeling of national unity in the country (see ch. 2, Historical Setting).

Organized military action also played an almost negligible part in attaining independence. Some revolutionary activity occurred during the rise of national feeling in the late nineteenth and early twentieth centuries. There were clashes between insurgents and Turkish forces as early as 1884 but, at the same time that the Albanians were resisting Turkish practices they considered oppressive against themselves, they were defending the Turks in their hostilities with the Greeks or the Slavs. They continued to be recruited into, and to serve in, the Turkish army.

By 1900 about 8,000 armed Albanians were assembled in Shkoder, but they were unopposed, and a situation resembling anarchy more than revolution prevailed in the country during the early 1900s. There were arrests, incidents of banditry and pillage, and many futile Turkish efforts to restore order. Guerrilla activity increased after about 1906, and several incidents occurred, which produced martyrs but which were not marked by great numbers of casualties. Nevertheless, although it was unorganized and never assumed the proportions of a serious struggle, the resistance was instrumental in maintaining the pressure that attracted international attention and led the great powers, when they intervened after the Balkan wars of 1912 and 1913, to recognize the independent state of Albania.

World War I began before the country could establish a viable governmental body—much less form, train, and equip a military establishment. During the war years it was occupied by the warring parties, and the last of them remained into 1920.

Ahmet Zogu—as minister of the interior and minister of war until 1922 and prime minister from 1922, except for a brief exile in 1924, until he became King Zog in 1928—created the first national forces of any consequence. Before 1925, so that he would have some assurance of their loyalty, these consisted of about 5,000 men from his home tribal district. Starting in about 1925 with Italian assistance and a considerable degree of Italian control over the forces, men were drawn through universal conscription. The first drafts called about 5,000 to 6,000 annually from the approximately 10,000 young men who became eligible for the draft each year. Italian aid equipped the forces, and Italian officers provided most of the training and tactical guidance, to the point that they had effective control over their employment.

At about the same time the Gendarmerie was formed with British assistance. It had an Albanian director, a British general who served as its inspector general, and a staff of British inspectors. The Gendarmerie became an effective internal security and police organization. It had a commandant in each of the ten prefectures, a headquarters in each of the subprefectures (up to eight per prefecture), and a post in each of the nearly 150 local communities. Its communications network was for many years the most complete telephone system in the country.

Although the Italians objected strenuously, King Zog used the Gendarmerie as a safeguard against the possible consequences of Italian domination of his regular armed forces. He kept the force under his direct control and retained its British advisers until 1938. Zog also retained a sizable armed group from his old tribal region.

King Zog's efforts to reduce Italian control over his forces were insufficient to save them from quick humiliation before World War II. The Italians attacked on April 7, 1939, and, although annual conscription had created a trained reserve of at least 50,000 men, it was never called. Resistance was overcome in about a week. Later in 1939 the Italians incorporated Albanian units into their forces. Little benefit was derived from the Albanians, who could see little point in fighting for the Italians, even against their traditional enemies, the Greeks. They deserted in large numbers (see ch. 2, Historical Setting).

Resistance to the occupation grew rapidly as signs of Italian weakness became apparent. At the end of 1942 guerrilla forces had numbered no more than perhaps 8,000 to 10,000. By the summer of 1943, when the Italian effort collapsed, almost all of the mountainous interior was controlled by various resistance groups.

The Germans took over the occupation from the Italians and inflicted near-decisive defeat upon the guerrillas in January 1944. Resistance grew again, however, as final defeat for the Axis powers appeared certain, and by the end of 1944 guerrilla forces probably totaled about 70,000 men. In addition, by their count, they had suffered about 28,000 casualties. The Communist-controlled National Liberation Movement had then solidified its hold over the guerrilla groups and was able to take over the country after the war. Enver Hoxha had been the chief political commissar of the General Staff that was created in July 1943. From that post he rose rapidly to leadership of the group and through it became the head of the Communist government that took over at the end of World War II.

Albania's first Communist military forces were equipped, trained, and modeled after Yugoslavia's. When Yugoslavia embarked on its separate road to socialism in 1948 and was expelled from the Communist Information Bureau (Cominform—see Glossary), Albania aligned directly with the Soviet Union. This did not involve an immediate change in materiel, organization, or training because the Soviet Union and Yugoslavia had had much the same relationship before their break.

Soviet aid included advisory personnel, a considerable amount of modern conventional armament, a few small World War II naval vessels, and a number of aircraft. This aid was halted entirely in 1961. The Soviet submarine flotilla that had been based on Sazan Island, off Vlore, passed Gibraltar in June 1961 on its way back to northern Soviet ports.

Communist China succeeded the Soviet Union as Albania's ally. Albania can provide China with little of tactical importance, but its value as an ally from a political standpoint has been sufficient to warrant continuation of aid in quantities sufficient to maintain the armed forces at about the same levels of personnel strength and equipment that they had achieved when they were supported by the Soviet Union, although interruptions in training are believed to have caused a deterioration in technical skills and know-how.

THE MILITARY ESTABLISHMENT

Position in the Government

The People's Army, which encompasses the ground, naval, and air arms of the regular armed forces, is under the Ministry of People's Defense, which, in turn, is within the Council of Ministers. The ministers are selected from the People's Assembly which, with its Presidium, is at the top of the governmental structure (see ch. 6, Government Structure and Political System).

In mid-1970 the minister of defense, Beqir Balluku, was also a deputy prime minister and a member of the Political Bureau (Politburo) of the Albanian Workers' Party. Balluku had a military career background and held the rank of colonel general in the army before its ranks were abolished in 1966. As defense minister he exercised direct operational and administrative control over all elements of the military establishment.

The People's Army

The army claims no antecedents in the forces of the pre-Communist regimes and dates itself from July 10, 1943, when a General Staff was formed within the guerrilla forces resisting the Italian occupation. Petrit Dume, its chief of staff in 1970, had commanded the People's Army for about twenty years. He was second only to Balluku in the defense hierarchy and was also a candidate member of the Politburo of the Party organization. Enver Hoxha, first secretary of the Albanian Workers' Party, held the rank of general of the army until rank designations were abolished but, although he could exercise personal direction of the armed forces as their commander in chief, he was not considered a member of the defense establishment.

All of the regular military forces are within the People's Army. The air and naval arms are usually treated separately because of their distinctive functions and equipment, but their men are sometimes referred to as naval and air soldiers. Major subcommands, such as the army's directorates of Political Affairs and Rear Services (Logistics), serve all service components. The same is the case with such organizations as the medical service that have functions applicable to all of the armed forces.

At lower levels, where the functions of the forces are specialized in relation to their weapons, organizational patterns appear to be similar to those in most of the other armed forces throughout the Communist world. During the post-World War II formative years, force structures were adapted from those of the Soviet Union. Realignments after 1961 to cooperate with the Communist Chinese are not believed to have affected them to any appreciable degree. Some unit designations, such as army division, are not used in the peacetime organization and, in other situations, the sizes of units may be scaled down somewhat from normal international practice.

Rank designations were abolished in 1966. Since then, according to the governmental decree that effected the change, position in the military hierarchy is based on the responsibilities stipulated in the relevant tables of organization of the armed forces. Most of the personnel who would have fallen into the lower rank categories are acquired by conscription. Men without highly skilled specialties are retained for two years; noncommissioned officers and others who receive special training are required to serve for longer periods.

The stated mission of the armed forces in general and the ground forces in particular is to defend the country and to secure its governing system. The stated mission notwithstanding, support of the system is primarily the responsibility of the security police forces and, against an external opponent, the armed forces are believed to have only a defensive capability. Unless Albanian forces engaged an enemy that was also committed against a third party in a more general conflict, they would, of necessity, revert to guerrilla fighting. Most of the training and much of the propaganda directed at the local population indicate that the leadership anticipates the possibility of guerrilla warfare.

The Party slogan, "the pick in one hand and the rifle in the other," also illustrates the dual use of service personnel in peacetime. They assist in the construction of industrial enterprises and hydroelectric plants and in land reclamation projects, crop harvests, and the like. They were used during the early 1960s, for example, in the construction of the oil refinery at Cerrik; in building a sugar factory, a lumber combine, and a textile factory; and in the draining of Lake Maliq to acquire additional agricultural land in a marshy lake district area north of Korce (see ch. 8, Economic System).

Ground Forces

The ground forces contain about three-quarters of the regular personnel and are the backbone of the armed forces. Consequently, many of the People's Army functions that apply to all of the service components are administered within the ground force organization.

Because the active personnel strength of the ground forces is around 30,000—sufficient to man only about two divisions—the brigade has been chosen as the basic tactical unit. The brigades are manned with approximately 3,000 men each, and there are probably one tank and five infantry brigades. The infantry brigades are believed to contain three infantry battalions and a lightly equipped artillery regiment. The tank brigade has Soviet-built weapons. Most of them are World War II T-34 medium tanks, but there are a few of the later model T-54s.

Almost all artillery is light and small caliber, since movement of heavy equipment is nearly impossible over much of the terrain. In addition, heavy weapons, their transport, or even their ammunition could not be produced locally, and little resupply from external sources could be expected in any lengthy conflict. In so small an area the rapid movement of forces would serve little purpose. The minimal amount of transport equipment available includes small numbers of Soviet-designed armored personnel carriers, command cars, and a few types of trucks.

Before 1961 training was based on Soviet methods, and specialized schools were scaled-down copies of those in the Soviet army. Training manuals were translated from the Russian. Although external support of the forces has been transferred from the Soviet Union to Communist China, the Chinese have apparently not required basic changes in the training programs. Most conscripts have been exposed to a considerable amount of drill and elementary basic training in school and in Communist youth organizations, permitting the forces to concentrate on tactical exercises. These consist mostly of small unit activities and involve fighting techniques appropriate to the defense of the mountainous interior. Physical conditioning, tactics involving light weapons, and operations using a minimum of materiel support are emphasized on a continuing basis. Political indoctrination, conducted or supervised by the political commissars, is heavily administered in all training programs.

Naval Forces

Naval units are subordinate to the Coastal Defense Command which, although a part of the People's Army, is operationally responsible directly to the Ministry of People's Defense. None of the pre-World War II navy survived the occupation and, as with the other branches of the service, the navy forgets any earlier ancestry and celebrates August 15, 1945, as its founding date. The senior naval officer is commander of naval forces, a deputy commander of coastal defense, and deputy minister of defense for naval affairs. In late 1969 Ymer Zeqir held these positions. As deputy commander of coastal defense he coordinated naval operations with those of the air defense and ground forces that would participate in defense of the coastal area. As deputy minister of defense he represented the naval forces in national defense planning and coordinated personnel, logistic support, and matters that are common to other branches of the armed forces.

Naval forces are divided into three commands: the Submarine Brigade, the Vlore Sea Defense Brigade, and the Durres Sea Defense Brigade. All combat ships are assigned to one of the three. The Submarine Brigade is based at the Pasha Liman anchorages south of the city of Vlore, at the extreme southwestern point in the bay. Main facilities of the Vlore Sea Defense Brigade are located on the island of Sazan, in the mouth of the bay about ten miles west of Vlore. This was the site of the Soviet submarine base before 1961. The Durres Sea Defense Brigade controls the units stationed at Durres and those that are locked within Lake Scutari. The Buene River is navigable between Lake Scutari and the Adriatic, but only the smallest of the ships in the lake can pass beneath the Shkoder city bridges.

The officially stated mission of the naval forces is to provide for the military security of coastal waters; to prevent smuggling; to prevent submarines from approaching the coast or harbors; to lay and sweep mines; to intercept enemy forces; to escort convoys along the coastline; and, together with police patrol boats, to control entries to, or exits from, the country. Original Soviet support for the navy was provided in order to secure a submarine and minelaying base with access to the Mediterranean Sea.

Forces available are considerably weaker than those of any one of the potential enemies and, with the exception of Vlore, Albanian harbors provide little natural protection. It is therefore probable that the leadership thinks in terms of peacetime shore patrols and would hope, in wartime, to use what units they were able to preserve to prevent totally uninhibited use of the seas adjacent to the country.

In mid-1970 naval ships included three or four submarines, eight minesweepers, twelve motor torpedo boats, one or two oilers, and perhaps twenty-five or thirty more ships, about one-half of which were classed as coastal patrol and one-half as auxiliary types. The submarines are obsolescent medium-range boats. Two of the minesweepers are oceangoing vessels; the other six can sweep harbors or inshore seas only. Most of the miscellaneous vessels were formerly Italian, of World War II and earlier vintages. Albanian sources claim that a dozen newer torpedo boats have been supplied by the Chinese, six of them hydrofoil types.

Naval personnel number approximately 3,000. Since many of the ships put to sea infrequently, many of the navy men do part-time fishing or agricultural work. Familiarity with ships helps a new conscript get a naval assignment, and many of those drafted are from the vicinities of Vlore or Durres and may serve their three years being only rarely out of sight of home. Their morale is only fair.

Officers are required to have a general education that includes at least some university credits. They receive specialized courses before going to sea. Before 1961 most officers and some of the higher noncommissioned officer ratings received some training in the Soviet Union. Without this training or a Chinese substitute for it, there has probably been some degradation in the technical capabilities of the officer and noncommissioned officer personnel.

Air Force

The Albanian Air Force is the youngest of the service branches, founded on April 23, 1951. As is the case with the navy, the air force is also a part of the People's Army, having organizational and logistic individuality only insofar as its equipment is different and requires different techniques and skills in its use. Arif Hasko, chief of the air force in mid-1970, was also a deputy minister of defense and, as was the case with his naval counterpart, advised on problems peculiar to his force and coordinated on matters of general interest to all branches of the service.

Air defense artillery and missile units are usually included with the air force and account for about two-thirds of its 5,000 to 7,000 personnel. Air defense units received Soviet equipment between 1948 and 1961, including that required at a few surface-to-air missile sites. Their Guideline missiles were paraded in Tirana on Army Day of 1964 and have been shown on occasion since. The original missiles supplied by the Soviets would have outlived their storage lifetimes by 1970. If a surface-to-air missile capability did exist at that time, the Chinese would have supplied the necessary replacements.

Aircraft in 1970 included sixty to seventy fighters and fighter-bombers and about the same number of transports, trainers, and miscellaneous noncombat types. All were of Soviet design. Fighter-bombers or ground attack aircraft were the jet MiG-15s and MiG-17s provided by the Soviet Union before 1961. Spare parts necessary to keep them operating since then have been supplied by Communist China. MiG-19s for the air defense interceptor role have also been furnished by the Chinese.

It is believed that the 1970 force included four ground support squadrons and probably two interceptor squadrons, with about ten or twelve aircraft per squadron. Air-to-air missiles are an integral part of the MiG-19 armament and are presumably being furnished in small quantities by the Chinese. Transport squadrons contain a few Soviet-built piston-engined Il-14s and AN-2s, some Soviet-built helicopters, and possibly a few helicopters built by the Chinese.

The five principal airbases are located near Tirana, Shijak (about twenty miles west of Tirana), Vlore, Sazan Island (at the mouth of Vlore Bay), and at Stalin (about forty miles south of Tirana). The base on Sazan Island that was built and used by the Russians has been used intermittently, if at all, since the Russians evacuated it in 1961. Helicopter bases have been, or are being, constructed at several inland cities as well as at Tirana, Shkoder, and as a part of the major base at Vlore. The forces had no surface-to-surface missile capability in 1970.

The missions assigned to the combat elements of the air force are to repel an enemy at the borders and to prevent the violation of Albanian airspace. Because the force is small, could not easily be resupplied, has exposed bases, and possesses no appreciable area to retreat into, however, it could not be expected to contribute significantly to any sustained combat effort. It serves mainly to provide the regime with ostensive evidence of its power and technological progress.

Mobilization Potential

In the event of total mobilization there are just under 500,000 males between the ages of fifteen and fifty. Of the total group approximately 75 percent, or nearly 375,000, are physically fit. More than half of these have had some military service, and a sizable group participates in military reserve activities (see ch. 4, The People).

Information as to how the existing establishment would be expanded is not available. Units active in 1970 could be enlarged to about double their peacetime strengths because all units are usually maintained at considerably below combat readiness strengths. New units would probably be created in infantry or guerrilla forces. Additional tank, air, and naval units would require more of their special equipment before they could become operational. Some women probably would be mobilized. The national economy, however, could not provide logistic support for the number of male personnel available, and external support would be necessary.

Political Indoctrination

At the time of the Communist takeover in 1944 and in the years immediately thereafter, political commissars were an integral part of the military organization. They were considered essential in order to assure that ideological beliefs were constant and were adhered to without deviation. As the years passed they lost their early importance and were eventually done away with, but they were reinstated in 1966 when alignment with Communist China brought renewed revolutionary fervor.

How much their organization and operations in 1970 differed from what they were in 1944 is not clearly understood, but the fact that they were still called political commissars was a strong indication that they performed basically the same functions. There is no question but that the justification for their existence was the same—that is, to ensure that the ideological and political orientation of the troops and of their leaders did not deviate from the Party line. The decree that reinstated the commissars stated that they would be assigned in all units, subunits, and military establishments. This presumably means that there are commissars in all base organizations and in tactical units down at least to the company level.

It is also known that Political Directorates in both the Ministry of People's Defense and the Ministry of the Interior control the commissars in the armed forces and the security forces, respectively. Political commissars are carefully selected from the standpoint of ideological reliability. Those appointed since 1966 must have had five years of unblemished Party membership. Those in the armed forces who are attached to the lower levels of the organizational structure are responsible to the Political Directorate and the Party organization rather than to superior officers within the military command channels. Hito Cako was chief of the People's Army Political Directorate in 1970.

In addition to the military court system, discipline is enforced as part of the educational and ideological training program by the political workers who act in conjunction with the Party organizations in service units. They are invited to take measures necessary against individuals whose attitude or conduct is considered harmful to the effectiveness of, or discipline within, the army.

Military Schools

Other than those that are set up for specialized training, there are three military schools providing curricula aimed at producing officer personnel or offering advanced military theory. The Skanderbeg military school is a secondary or preparatory school. It is attended by children of top Party, government, and military leaders and prepares them for entrance into the Enver Hoxha United Army Officers School. The Hoxha school is the oldest military educational institution in the country. It started a formal curriculum in 1945 but, according to Party claims, was in operation before the World War II occupation forces left the country in 1944. It is the military academy that provides a university level curriculum and whose students become commissioned officers upon graduation.

The Mehmet Shehu Military Academy is named for the man who in 1970 was premier (chairman of the Council of Ministers) and also a member of the Party Politburo. Shehu was a lieutenant general before 1966 and was considered one of the country's most capable military leaders. The academy is the advanced military institution that offers career training equivalent to that of command and staff or war college institutions in Western military establishments.

Military Medicine

The medical services were organized during the 1950s along the lines of those in the Soviet and East European Communist forces in order to facilitate cooperation among them. Although there has been no such cooperation since 1961, the basic organization was unchanged in 1963 and probably remained basically the same in 1970.

The head of the medical establishment has the title of chief, Albanian Armed Forces Medical Service. He is responsible to the chief of the Rear Services, which is one of the unified directorates directly beneath the Ministry of People's Defense. Naval, air force, and ground force staffs are responsible to him, but the naval and air force groups appear to have a largely advisory capacity, except as they work to secure the services required by their branches of the service. The hospital, pharmaceutical, and personnel sections, however, are operated by the deputy chief of medical services, who is also head of the ground forces' medical department.

Albanian sources state that there is close cooperation between the military medical service and the Ministry of Health. The forces' medical personnel, facilities, equipment, and medicines have been used to improve sanitary and medical conditions in less developed areas and to provide assistance in flood, earthquake, and other emergency situations.

Decorations

Recognition for high standards of conduct, exceptional effort, or noteworthy accomplishment is bestowed lavishly. Highly prized decorations include the Partisan Star, Order of the Albanian Flag, Order of the National Hero, and Order of Skanderbeg. Other decorations that are worn by a few of the highest military and Party officials include the Memorial Medal, the Order of Liberty (or Order of Freedom), the Liberation Medal, Order of the People's Hero (or Hero of the People), and Order of Valor. Some of the decorations, including the Partisan Star and Order of Skanderbeg, are awarded in three classes. This group of decorations is usually awarded individually, but on rare occasions some can be presented to a group.

The Order of Labor (or Hero of Socialist Labor) and the Red Flag Order (or Red Banner) may be presented to individuals, usually civilians, but are most frequently reported when awarded to a group or an enterprise.

Typical recipients would be a factory for overfulfilling its quotas, a ship after completing an unusual voyage, or a military unit that had performed well in some civic project or in an emergency relief situation.

Paramilitary Training

In November 1944, when partisan resistance forces were at their peak strength of about 70,000, about 6,000 of them were women and 1,000 were boys under fifteen years of age. Formal paramilitary training was undertaken in 1945, shortly after the Hoxha regime gained control, and was made obligatory for all young people in 1953. Training has been developed to the point that fifteen- to nineteen-year-old youths can be organized into their own auxiliary units in emergencies.

Major revisions to the secondary school and university military training programs were announced in 1969 in preparation for implementation during the ensuing school year. The extent of training, what it would include, and aims of the new program were given wide publicity throughout 1969 in order to ease the transition. The purpose of the programs is to provide the armed forces with conscripts who are in good physical condition and who have sufficient basic military training to permit them to step directly into a military unit and perform usefully with a minimum of adjustment and little additional training.

Beginning in 1970 the secondary school year was to consist of 6-1/2 months of academic work, 2-1/2 months of physical work in agriculture or industry, 1 month of military training, and 2 months of relaxation. According to official guidance, however, the youths are encouraged to use their relaxation period for "ideological and physical steeling." The university year would consist of 7 months of academic work, 2 months of military training, 1 month of physical work, and 2 months of ideological and physical steeling.

Physical training of the type that contributes most to future military service is encouraged. Specific goals to be derived from it are basic physical improvement in speed, agility, strength, and resistance and the moral attributes of bravery, strong will, and personal discipline. Light sports, such as volleyball, are discouraged. Track, wrestling, and body contact sports are advised. Swimming and skiing are also considered to have military applications. It is recommended that calisthenics and physical culture activities be carried on in large groups.

Military instruction includes close order drill, crawling and obstacle penetration, storming techniques, and hand-to-hand combat. Academic courses in the military area train in the care and use of various types of weapons, the theories of military art, and the techniques of conventional and guerrilla warfare. Schools organize marches and excursions that are combined with tactical military exercises to give them a wholly military character. Most of these are designed to teach guerrilla warfare tactics. Overnight stalking exercises feature searches for intruder groups, a simulated target demolition, or some such objective. Girls as well as boys are required to participate. Tirana press photographs have shown some groups of girls engaged in mortar training, others in target shooting. In the 1969 Tirana May Day parade girls, in ranks of fifteen abreast, carried submachineguns.

When the programs have been completely implemented, students in the first and second years of secondary schooling will receive all of their physical and military training at their schools. It will be supervised by teachers and military officers assigned to the schools. Third- and fourth-year students will have part of the training at their schools, but with entire day or week periods devoted to the program. They will also spend a part of the allocated month in military units to which the school is attached for the purpose.

Facilities are not adequate in many schools, and in many areas military units are not immediately available to assist in training. It will be several years before the complete revised programs can be implemented. The first year's effort, however, involves about 10,000 university students and about 170,000 other people. The latter figure includes schoolteachers, military personnel who cooperate in the training, and others who provide miscellaneous voluntary or part-time assistance, in addition to those who receive the training. Students in the program have been compared with those in the Communist Chinese Red Guard, but the organization of the Albanian program is designed to keep it closely aligned with the school curriculum and with active military units to prevent large-scale independent action by youth groups.

Paramilitary programs of Party-sponsored youth organizations are similar in many ways to those in the school system. Pioneers take children, both boys and girls, between the ages of seven and fourteen. A group of these young Pioneers carried rifles and submachineguns in the 1968 Tirana May Day parade. From ages fifteen to twenty-five they may belong to the Union of Albanian Working Youth, frequently called the Communist Youth Movement. The Union of Albanian Working Youth had 210,000 members in 1967. Nearly all personnel drafted into the armed forces fall within the youth movement's age brackets, and its units within the services are active. Political and ideological indoctrination is intensive in these organizations and prepares the youth for possible membership in the Party in later years (see ch. 6, Government Structure and Political System).

Military Justice

There is no distinction between the civil judicial order in general and the military order in particular, but military crimes are treated in a separate chapter of the penal code. That chapter treats those acts, committed by persons under the jurisdiction of military courts, that are directed against military discipline, military orders, and the like. They include a broad variety of violations against persons, property, or the state.

A military crime, in the Albanian system, has two characteristics distinguishing it from nonmilitary crimes. The crime is committed against regulations established for the performance of military service, and the defendant is a member of the armed forces. For criminal justice the security forces under the Ministry of the Interior and all local police are considered armed forces and are subject to military law and to trial in military courts, as are reservists or persons called to military or police duty for short periods. Also, military violations are believed to include a variety of crimes against the state that might not be classed as military in Western countries, including some in the so-called socially dangerous category. As is the case in the Soviet Union, persons who fail to report on others committing crimes are themselves liable.

Military courts are selected by the People's Assembly or by its Presidium when it is not in session. Members are military personnel and ordinarily serve on a court for three years. Each court has a chairman, vice chairman, and a number of members called assistant judges. The chairman and at least one of the assistant judges must be military superiors of the defendant.

In exceptional circumstances the People's Assembly may appoint a special court for a particular case or a group of cases. A special court may be all or only partially military. Such a court was appointed, for example, when Vice Admiral Teme Seyko, commander of the naval forces, was accused in 1961 of "having been in league with the imperialist Americans, Greek monarcho-fascists and Yugoslav revisionists." The admiral was executed.

When crimes are committed during military operations, sentences are heavier than when the same offenses are committed under conditions where duress is not a factor. During combat or wartime circumstances, legislative acts call for the most severe penalties.

THE MILITARY ESTABLISHMENT AND THE NATIONAL ECONOMY

According to official government pronouncements relating to the state budget, 471 million leks (5 leks equal US$1) were appropriated for defense expenditures in 1970. That amount is 9.2 percent of the total planned expenditures of 5,110 million leks, or about 225 leks per inhabitant during the year. Whether or not all expenses that would fall within the defense category in Western countries are included in these figures is not known. It is the practice in some Communist governments to distribute peripheral defense costs among other agency appropriations (see ch. 8, Economic System).

The defense budget was increased drastically in 1969 and 1970 over the levels of earlier years, apparently in reaction to the Soviet invasion of Czechoslovakia. The midyear calculated expenditures for 1969 represented an increase of about 38 percent over those of 1968, and 1970 projections showed another 12.2 percent anticipated increase over 1969.

The burden represented by 225 leks per person can be illustrated by relating it to income and costs of living. In 1967, for example, a typical head of family worker earned about 7,200 leks per year. The average family group consisted of between five and six persons, and about 90 percent of its earnings was required for food and housing. In the preponderant majority of situations where there was only one wage earner per family, therefore, per capita defense costs exceeded everything that the family had available for all uses except food and shelter.

The 50,000 men in the regular and security forces represent about 2.4 percent of the population, but each annual draft takes a number that is equal to roughly one-half of the young men that become nineteen years old during the year. There is no reliable information as to how willingly the average citizen performs his military service or whether or not his contribution is appreciated by the remainder of the people. The controlled-communications media do everything possible to promote good morale among those in the service and to show that the public supports them.

FOREIGN MILITARY RELATIONS

Small, underdeveloped, and suffering continually from an unfavorable balance of trade, Albania has always needed assistance to maintain even a small military force. Accepting aid from Italy before World War II resulted in a severe curtailment of national initiative in the employment of the forces and probably contributed to their immobility at the time of the Italian invasion in 1939.

Between 1945 and 1948 Yugoslavia's control over Albania's forces was tighter than Italy's had been. In addition to technical advisers and instructors in regular service units, the Communist Party organization provided an effective vehicle for controlling the reliability of personnel, particularly the military leadership.

Because the Soviet Union, like Italy, was physically separated from the country it was a more desirable ally than neighboring Yugoslavia had been. It was nonetheless able to maintain tighter controls over Albanian forces than either Yugoslavia or Italy had achieved. General Petrit Dume, who was commander of the People's Army during its dependence on the Soviet Union and still was in 1970, had said in November of 1952 that his force was an integral part of the Soviet Army.

Albania became one of the original Warsaw Treaty Organization members in 1955. Separated from the other signatories, its forces were unable to participate in the pact's field exercises and after 1961, because of its rift with the Soviet Union, was not invited to attend the organization's meetings. In 1968, protesting the Soviet invasion of Czechoslovakia, Albania formally withdrew from the pact.

Communist China was Albania's only military ally in 1970. In 1970 the Chinese were believed to be enabling Albania to maintain its forces at approximately the same levels that had been reached by 1960 with Soviet assistance (see ch. 6, Government Structure and Political System).

SECURITY FORCES

Albanian sources publish little concerning the security police except for some articles expressing gratitude for their services and a smattering of information relative to their responsibilities. Few of the observers who have visited the country since 1945 have been in positions to see, or have been qualified to judge, their actual performance. It is undoubtedly true that the Albanian leadership emulated many of Joseph Stalin's techniques for controlling the population, that it modified its attitudes and practices less than did the other East European Communist countries after Stalin's death, and that it has maintained a high degree of Stalinism since its break with the Soviet Union and alignment with Communist China (see ch. 6, Government Structure and Political System).

There is probably credibility in reports stating that no other Communist country has as extensive a police and security organization relative to its size as that which operates in Albania. Hoxha has regarded the security police as an elite group, and they have been the mainstay of his power. By 1961, although arrests had tapered off from earlier levels, fourteen concentration or labor camps were still in use. Foreign visitors in Tirana have reported that it is impossible to move around the city without escorts and that conversations with ordinary citizens are discouraged. Local police, servicemen, and security police are in evidence everywhere.

All security and police forces were responsible in the governmental structure to the Ministry of the Interior. The minister in 1970 was Kadri Hasbiu. Each organization—the Directorate of State Security, the People's Police, and the Frontier Guards—constituted a separate directorate of the ministry. The total regular uniformed security personnel numbered approximately 12,500. This figure did not include the plainclothes security police, informers, or the citizens who were performing their two months of mandatory auxiliary duty attached to local police units.

A larger proportion of personnel in the security forces are Party members than is the case in the regular military forces. In the state security organization, nearly all of those who serve in important positions are believed to be Party members. In the Frontier Guards the officers and many of the men are Party members.

The Directorate of State Security

The Directorate of State Security (Drejtorija e Sigurimit te Shtetit—commonly abbreviated to Sigurimi) is organized into four battalions and has more plainclothes personnel than uniformed. It celebrates March 20, 1943, as its founding day and is credited by Hoxha and others of the Party leadership as having been instrumental in the victory of his faction of the partisan effort. Actually the People's Defense Division, from which the Sigurimi evolved, was formed in 1945. Composed at that time of some 5,000 of the most reliable of the resistance fighters, it was headed initially by Koci Xoxe, who was executed as a Titoist four years later. Mihalaq Zicishti was its chief in 1970.

The stated missions of the security police are to prevent counterrevolution and to eliminate opposition to the Party and government. Its interests are directed toward political and ideological opposition rather than crimes against persons or property unless such crimes appear to have national implications.

In the late 1950s the Sigurimi had seven sections: political, censorship, public records, prison camp, two sections for counterespionage, and a foreign service. The political section's primary function was the penetration of opposition political factions. One of the counterespionage sections was specialized and had only a responsibility for eliminating underground organizations. The censorship section operated not only with the press, radio, publications, and other communications media but with cultural societies, schools, and schoolteachers. The public records section was also charged with ideological supervision of economic agencies.

Sigurimi personnel at labor camps attended to the political reeducation of the inmates and evaluated the degree to which they remained socially dangerous; camp guards were local police. The foreign service section placed its personnel as widely as possible in order to maintain contact with aliens or foreigners in the country and in diplomatic and visiting groups.

Sigurimi personnel may be conscripts called during the annual draft or may be career volunteers. Personnel are screened, and the conditions of service are made sufficiently attractive to secure as reliable and dedicated men as possible.

Frontier Guards

The Frontier Guards are organized into five battalions. Individual units are manned with fewer personnel than Sigurimi battalions, however, and the total strength of the force is lower. Although the force is organized strictly along military lines, it is under the Ministry of the Interior and is more closely associated with the security police than with the regular armed forces.

The stated mission of the Frontier Guards is to protect the State's borders and to take action against spies, criminals, smugglers, and infiltrators along the boundaries. In the process they also prevent Albanians from leaving the country.

Frontier Guards personnel, like those of the Sigurimi, may be acquired during the annual conscription. Career personnel are often those who have served tours in the regular services. A guards' school was established in 1953 in Tirana. Its students, as well as others allowed in the force, are carefully screened for political reliability.

People's Police

The People's Police has five branches—the Police for Economic Objectives, Communications Police, Fire Police, Detention Police, and General Police. The Police for Economic Objectives serve as guards for state buildings, factories, construction projects, and similar enterprises. Communications Police guard bridges, railways, and wire lines. Firefighting is a police function, accomplished by the Fire Police. Detention Police are prison and camp guards. The fifth branch, the General Police, attend to traffic regulation, local crime, and other duties usually performed by local or municipal police.

General Police functions overlap those of the security police to some extent, but the force operates in the local, as opposed to the national, environment. Headquarters in the larger towns have security sections that maintain records on suspected anti-Communists, an alien section that maintains contact with Albanians outside their own districts as well as aliens, and a political commissar who is so placed as to assure the proper political orientation of all other personnel.

Citizens are required to carry identification cards. These contain family and employment data and, as they are needed even for intervillage travel, constitute an effective control over movement of the population.

Minimum service on the police force is for three years. Individuals with earlier service in the armed forces, security police, or Frontier Guards are preferred.

Auxiliary Police

A 1948 law requires that all able-bodied men serve two months assisting the local police. They perform with the regular People's Police of their localities, wear the police uniform made distinguishable only by a red armband, and serve without pay. The auxiliary police program serves a dual purpose. It provides additional help for the police forces. Of more overall value, it gives a sizable portion of the population some familiarity with, and presumably a more sympathetic understanding of, police activities and problems.

BIBLIOGRAPHY

RECOMMENDED SOURCES

"Albania: First Atheist State in the World," *Radio Free Europe Research Departments: Communist Area*, October 1967, 1-3.

Albania: Geographical, Historical and Economic Data. Tirana: Naim Frasheri State Publishing House, 1964.

Albanian Historical Society of Massachusetts. *The Albanian Struggle in the Old World and New.* (Works Progress Administration Series.) Boston: Writer, 1939.

Amery, Julian. *Sons of the Eagle: A Study in Guerrilla War.* London: Macmillan, 1948.

Brezezinsky, Zbigniew K. *The Soviet Bloc: Unity and Conflict.* (Rev. ed.) Cambridge: Harvard University Press, 1967.

Conti, Massimo. "L'Albania," *La Stampa* (Turin), August 31-September 12, 1969.

Coon, Carleton S. *The Mountain of Giants: A Racial and Cultural Study of the North Albanian Mountain Ghegs.* Cambridge: Harvard University Press, 1950.

Dhima, Dhimo M. *E Drejta Kushtetuese e Republikes Popullore te Shqiperise.* Tirana: N.I.S.H. Shtypshkronjave "Mihal Duri," 1963.

"Dog Wags Tail," *Economist*, CCXIX, No. 6404, May 21, 1966, 814.

Europa: The World of Learning, 1969-70. London: Europa Publications, 1970, 57.

Europa Year Book, 1969, I. London: Europa Publications, 1969, 454-458.

The Facts About Soviet-Albanian Relations. Tirana: Naim Frasheri State Publishing House, 1964.

"4 Albanians End Athens Trade Visit, First in 20 Years," *New York Times*, June 30, 1970, 9.

Gardiner, Leslie. "Albania: Last Lonely Stronghold," *U.S. Naval Institute Proceedings*, XCIII, No. 10, October 1967, 53-59.

Gegaj, Athanas, and Krasniqi, Rexhep. *Albania.* New York: Assembly of Captive European Nations, 1964.

Great Britain. Admiralty. Naval Intelligence Division. *Albania.* (Geographical Handbook Series.) London: n.pub., 1945.

Griffith, William E. *Albania and the Sino-Soviet Rift.* Cambridge: Massachusetts Institute of Technology Press, 1963.

Grovski, Vladimir, and Grzybowski, Kazimierz. *Government, Law, and Courts in the Soviet Union and Eastern Europe,* I and II. New York: Praeger, 1959.

Hamm, Harry. *Albania: China's Beachhead in Europe.* New York: Praeger, 1963.

Hoffman, Paul. "Albania Signs New Trade Pact with China and Condemns U.S.," *New York Times,* January 21, 1970, C-8.

Hoxha, Enver. "Ne Cdo Pune te Zbatojme nje Metode dhe Stil Leninist Revolucionar," *Rruga e Partise* (Party Path), XVI, No. 7, July 1969, 4-15.

———. *VEPRA,* I. Tirana: Shtepia Botonjese "Naim Frasheri," 1968.

Illustrated Library of the World and Its Peoples: Yugoslavia, Rumania, Bulgaria, Albania. New York: Greystone Press, 1965.

Instituti i Studimeve Marxiste-Leniniste Prane KQ te PHSH. *Mbi Klasat dhe Luften e Klasave.* Tirana: Shtepia Botonjese "Naim Frasheri," 1967.

Kertesz, Stephen D. *East Central Europe and the World: Developments in the Post-Stalin Era.* Notre Dame: University of Notre Dame Press, 1962.

Kodifikimi i Pergjithshem i Legjislacionit ne Fuqi te Republikes Popullore te Shqiperise, I. Tirana: Shtepia Botonjese "Naim Frasheri," 1958.

Koliqi, Ernesto. "Albania." Pages 370-531 in *Enciclopedia dei Popoli d'Europa,* I. Milan: M. Canfalonieri, 1965.

Kongresi i Peste i Partise se Punes te Shqiperise. Tirana: Shtepia Botonjese "Naim Frasheri," 1966.

Krasniqi, Rexhep. "Persecution of Religion in Communist Albania," *Acen News,* No. 128, March-April 1967, 17-20.

Kristo, Frasheri. *The History of Albania: A Brief Survey.* Tirana: n.pub., 1964.

May, Jacques M. (ed.) *The Ecology of Malnutrition in Five Countries of Eastern and Central Europe*, IV: East Germany, Poland, Yugoslavia, Albania, Greece. New York: Hafner, 1963.

Pano, Nicholas C. *The People's Republic of Albania*. Baltimore: John Hopkins Press, 1968.

Pipa, Fehime. *Nji Shekull Shkolle Shqipe, 1861-1961*. Rome: Arti Grafiche Editoriali A. Urbanite, 1961.

Plasari, N.; Mara, H.; and Misja, V. *Partia e Punes s Shqiperise*. Tirana: N. Sh. Botime "Naim Frasheri," 1962.

Pounds, Norman J.G. *Eastern Europe*. Chicago: Aldine, 1969.

Prybyla, Jan S. "Albania's Economic Vassalage," *East Europe*, XVI, No. 1, January 1967, 9-14.

Republika Popullore e Shqiperise. "Aresimi dhe Kultura." Pages 115-130 in *Vjetari Statistikor i R. P. Sh.*, 1967-1968. Tirana: 1968.

———. "Mbi Sistemin Aresimor," *Gazeta Zyrtare* (Tirana), No. 10, December 31, 1969, 112-117.

Roucek, Joseph S., and Lattich, Kenneth V. *Behind the Iron Curtain*. Coldwell: Caxton Printers, 1964.

Shehu, Mehmet. "Mbi Konklusionet e Diskutimit Popullor per Revolucionarizimin a Metejshem te Shkolles Tone," *Arsimi Popullor* (People's Education), No. 4, July-August 1969, 21-103.

Skendi, Stavro. *The Albanian National Awakening, 1878-1912*. Princeton: Princeton University Press, 1967.

———. *The Emergence of the Modern Balkan Literary Languages—A Comparative Approach*. (School of International Affairs, Institute on East Central Europe, Columbia University.) Wiesbaden: Otto Harrassowitz, 1964.

———. "The History of the Albanian Alphabet: A Case of Complex Cultural and Political Development," *Sudost Forschungen* (Munich), XIX, 1960, 263-284.

———. *The Political Evolution of Albania, 1912-1944*. New York: Mid-European Studies Centers, March 8, 1954.

Skendi, Stavro (ed.). *Albania*. New York: Praeger, 1956.

Statistical Yearbook, 1967. Paris: United Nations Educational, Scientific and Cultural Organization, 1968.

Statistical Yearbook of the German Democratic Republic, 1969. Berlin: State Publishing House, 1969.

Stokes, William Lee. *Essentials of Earth History.* Englewood Cliffs: Prentice-Hall, 1966.

Thomas, John I. *Education for Communism: School and State in the People's Republic of Albania.* (Hoover Institution Studies, XXII.) Stanford: Hoover Institution Press, 1969.

Triska, Jan F. (ed.) *Constitutions of the Communist Party-States.* (Hoover Institution Publications 70.) Stanford: Hoover Institution on War, Revolution, and Peace, 1968.

Twenty Years of Socialism in Albania. Tirana: Naim Frasheri State Publishing House, 1964.

U.S. Congress. 83d, 1st Session. Senate. Committee on Foreign Relations. *Tensions Within the Soviet Captive Countries: Albania.* (Document No. 70, Part 6.) Washington: GPO, 1954.

U.S. Department of Commerce. Bureau of the Census. Foreign Demographic Analysis Division. *Projections of the Population of the Communist Countries of Eastern Europe, by Age and Sex, 1969 to 1990.* (International Population Reports Series, P91, No. 18.) Washington: GPO, 1969.

U.S. Department of Commerce. Office of Technical Services. Joint Publications Research Service (Washington). The following publications are JPRS translations from foreign sources:

"Abuses of Principle of Compensation According to Labor," by Dervish Gjiriti, in *Puna* (Labor), Tirana, 1970. (JPRS: 50,847, *Translations on Eastern Europe, Economic and Industrial Affairs,* No. 310, 1970.)

"Advanced Technology: An Important Factor in Surmounting the Artisan Stage of Industrial Production," by Koco Theodhosi, in *Zeri i Popullit* (Voice of the People), Tirana, 1969. (JPRS: 47,891, *Translations on Eastern Europe, Economic and Industrial Affairs,* No. 114, 1969.)

"Against the Handicraft Method of Management in the Engineering Industry," by Vangjush Gambeta, in *Zeri i Popullit* (Voice of the People), Tirana, 1968. (JPRS: 47,544, *Translations on Eastern Europe, Economic and Industrial Affairs,* No. 92, 1969.)

"The Agricultural Tasks of 1970 Demand Greater Use of Organic Fertilizer," by Xhemal Barushi, in *Bashkimi* (Unity), Tirana, 1970. (JPRS: 50,065, *Translations on Eastern Europe, Economic and Industrial Affairs,* No. 265, 1970.)

"Bank Activities and Bank Control as a Component Part of State Control Must be Improved," by Zeqir Lika, in *Ekonomia Popullore* (People's Economy), Tirana, 1969. (JPRS: 48,892, *Translations on Eastern Europe, Economic and Industrial Affairs*, No. 186, 1969.)

"Concentration and Specialization Cannot be Accomplished Without a Struggle Against Outdated Concepts," by Fejzo Rino, in *Zeri i Popullit* (Voice of the People), Tirana, 1968. (JPRS: 46,647, *Translations on Eastern Europe, Economic and Industrial Affairs*, No. 41, 1968.)

"Control by the Working Class and Problems of Finance and Accounting," by Mensur Saraci, in *Zeri i Popullit* (Voice of the People), Tirana, 1968. (JPRS: 46,647, *Translations on Eastern Europe, Economic and Industrial Affairs*, No. 41, 1968.)

"The Country's Power Resources and the Ways to Use Them More Economically," by Harilla Nishku, in *Ekonomia Popullore* (People's Economy), Tirana, 1970. (JPRS: 50,784, *Translations on Eastern Europe, Economic and Industrial Affairs*, No. 305, 1970.)

"Development of the Machine Industry," by Thoma Afezolli, in *Zeri i Popullit* (Voice of the People), Tirana, 1969 (JPRS: 48,685, *Translations on Eastern Europe, Economic and Industrial Affairs*, No. 171, August 26, 1969.)

"Disappearance and Reduction of Social and General Diseases, Great Victory of the Party in the Health Field," by Josif Adhami, et al., in *Shendetesia Popullore* (People's Health), Tirana, 1969. (JPRS: 50,302, *Translations on Eastern Europe, Economic and Industrial Affairs*, 1969.)

"Elements of Internal Democracy in the Agricultural Cooperatives in Berat District," by Omer Mero, in *Bashkimi* (Unity), Tirana, 1968. (JPRS: 46,439, *Translations on Eastern Europe, Economic and Industrial Affairs*, No. 34, 1968.)

"Expansion of Mechanization in Agriculture," by Xhelal Shkreta, in *Ekonomia Popullore* (People's Economy), Tirana, 1968. (JPRS: 47,515, *Translations on Eastern Europe, Economic and Industrial Affairs*, No. 90, 1969.)

"The Extension and Protection of the Forests is the Responsibility of All the People," by Thoma Dine, in *Rruga e Partise* (Party Path), Tirana, 1969. (JPRS: 48,096, *Translations on Eastern Europe, Economic and Industrial Affairs*, No. 129, 1969.)

"For the Implementation of the Tasks Concerning the Further Revolutionization of Our Schools," by Mehmet Shehu, in *Zeri i Popullit* (Voice of the People), Tirana, 1968 (JPRS: 45,432, *Translations on Eastern Europe, Economic and Industrial Affairs*, No. 256, 1968.)

"The Great Revolutionary Transformations in the Development of Our Socialist Health on the Twenty-fifth Anniversary of the Victory of the People's Revolution and the Establishment of the Dictatorship of the Proletariat," by Ciril Pistoli, in *Shendetesia Popullore* (People's Health), Tirana, 1969. (JPRS: 50,345, *Translations on Eastern Europe, Political, Sociological, and Military Affairs*, No. 207, 1970.)

"Immediate Interests Must be Correctly Combined With Long-Term Ones," by Perikli Samsuri, in *Bashkimi* (Unity), Tirana, 1969. (JPRS: 49,222, *Translations on Eastern Europe, Economic and Industrial Affairs*, No. 221, 1969.)

"Improper Use of Investment Funds," by Andrea Nako, in *Bashkimi* (Unity), Tirana, 1968. (JPRS: 46,570, *Translations on Eastern Europe, Economic and Industrial Affairs*, No. 38, 1968.)

"The Improvement of Fodder: A Fundamental Condition of the Development of Livestock," by Andrea Shundi and Petrit Disdardi, in *Zeri i Popullit* (Voice of the People), Tirana, 1970. (JPRS: 49,941, *Translations on Eastern Europe, Economic and Industrial Affairs*, No. 256, 1970.)

"Increased Savings Deposits: An Index of Growing Prosperity," by Ramadan Citaku, in *Zeri i Popullit* (Voice of the People), Tirana, 1969. (JPRS: 49,222, *Translations on Eastern Europe, Economic and Industrial Affairs*, No. 211, 1969.)

"Labor Productivity in Industry Must be Raised," by Jonuz Drishti, in *Ekonomia Popullore* (People's Economy), Tirana, 1968. (JPRS: 46,163, *Translations on Eastern Europe, Economic and Industrial Affairs*, No. 21, 1968.)

"Let Us Expand and Perfect Our Labor Force Plans," by Besim Bardhoshi, in *Zeri i Popullit* (Voice of the People), Tirana, 1968. (JPRS: 46,940, *Translations on Eastern Europe, Economic and Industrial Affairs*, No. 57, 1968.)

"Let Us Further Develop the Struggle for the Mechanization of Work Processes," by Pjeter Kosta, in *Zeri i Popullit* (Voice of the People), Tirana, 1969, (JPRS: 48,647, *Translations on Eastern Europe, Economic and Industrial Affairs*, No. 166, 1969.)

"Let Us Further Intensify the Participation of the Working Masses in Reinforcing the Savings Regimen," by Aleks Verli, in *Rruga e Partise* (Party Path), Tirana, 1969. (JPRS: 48,349, *Translations on Eastern Europe, Economic and Industrial Affairs*, No. 143. 1969.)

"Let Us Strengthen the Movement of the Working Class for the Overall Development of the Villages," by Sotir Kamberi, in *Rruga e Partise* (Party Path), Tirana, 1968. (JPRS: 45,815, *Translations on Eastern Europe, Political, Sociological, and Military Affairs*, No. 9, 1968.)

"Let Us Take All Necessary Measures to Organize Better the Export of Vegetables and Fruit," by Thechar Fundo, in *Zeri i Popullit* (Voice of the People), Tirana, 1968. (JPRS: 45,432, *Translations on Eastern Europe*, No. 256, 1968.)

"Massive Scientific Experimentation is an Important Factor in the Socialist Transformation of Our Agriculture," by Pirro Dodbiba, in *Bashkimi* (Unity), Tirana, 1969. (JPRS: 47,948, *Translations on Eastern Europe, Economic and Industrial Affairs*, No. 118, 1969.)

"The Maximum Utilization of Labor Time Demands Regular Material and Technical Supply," by Pjeter Kosta, in *Zeri i Popullit* (Voice of the People), Tirana, 1970, (JPRS: 50,112, *Translations on Eastern Europe, Economic and Industrial Affairs*, No. 286. 1970.)

"On Fulfillment of the 1969 State Plan and Budget and on Tasks of the 1970 Draft State Plan and Budget," by Abdyl Kellezi, in *Zeri i Popullit* (Voice of the People), Tirana, 1970, (JPRS: 50,060, *Translations on Eastern Europe, Economic and Industrial Affairs*, No. 264, 1970.)

"On Some of the Problems of Setting Work Norms in Agricultural Cooperatives," by Lefter Peco, in *Zeri i Popullit* (Voice of the People), Tirana, 1969. (JPRS: 49,190, *Translations on Eastern Europe, Economic and Industrial Affairs*, No. 209, 1969.)

"On the Work of the Party and Mass Organizations and of Economic and State Organs for a Further Increase of Productivity and Strengthening of Proletarian Discipline at Work," by Xhafer Spahiu, in *Zeri i Popullit* (Voice of the People), Tirana, 1969. (JPRS: 49,716, *Translations on Eastern Europe, Economic and Industrial Affairs*, No. 242, 1969.)

"Powerful Fraternal Aid in the Spirit of Proletarian Internationalism," by Pupo Shyti, in *Ekonomia Popullore* (People's Economy), Tirana, 1968. (JPRS: 47,677, *Translations on Eastern Europe, Economic and Industrial Affairs*, No. 100, 1969.)

"Problems of Mechanization in Raising Livestock and of Farm Machinery Repair and Maintenance Bases," by Xhelal Shkreta, in *Ekonomia Popullore* (People's Economy), Tirana, 1968. (JPRS: 47,677, *Translations on Eastern Europe, Economic and Industrial Affairs*, No. 100, 1969.)

"Progress of the Machine Industry" by Tago Adhami, in *Ekonomia Popullore* (People's Economy), Tirana, 1968. (JPRS: 46,163, *Translations on Eastern Europe, Economic and Industrial Affairs*, No. 21. 1968.)

"Proper Utilization of Work Time: An Important Factor for Fulfilling and Surpassing Planned Tasks," by Hajredin Celiku, in *Zeri i Popullit* (Voice of the People), Tirana, 1969. (JPRS: 47,550, *Translations on Eastern Europe, Economic and Industrial Affairs*, No. 93, 1969.)

"Protection of Mother and Child Health, the High Expression of Socialist Humanism, Realized by the Party During the 25 Years of People's Power," by Vera Ngjela et al., in *Shendetesia Popullore* (People's Health), Tirana, 1969 (JPRS: 50,302, *Translations on Eastern Europe, Political, Sociological, and Military Affairs*, No. 204, 1970.)

"The Ratio Between Means of Production and Consumer Goods," by Besim Bardhoshi, in *Zeri i Popullit* (Voice of the People), Tirana, 1968. (JPRS: 47,242, *Translations on Eastern Europe, Economic and Industrial Affairs*, No. 77, 1969.)

"Rebuilding: One of the Most Important Ways to Modernize Industry," by Harilla Papajorgji, in *Rruga e Partise* (Party Path), Tirana, 1970. (JPRS: 50,304, *Translations on Eastern Europe, Economic and Industrial Affairs*, No. 378, 1970.)

"Relations of Collective Ownership in Agricultural Cooperatives are Improving," by Munir Como, in *Rruga e Partise* (Party Path), Tirana, 1970. (JPRS: 50,304, *Translations on Eastern Europe, Economic and Industrial Affairs*, No. 278, 1970.)

"Rising Labor Productivity: An Economic Law of Socialism," by Zeqir Lika, in *Zeri i Popullit* (Voice of the People), Tirana, 1970. (JPRS: 50,201, *Translations on Eastern Europe, Economic and Industrial Affairs*, No. 272, 1970.)

"Shortcomings of the Vegetable Supply," by Avni Oktrova, in *Zeri i Popullit* (Voice of the People), Tirana, 1968 (JPRS: 46,205, *Translations on Eastern Europe, Economic and Industrial Affairs*, No. 22, 1968.)

"Some of the Problems of the Socialist Organization of Labor," by Koco Stefani, in *Bashkimi* (Unity), Tirana, 1969. (JPRS: 49,305, *Translations on Eastern Europe, Economic and Industrial Affairs*, No. 214, 1969.)

"The Strengthening and Growth of the Various Branches and Sectors: Important Factors in Cooperation Between and the Overall Development of Cooperative Villages," by Baki Karalliu, in *Rruga e Partise* (Party Path), Tirana, 1968. (JPRS: 47,134, *Translations on Eastern Europe, Economic and Industrial Affairs*, No. 71, 1968.)

"The Struggle to Raise Healthy Children and Reduce the Mortality Rate: A Great Social and Medical Problem," by Sh. Josa, R. Cikuli, and Xh. Basha, in *Shendetesia Popullore* (People's Health), Tirana, 1969. (JPRS: 50,345, *Translations on Eastern Europe, Political, Sociological and Military Affairs*, No. 207, 1970.)

"Why are Unnecessary Materials Imported?," by Gaslli Vllamasi, in *Zeri i Popullit* (Voice of the People), Tirana, 1968. (JPRS: 46,876, *Translations on Eastern Europe, Economic and Industrial Affairs*, No. 53, 1968.)

"The Youth Discharged from the Army: A Great Force for the Development of Subsidiary Activities in Our Socialist Villages," by Vasil Premti, in *Rruga e Partise* (Party Path), Tirana, 1968. (JPRS: 47,134, *Translations on Eastern Europe, Economic and Industrial Affairs*, No. 71. 1968.)

Vjetari Statistikor i R. P. Sh. Tirana: Republika Popullore e Shqiperise, Drejtoria e Statistikes, 1967-68.

Vokopola, Kemal. "The Albanian Customary Law," *Quarterly Journal of the Library of Congress*, XXV, No. 4, October 1968, 306-315.

——. "Church and State in Albania," *Committee on the Judiciary, United States Senate*, II, April 2, 1965, 33-47.

Whitaker, Ian. "Tribal Structure and National Politics in Albania, 1910-1950." Pages 253-293 in *A.S.A. Monographs, No. 7: History and Anthropology*. London: Tavistock Publications, 1968.

"With a Hand Across Your Lens," *Economist*, CCXXIV, No. 6,464, July 15, 1967, 210.

World Radio-TV Handbook, 1970. (Ed., J.M. Frost.) (24th ed.) Soliljevej: H.P.J. Meakin, 1970.

Worldmark Encyclopedia of the Nations, V: Europe. New York: Harper and Row, 1967.

Yearbook on International Communist Affairs, 1968. (Ed., Richard V. Allen.) Standford: Hoover Institution Press, 1969.

Zavalani, T. *Histori e Shqipnis*, II. London: Poets and Painters Press, 1966.

OTHER SOURCES USED

"Albanian Drama Under Foreign Influences," *Radio Free Europe: Research Departments*, May 6, 1965.

"Albania's 1969 Plan Fulfillment and the 1970 Plan," *Radio Free Europe Research: Communist Area*, March 2, 1970, 1-11.

"Albania's Rapid Economic Growth at the Expense of the Consumer," *Radio Free Europe Research: Communist Area*, January 10, 1970, 1-5.

Capps, Edward. *Greece, Albania, and Northern Epirus.* Chicago: Arganout, 1963.

Churchill, Winston S. *The Second World War: VI: Triumph and Tragedy.* Cambridge: Riverside Press, 1953.

Ciano, Galeazzo. *The Ciano Diaries, 1939-1943.* Garden City: Doubleday, 1946.

Cusack, Dymphna. *Illyria Reborn.* London: Heinemann, 1966.

Djilas, Milovan. *Conversations with Stalin.* New York: Harcourt, Brace and World, 1962.

Fjalor i Gjuhes Shqipe. Tirana: Instituti i Shkencavet Sekcioni i Gjuhes e i Letersise, 1954.

Foreign Broadcast Information Service. *Broadcasting Stations of the World.* Part I: Amplitude Modulation Broadcasting Stations According to Country and City. Washington: GPO, September 1, 1969.

Frasheri, Kristo. *The History of Albania.* Tirana: n.pub., 1964.

Gazeta Zyrtare (Tirana), No. 6, September 29, 1966, 151-169.

Instituti i Studimeve Marksiste-Leniniste Prane KQ te PHSH. *Historia e Partise se Punes te Shqiperise.* Tirana: Shtepia Botonjese "Naim Frasheri," 1968.

Jacomoni de San Savio, Francesco. *La Politica dell' Italia in Albania.* Rocca San Casciano: Cappelli Editore, 1965.

Kasneci, Lefter. *Rruga e Lavdishme e Ushterise Popullore.* Tirana: "Naim Frasheri," 1963.

Koliqi, Ernesto. "Albania." Pages 370-531 in *Enciclopedia dei Popoli d'Europa,* I. Milan: M. Canfalonieri, 1965.

Kondi, Piro. "To Follow the Experience of Work in Studying the History of the Party," *Zeri i Popullit,* February 3, 1970, 2.

Lendvai, Paul. *Eagles in Cobwebs—Nationalism and Communism in the Balkans.* Garden City: Doubleday, 1969.

Logoreci, Anton. "Politics in Flux; Albania: The Anabaptist of European Communism," *Problems of Communism,* XVI, No. 3, May-June 1967, 22-28.

1970 World Population Data Sheet. Washington: Population Reference Bureau, 1970.

Omari, Luan; Dode, Petro; and Beqja, Hamit. *20 Vjetori Shqiperi Socialiste*. Tirana: N. Sh., Botime "Naim Frasheri," 1964.

"Opposition to the Albanian Cultural Revolution," *Radio Free Europe: Research Departments*, September 22, 1966.

Organizatat-Baze te Partise per Revolucionarizimin e Metejshem te Jetes se Vendit. Tirana: Shtepia Botonjese "Naim Frasheri," 1968.

Pacrami, F. "Duke Kaluar nga Diskutimi ne Zbatim per Revolucionarizimin e Metejshem te Shkolles, Rruga e Partise," XVI, No. 8, July 1969.

Political Handbook and Atlas of the World: Parliaments, Parties, and Press. (Ed., Walter H. Mallory.) New York: Simon and Schuster, 1968.

The Road to Communism. (Documents of the 22nd Congress of the Communist Party of the Soviet Union, October 17-31.) Moscow: Foreign Languages Publishing House, n.d.

"Situation Report," *Radio Free Europe: Research Departments*, April 19, 1967.

Sphiu, Xh. "Mbi Disa Probleme te Punes se Partise ne Fshat per Ngushtimin e Dallimeve Esenciale Midis Qytetit dhe Fshatit, Midis Zonave Fushore dhe Atyre Malore," *Rruga e Partise*, XVI, No. 8, August 1969, 1-20.

"The State of Wall Posters in Albania," *Radio Free Europe: Research Departments*, April 13, 1967.

Stickney, Edith Pierpont. *Southern Albania or Northern Epirus in European International Affairs, 1912-1923*. Stanford: Stanford University Press, 1926.

Swire, Joseph. Albania: *The Rise of a Kingdom*. London: Williams and Norgate, 1929.

Twenty Years of Socialism in Albania. Tirana: Naim Frasheri State Publishing House, 1964.

United Nations Educational, Scientific and Cultural Organization. *World Communications*. New York: 1964.

U.S. Congress. 83d, 2d Session. House of Representatives. *Communist Takeover and Occupation of Albania*. (Special Report No. 13.) Washington: GPO, 1954.

U.S. Department of Commerce. Office of Technical Services. Joint Publications Research Service (Washington). The following publications are JPRS translations from foreign sources:

"The Class Struggle—the Dividing Line between Marxism and Revisionism," by Bujar Hoxha, in *Zeri i Popullit* (Voice of the People), Tirana, 1968. (JPRS: 45,815, *Translations on Eastern Europe, Political, Sociological and Military Affairs*, No. 9, 1968.)

"The Elimination of Backward Customs Requires Continued and Persistent Work," by Kol Tollumi, in *Rruga e Partise* (Party Path), Tirana, 1968. (JPRS: 45,815, *Translations on Eastern Europe, Political, Sociological and Military Affairs*, No. 9, 1968.)

"Let Us Strengthen the Movement of the Working Class for the Overall Development of the Villages," by Sotir Kamberi, in *Rruga e Partise* (Party Path), Tirana, 1968. (JPRS: 45,815, *Translations on Eastern Europe, Political, Sociological and Military Affairs*, No. 9, 1968.)

"The Problems Raised by Comrade Enver in His Speech 'The Rights and Freedoms of Women Must be Fully Understood and Protected by All' and What Should be Done to Solve Them," by Piro Kondi, in *Rruga e Partise* (Party Path), Tirana, 1970. (JPRS: 50,462, *Translations on Eastern Europe, Political, Sociological and Military Affairs*, No. 214, 1970.)

"Remnants of Patriarchalism in the Family and Society: A Serious Hindrance to The Complete Triumph of the Socialist Way of Life," by Kol Gjoka and Lluke Pashko, in *Rruga e Partise* (Party Path), Tirana, 1968. (JPRS: 46,588, *Translations on Eastern Europe, Political, Sociological and Military Affairs*, No. 32, 1968.)

"Social and Family Relations: A Broad Field for the Class Struggle," by Hysni Kapo, in *Rruga e Partise* (Party Path), Tirana, 1970. (JPRS: 50,200, *Translations on Eastern Europe, Political, Sociological and Military Affairs*, No. 198, 1970.)

"Some Problems of the Academic, Cultural, and Aesthetic Education of Youth," by Ismail Hoxha, in *Nendori* (November), Tirana, 1967. (JPRS: 43,672, *Translations on Eastern Europe, Political, Sociological, and Military Affairs*, 1967.)

(The periodical, *Ekonomia Popullore* [Tirana], November to December 1965, was used in the preparation of this book.)

GLOSSARY

Albanian Workers' Party—The Communist Party of Albania. This name adopted by the First Party Congress in 1948.

basic party organization—The Albanian Workers' Party unit established in state enterprises and institutions, on collective or cooperative farms, and in military organizations. In some Communist states—for example, the Soviet Union—the equivalent is a primary party organization.

Bektashi—A dervish order, offshoot of the Shia branch of Islam, emphasizing abstinence from violence and charity to all people.

besa—A pledge to faithfully fulfill an obligation or promise. Formerly used to effect a truce during hostilities involving clans or conflicts between individuals.

bey—The head of a feudal estate or an administrative official under the Turks. Became the dominant class after Albanian independence in 1912. Also formerly used as a title of respect.

CEMA—Council for Economic Mutual Assistance; members: Bulgaria, Czechoslovakia, East Germany, Hungary, Mongolia, Poland, and the Soviet Union.

civil war—The hostilities from September 1943 to November 1944 in which partisans of the Communist-led National Liberation Front fought the two principal anti-Communist organizations, Balli Kombetar (National Front) and Levizja e Legalitetit (Legality Movement).

clan—An organization that included several families and provided controls as stipulated by unwritten codes. In 1945 the clans were broken up by the Communist regime.

collective or cooperative—An organization in which members retain only their personal effects; all other belongings become community property. Production from group efforts goes into a common fund. Members are paid on the basis of their contribution of work units.

Cominform—Communist Information Bureau. International organization of Communist parties, established in 1947 and dissolved in 1956.

Democratic Front—The largest and most important social organization utilized by the Albanian Workers' Party to gain the support of the masses for their objectives. Its work includes political, economic, social, and cultural tasks. It succeeded the National Liberation Front in 1945.

district—The major subdivisions of the country. There were twenty-six in 1970.

Gegs—The larger of the two subgroups of Albanians. They inhabit the area north of the Shkumbin River. Differentiated until World War II by their tribal organization and primitive life style; also have distinctive physical features.

Kosovo—An autonomous region within the Serbian Republic of Yugoslavia. This area previously called Kosovo-Metohija and frequently referred to as Kosmet.

lek—The standard monetary unit. Does not have an international official exchange rate. Nominally valued in Tirana at 5 leks to 1 United States dollar; the tourist rate in early 1970 was 12.5 leks to US$1. Devalued in August 1965 by exchanging 1 new lek for 10 old leks.

Marxism-Leninism—From the Albanian Communist viewpoint, the ideology of Karl Marx and Vladimir Lenin as reflected in the experience of the Soviet Union until the death of Joseph Stalin.

mass organization—Generally of a social or professional nature with broad membership designed to link the Party with the masses and to gain support for Party objectives.

National Liberation Front—Created in 1942; Communist-led; fought Italian and German occupying forces and immobilized other Albanian factions to seize power in 1944.

Ottoman—Relating to the Turks or to Turkey. Derived from name of fourteenth-century founder of the Ottoman Empire.

party cadre—A thoroughly indoctrinated and reliable Party group. Utilized wherever deemed necessary to maintain efficiency and performance. Frequently specially trained in management.

pasha—A person of high rank; formerly used as a title of respect; title given to appointed provincial heads during the Ottoman period.

People's Army—The armed forces of Albania. Composed of ground, air, and navy elements.

People's Council—The highest government organ at district and lower echelons. Members are elected for three-year terms.

Politburo—The highest and most powerful executive body of the Albanian Workers' Party. In early 1970 it consisted of eleven full members and five candidate members.

Presidium of the People's Assembly—Administers and conducts governmental functions between Assembly meetings. Issues decrees and judges constitutionality of laws. In early 1970, composed of a president, two vice presidents, and ten members.

revisionism—As interpreted by Albanian Communists, the actions and ideologies of Communist states that are inconsistent with Albanian interpretations of Marxism-Leninism.

Sigurimi—Name applied to state security police under the Communist regime; derived from the Directorate of State Security (Drejtorija e Sigurimit te Shtetit).

Sunni—One of the two major branches of Islam.

Tosks—The smaller of the two subgroups of Albanians. They live south of the Shkumbin River. Differences in social organization between the two groups lessened under Communist rule. They abandoned their tribal pattern of life earlier and were more influenced by foreign cultures before 1945 than were the Gegs.

Zogu, Ahmet—Served as prime minister and president during the early 1920s; then ruled as King Zog from 1928 until 1939. Was leader of conservative forces composed of landowners, former Ottoman bureaucrats, and tribal chiefs.

Printed in the USA
CPSIA information can be obtained
at www.ICGtesting.com
LVHW091922260923
759422LV00005B/127